Southern Living
LANDSCAPE BOOK

Edited by Steve Bender
Senior Writer, *Southern Living*

Oxmoor
House®

Southern Living® Landscape Book

Editor: Steve Bender
Project Editor: Fiona Gilsenan
Managing Editor: Pamela Cornelison
Art Director: Alice Rogers
Consulting Art Director: James Boone
Consulting Editor: Bob Doyle
Associate Editor: Dawn P. Cannon
Garden Design Editor: Tom Wilhite
Writers: Evan Elliot, Laura Tringali
Photo Editor: Melinda Anderson
Photo Research Assistants: Tracy Duncan, Laurl Self
Editorial Assistants: Claudia Blaine, Lynne Long,
    Zophia Rendon
Production Coordinator: Patricia S. Williams
Copy Editors: Christine Miklas, Carol Whiteley
Proofreaders: Desne Border, Lura Dymond,
    Marianne Lipanovich, David Sweet
Indexer: Thérèse Shere
Computer Production: Linda M. Bouchard, Joan Olson
Illustrators: Deborah Cowder, Peter Eckert, Lois Lovejoy, Rik Olson,
    Mimi Osborne, Reineck & Reineck, Wendy Smith, Jenny Speckels, Elisa Tanaka

Southern Living®

Editor: John Alex Floyd, Jr.
Executive Editor: Eleanor Griffin
Garden Editor: Linda C. Askey
Associate Garden Editor: Charles Thigpen
Assistant Garden Design Editor: Troy Black
Assistant Garden Editors: Liz Druitt, Ellen Riley
Building Editor: Louis Joyner
Senior Garden Photographer: Van Chaplin
Photographers: Jean Allsopp, Ralph Anderson, Tina Cornett,
    Sylvia Martin, Art Meripol, Allen Rokach, Laurey Weigant

Copyright © 2000 by Oxmoor House, Inc.
Book Division of Southern Progress Corporation
P.O. Box 2463, Birmingham, Alabama 35201

Southern Living® is a federally registered trademark of Southern Living, Inc.

10
First printing January, 2000
Library of Congress Catalog Card Number: 99-65883
Hardcover edition: ISBN 0-376-03876-4. Softcover edition: ISBN 0-376-03877-2

For additional copies of the Southern Living Landscape Book or other Southern Living books, call our distribution partners at Leisure Arts, 1-800-526-5111.

Printed in the United States.

Cover photograph: Barbara Ashford garden, Birmingham, Alabama; Van Chaplin

Title page photograph: Mary and Clinch Belser garden, Columbia, South Carolina; Jean Allsopp

Copyright page photograph: David Dempsey and Lawrence Adkins garden, Atlanta, Georgia; Van Chaplin

Foreword

This book will help you take your home landscape to new heights of beauty. It is not a reference for folks who want clipped balls of shrubs marching across the front of their house or clashing colors in a hodgepodge of flowering plants. Instead it is a complete guide to making your home and garden the beauty spot of the neighborhood.

Each part of a well-designed landscape has its own function. The front yard reflects how you present yourself to friends, neighbors, and passersby. It should clearly guide guests to the entry. It should also anchor the house so it blends well with the natural landscape. The backyard—whether it contains a child's play area, a lush perennial border, a treasured collection of plants, beautiful garden accessories, or simply a comfortable sitting area—should be your private space. And finally, all houses need practical service areas where you can conceal items such as trash receptacles, potting benches, and tools.

These are not just *Southern Living* concepts, they are also basic principles followed by most of America's great landscape designers. So how can you replicate the Southern garden style? Use the advice and examples in this book. Then apply your own personal touches and get to work. But don't be afraid to experiment. My old friend landscape architect Dan Franklin of Atlanta said to me many years ago, "One of the beauties of any garden is that it is okay for plants to have feet and be moved around until you get just the right look." It is part of the personal design process.

Thank you for allowing *Southern Living* to be part of your landscape planning. I hope you enjoy using this book.

John Alex Floyd, Jr.
Editor, *Southern Living*

EXPLORING THE SOUTHERN STYLE

It's easy to do an ordinary project," says Robert Marvin of Walterboro, South Carolina, considered by many to be the "dean" of Southern landscape architects. "But you can never settle for the ordinary, even once. There are 100 good design solutions to a project, but there are only two or three truthful breakthroughs that are right."

This is a book of extraordinary gardens—extraordinary not because of size or sheer magnificence, but because they represent breakthroughs that are right. They pay homage to their surroundings. They meet the needs of their owners. They solve common problems. They beautify their communities. They reflect the dynamic power of pure creativity. And above all, they express that quality so easy to recognize but so hard to describe—what we at *Southern Living* call "Southern garden style."

The Southern garden style springs from concepts that originated in 18th- and 19th-century Europe. Two countries in particular affected its development. From France came geometric gardens intersected by straight lines, formal parterres, and clipped hedges. Often concealed behind walls, these gardens depended on evergreen foliage, patterned stonework, fountains, and ornamental iron for visual impact. The French garden influence thrives today in old port cities such as New Orleans, Mobile, Savannah, and Charleston.

England, however, had an even greater influence. English garden designer Lancelot "Capability" Brown pioneered the idea of the landscape park, which integrated the house with its natural surroundings. Because Brown's schemes mainly involved gigantic manor houses and hundreds of acres of lawns and woodlands, this notion was of little use to average gardeners at the time. But it did establish the premise that a house and garden should work together—a concept central to today's Southern gardens.

Even more telling was the English love of color and flowering plants. The advent of the English cottage garden saw a frenzy of flowers seemingly thrown together. But within that "chaos" existed carefully planned vignettes—combinations of colors and shapes conceived almost as paintings.

On the opposite end of the spectrum stood the English mixed border, a carefully orchestrated blend of annuals, perennials, bulbs, shrubs, and even trees. Both cottage gardens and mixed borders flourish in the South today, even though our climate isn't at all like that of England. We've adjusted these styles to the plants that grow here. And like the Victorians, we've adopted non-native plants from all over the world, including azaleas, camellias, daffodils, roses, wisteria, and palms.

Just as our ideas of how gardens should look and what plants to include have evolved over the years, so too has our idea of exactly where the garden should be. During colonial times, the front of the house was practically devoid of plants, save perhaps for boxwoods at the corners and beside the front door. Such minimalist planting is sometimes referred to as the "Williamsburg style." It worked because it was thought that the handsome house facades of prosperous merchants and landowners of that era needed little embellishment.

Colonial gardens focused on practical plants, such as vegetables, herbs, and fruits, rather than ornamentals. These gardens grew out back, separated from the house by a fence and service area. The emphasis on utility extended even to the courtyards of Charleston and Savannah where you were more likely to encounter chickens or a privy than roses or a fountain.

It wasn't until the advent of suburbs in the 20th century that gardening out front really came into its own. This newfound enthusiasm spawned a pair of regrettable trends that persist to this day. One was the planting of maniacally pruned evergreens meant to hide ugly, concrete foundations. The other was the boundless lawn, which chained its owner to a mower for hours every weekend.

Lady Banks's rose
Savannah, Georgia

About this book

The Southern Living Landscape Book *has a three-fold purpose— to inspire, provide examples, and offer practical information you can use to create the garden you've always wanted. For more about the plants mentioned in its pages, turn to its best-selling companion, the* Southern Living Garden Book. *There you'll find more than 5,000 plants listed by both common and botanical names. Each plant description includes a climate zone rating, telling you where in the South it grows well, along with helpful information about how to plant and care for it.*

Fortunately the evolving Southern garden style, as expressed by the gardens in this book, addresses both problems. First, it considers the garden an extension of the house—a well-designed garden flows from a well-designed house. Second, it encourages the use of mixed plantings, ground covers, and paved areas to reduce maintenance, separate the lawn from those of the neighbors, and deal with practical everyday landscape problems. Solutions to these problems include adding privacy, providing convenient parking, getting people comfortably to the front door, and leaving room for recreation.

But perhaps the most pivotal feature of the Southern garden style is the way it establishes a sense of place. Though tied together by history and culture, the American South is a disparate region of unique habitats and environments. The best gardens speak of those environments through the use of local plants and materials. For example, limestone and mesquite tell you you're in Texas; coquina and bird of paradise say you're in Florida. By designing gardens that truly fit their surroundings, we can ensure the survival of the Southern style.

Steve Bender

CONTENTS

Peg and Truman Moore garden
Charleston, South Carolina

GARDENS OF THE SOUTH

This chapter showcases some of the finest gardens in the South that Southern Living *has been privileged to visit. What's their recipe for success? Start with a strong design that defines space, focuses the eye, and frames a view. Add a good dose of color for interest and emotional appeal. Mix in attention to detail that reveals the owner's personality. Then top it off with plants and materials that suit the climate and region.*

Though diverse in design and terrain, the gardens in this chapter illustrate solutions to many common problems homeowners face: How can I create privacy? How can I frame or open up a view? How can I create an appealing garden year-round?

While you may not be able to replicate these gardens, you can still put many of their innovative and practical ideas to good use when creating or redesigning your own garden.

PERFECT UNION
Joining indoors and out

Blurring the distinction between indoors and outdoors is the goal of this unforgettable house and garden. Here, East meets West in a remarkable design that blends Texas limestone foundations and cedar framing with copper roofs reminiscent of Japanese pagodas.

Exterior walls made mostly of glass invite the outdoors inside, so the design of the garden had to be as spectacular as the home itself. "In Japan, the landscape reflects nature," says landscape architect Rosa Finsley. "So we thought if you're going to do a Texas/Japanese-style house, you should also do a naturalistic landscape."

Finsley carries out this theme with plants adapted to the unforgiving climate and soil of North Texas. Though modest in size, the garden feels larger thanks to pockets of plants you can't see all at once. As you turn a corner or sit in a different spot, the view opens up and changes.

A steady progression of color characterizes this garden. Autumn, often overlooked elsewhere in the region, is beautiful here. Paths wind past sweeps of aromatic aster and an assortment of flowering salvias. Graceful plumes of ravenna grass, 'Gracillimus' maiden grass, and Lindheimer's muhly grass (*Muhlenbergia lindheimeri*) punctuate the air. In late afternoon, the pink sprays of Gulf muhly grass (*Muhlenbergia filipes*) glow in the setting sun.

FAR LEFT *At one corner of the house, water wells up from a hole bored into a native stone and trickles over the sides. A pump in a basin hidden by river stones recirculates the water through the fountain.*

ABOVE *This remarkable house and garden reflect the Japanese tradition of unity of home and garden. Exterior walls made mostly of glass blur the distinction between indoors and out.*

ABOVE *An arbor covered with crossvine shades a limestone terrace. Compacted decomposed granite gives the adjacent courtyard a natural look. Both areas offer ample seating for guests.*

RIGHT *This multitextured blend of hardy ground covers, succulents, grasses, roses, ferns, and shrubs greets visitors on their way to the front door.*

DESIGN TIPS

❧ Consider the architecture of your home when planning your garden. A naturalistic garden would look out of place with a formal home.

❧ Native plants adapted to the region are easy to grow, and many also attract birds and other local wildlife.

❧ Pockets of plants that can't be seen all at once make a small garden appear larger.

ABOVE *Stacked native limestone magnifies the soothing sound of water pouring from a spillway near the back of the house.*

RIGHT *Native and ornamental grasses as well as perennials echo the look of the original prairie and provide a haven for native bees, birds, and other wildlife.*

MORE THAN ROSES
A structured approach

When garden designer Norman Kent Johnson planned this Birmingham garden, his main task was giving it a sufficient framework to extend its appeal beyond the unstructured and erratic nature of most of its roses.

He constructed an arbor to serve as a wall for the outdoor "room." The structure echoes the lattice and brick arches on the back of the house. An ornate toolshed at the garden's far end anchors the center line of the garden. Looking out from the shed door gives a clear

view across a gurgling fountain to a wall ornament between the lattice arches.

Key to the design is a network of perpendicular gravel paths edged in brick. The straight lines of the paths lend formality, while the gravel allows spreading herbs and wayward perennials to tumble onto the paths and soften the beds' rigid lines. The garden's strong lines also allow the owner to experiment with new and different plants without compromising the design.

FACING PAGE *Roses are the stars of this well-ordered garden, but perennials such as hostas, lamb's ears, coreopsis, and thyme maintain interest when the roses are resting.*

BELOW *Aligning ornaments and structures for strong sight lines produces a sense of formality in a garden. Here, a handsome fountain directs the eye to a wall ornament between a pair of lattice arches.*

DESIGN TIPS

∽ A structured design allows you to experiment with plants without ruining the lines of the garden.

∽ Tuck in annuals, ground covers, and other plants for color and bloom when the roses wane.

∽ To give a structured garden a more natural feel, allow plants to grow beyond the design's formal lines.

ALL IN THE DETAILS
Room for fresh air

Nowhere in the South do details take on greater significance than in the historic courtyards of Charleston. The trickle of water, the cool feel of old brick underfoot, the tracery of vines on stucco walls all play an intimate part. This garden, the work of owner and landscape architect Robert Chesnut, captures all the historic details.

A need for privacy mandated high walls. But rather than making the area seem confined, the effect is quite the opposite. "You have to keep the viewer's eye inside the courtyard to create the feeling of a room," Robert says. Glossy privets that rise above the walls keep the view within the courtyard and provide privacy.

Illusion is the key to furnishing this courtyard. To make the garden seem larger, Robert used a modified herringbone pattern for the brick paving. A second trick involved a curved panel of lattice that contains a wall fountain spouting water into a pond below. "To give the illusion of more space and to make the wall behind the fountain appear open, I painted the stucco behind the lattice black," he says.

Creating a sitting area without obstructing movement presented another challenge. A stone shelf, sconce, and a pair of chairs are the perfect solution.

ABOVE *This well-planned courtyard extends the home's living space into the outdoors and creates a private, fresh-air "room." The long, narrow courtyard has a cozy sitting area that can be viewed from the kitchen, a fountain seen from the breakfast room, and a statue and trellis seen from the dining room.*

TOP RIGHT *The sitting area features a wall-mounted candelabra sconce with votive candles and a shelf made of coquina stone, a limestone made of crushed shells and coral, supported by antique iron corbels. Creeping fig softens the look of the stucco wall.*

RIGHT *Curved stucco edging, lattice, and a pond echo the shape of the fountain made from a metal chandelier canopy. The stucco wall behind the lattice is black, giving the illusion of space behind the fountain.*

DESIGN TIPS

❧ Vines on walls add texture and create a feeling of age.

❧ Repeating architectural elements and shapes unifies a small garden.

❧ An intricate pattern of brick flooring can visually enlarge an enclosed space.

❧ The smaller the space, the more important the details.

HEAVEN ON A HILLTOP
Living a dream

Nancy Gunn Porter built her dream home on a wooded hilltop just outside Little Rock, Arkansas. Once she finished the last details of the 1730s-style New England salt-box, she was ready to create her dream garden.

Today, a rustic picket fence encircles the house and Nancy's luxuriant garden of mixed borders, visually connecting the property to its wooded surroundings. Soft pine-straw paths provide for a cushioned stroll through the garden. Nancy started her garden with Southern heirloom flowers first grown in Arkansas in the 1730s, such as larkspur, old roses, foxglove, and hollyhock. She eventually broadened her plant palette to include perennials such as peonies, pinks, irises, and Shasta daisies.

Over the years, Nancy has learned what works best in her garden, but she also enjoys experimenting with new plants. The result is a garden that looks a little different each year. She has a great sense of design and accepts a little help from Mother Nature as well. Seedlings sprout wherever seeds fall, giving the garden a free and more natural look.

RIGHT AND ABOVE *This cottage-style garden gently flows into the wooded surroundings. In spring and summer, larkspur, roses, foxglove, butterfly bush, white phlox, cosmos, and verbenas create bursts of color against a dramatic backdrop of native evergreens. In autumn, sugar maples rain golden leaves on the purple asters and Mexican bush sage blooming below.*

LEFT *Visitors who look over the picket fence are immediately drawn into this flower-filled garden. Roses, Louisiana and Siberian irises, French hollyhocks* (Malva sylvestris), *lamb's ears, pinks, and Shasta daisies are just a few of the plants that line this thickly mulched path.*

ABOVE *The garden features many heirloom plants, such as old roses and larkspurs, known to have been grown in the South in the early 18th century. The peonies shown here were dug from the garden of the owner's mother and are more than 50 years old. Such historical plants complement the colonial style house.*

DESIGN TIPS

❧ Match a garden's style to that of the house. A rustic fence and cottage garden can highlight a saltbox home.

❧ Indigenous materials such as pine straw on paths reinforce the rustic feel of a garden.

❧ Allowing flowers to reseed adds to the natural look of a garden and can create pleasing drifts of color.

FORMAL AND NATURAL
When opposites attract

Today, this lovely backyard beckons, but it wasn't always so. A few years ago, it consisted of little more than a strip of grass between the house and the surrounding woods. Then garden designer Chip Callaway superimposed a formal framework of straight lines and circles over the informal setting. He saved the existing trees and succeeded in marrying both structured and natural design elements.

The terrace steps down to a grassy path and then to a small lawn with a fish pond in its center. Garden paths radiate from the pond in four directions. Turning right or left takes you through elaborate understory plantings of hydrangeas, viburnum, witch hazel, boxwoods, deciduous hollies, camellias, rhododendrons, and dogwoods. Astilbes, hostas, columbines, ferns, and impatiens carpet the garden floor.

Walking straight back from the pond, you'll reach the garden's landmark feature—a pergola inspired by Beatrix Farrand's pergola at Dumbarton Oaks in Washington, D.C. This elaborate garden structure supports an abundance of sweet autumn clematis, silver lace vine, and Carolina jessamine flowers. Fiveleaf akebia thrives in the shade and adds handsome evergreen foliage.

ABOVE *The center of both the pergola and the fountain lies on an axis with the home's back doors and porch, creating formality in a natural setting.*

RIGHT *The fountain, pond, and ornate pergola give the wooded backyard focus and depth. Grassy paths radiating from the pond travel through lush understory plantings of shade-loving shrubs, trees, and flowers.*

SALVAGING A TREASURE
Linking past and present

Before the owners of this Florida property could design their garden, they had to choose between two options: save a crumbling arbor that was nearly a century old or bulldoze it and start from scratch. Fortunately, they consulted with landscape architect John Adams, who recognized the beauty of the structure. "I saw it not as a liability, but as a treasure we ought to work the entire garden around," Adams says.

His first task was linking the arbor to the house. He did this by running a brick walk from between a rear deck and the guest parking area down to the arbor. A handsome brick archway straddles the walk and guides a visitor's view to the arbor beyond. To contain the view and give the garden a visual stopping point, Adams designed a short, curved wall at the walk's end, just beyond the arbor. A recirculating fountain set into the top of the wall gently drips water into a tiny pool.

Simple concrete benches supply seating nearby for listening to the fountain, admiring the surrounding blossoms, or chatting with friends. Lights located along the walk and directed into massive oaks overhead extend the enjoyment of the garden into the evening.

ABOVE *This reclaimed arbor is the centerpiece of the garden. Just beyond, benches and a low wall of native stone offer a destination point. A fountain set into the top of the wall creates a feeling of privacy and calm. The arbor's columns (far right) are made of the same native stone.*

LEFT *A new brick archway and walk direct attention to the treasured arbor beyond. Shade cast by massive live oaks keeps the area cool for entertaining.*

RIGHT *Caladiums and Asian star jasmine carpet the ground beneath the arbor's new cedar timbers that were added to stone columns nearly a century old.*

WELCOMING CHANGE
Enjoying the garden life

Even after more than 30 years, each day in the garden is a shared delight for Jack and Russell Huber. When these lifelong gardeners bought the property in 1968, it was truly a diamond in the rough. Years of renovation have brought welcome renewal to their backyard retreat.

A critical change occurred when they tore down an old stable they had been using as a greenhouse and redesigned the garden. They decided to replace the old structure with an elegant garden house. "I knew we were in trouble when my husband, Jack, brought home the stained glass windows," Russell recalls.

The new stone garden house weaves a thread of architectural continuity from the home to the garden. "That was the pivotal change in our garden," says Jack, of adding the outbuilding. "It freed some adjoining land and allowed us to build walls, bring in topsoil, make walks, and give [the garden] structure."

With the garden's framework now in place, plantings just seem to evolve. Louisiana irises sprout from a circular fish pond at the hub of the paths. Carefree daylilies and hydrangeas add early summer color. Sweeps of Japanese pachysandra, mondo grass, ajuga, creeping Jenny, and other shade-loving ground covers carpet the soil beneath tall hardwoods.

Though Jack and Russell appreciate the exercise, they no longer enjoy long days working in the garden as they once did. To reduce maintenance, they plan to remove finicky plants, such as hybrid tea roses, and emphasize hardy plant favorites, such as Lenten roses *(Helleborus orientalis)*. "I think we'll always be changing plants," says Jack. "Gardens are always in a state of becoming. That's good because it energizes and inspires us."

FAR LEFT *All the paths, including this one lined with daylilies and 'Annabelle' hydrangeas, radiate from a circular fish pond in the garden's center.*

CENTER *This beautiful stone garden house provides a focal point and the framework for the owners' plantings. A bench tucked beneath a common snowball bush* (Viburnum opulus 'Roseum') *offers a quiet place to relax.*

BELOW *Planted amid mondo grass, this Japanese maple combines handsome architectural trunks with colorful seasonal foliage.*

DESIGN TIPS

❧ Adding an elegant touch such as a stained glass window to a garden house can turn the structure into a focal point.

❧ Replace high-maintenance plants with hardy favorites to reduce garden maintenance.

❧ Constructing an outbuilding can also add design structure to the garden.

LEFT *A stone walk winds beneath an arch covered with Armand clematis, then past mixed borders of impatiens, daylilies, hydrangeas, and bamboo.*

ABOVE *The sound of water pouring from the fish pond's spillway is magical and adds another dimension to the garden. Sweeps of ground covers in various shades of green are not only lovely, they also serve to reduce maintenance.*

AN ELEGANT SETTING

Where memories flow

Tucked into a quiet corner, this classical garden began with a memory. When the owner inherited a beloved bronze fountain from her mother, she fondly recalled her

mother's garden and wanted to create a setting worthy of this special gift.

The owner called on landscape designer Carrington Brown to create an elegant sitting area for the purpose of viewing the fountain. A 10-inch-wide strip of mondo grass forms a green frame within the brickwork of the new patio. The 15-square-foot space includes a circle of hexagonal bricks in the center that echoes a pattern found in older parts of the property. Though the six-sided bricks are new, all of the traditional bricks were salvaged, giving the garden an aged look. A brick wall that encloses the area lends a sense of seclusion.

In the perennial border, the light-colored blooms of bleeding-heart, dianthus, and balloon flower stand out against darker foliage with contrasting textures. Ornately carved wooden chairs offer an inviting place to sit and enjoy the fountain and garden.

LEFT *Delightful perennial combinations abound. Here, the white blooms of bellflowers keep company with alum root and cranesbill.*

ABOVE *An heirloom bronze statue inspired this lovely formal garden and sitting area. The garden walls enclose a wide variety of plants, including ferns, hostas, lamb's ears, sedum, impatiens, and purple alum root.*

Give special ornaments a place of prominence in the garden where you can sit and enjoy them.

Use salvaged brick or mix new paving with old to give a space a timeless look.

Plant light-colored blooms in front of darker foliage for contrast and interest.

BELOW *A circle of hexagonal bricks in the terrace's center repeats the brick pattern of other areas in the garden.*

DELIGHTFUL DIMENSIONS
Enchanting garden "rooms"

One way to make a narrow courtyard look bigger is to divide it into a series of spaces. That's what landscape architects Richard Dawson and Lawrence Estes did here.

To shield this garden from hot afternoon sun, Dawson and Estes located it on the east side of the house and enclosed it with a high brick wall. An elegant raised fountain serves as a focal point viewed from the large, central terrace and living areas of the house. Recessed herringbone-pattern brick panels call attention to the fountain's three low water jets.

Just beyond the fountain, a large arbor with benches placed between its columns forms a separate sitting area.

From there, a pair of steps lead down to the pool. "The land around Houston is so flat, even a minor change in elevation can be dramatic, especially in a small garden," Dawson says.

A brick retaining wall at the back of the pool houses spray jets that transform the pool from recreational to decorative at the flip of a switch. A small dining terrace appears to float on the pool's surface. To add a splash of adventure, stepping pads completely surrounded by water are the only way to access this brick and stone peninsula—another detail that makes this garden so enchanting.

DESIGN TIPS

∾ To unify a design, repeat materials throughout the landscape.

∾ The sound of falling water has a soothing effect and masks surrounding noise.

∾ In flat terrain, even a minor grade change can be dramatic.

∾ A series of garden areas can make a small yard seem large.

FACING PAGE *A plant-covered arbor made of rough cedar beams and smooth stone columns becomes a separate space within the long, narrow courtyard. Benches tucked between the columns offer cool seating for quiet conversations.*

ABOVE *This raised fountain lends the refreshing sound of splashing water to the garden. Herringbone panels in the brick wall call attention to the fountain's three water jets. Ferns cascade from terra-cotta pots atop the brick wall.*

RIGHT *The main walkway to this "floating" terrace above the pool is made of stepping pads surrounded by water. Each pad is a single stone paver framed with brick. The pavers with brick banding are repeated throughout the garden.*

SIMPLE SYMMETRY
A bird's-eye view

Looking out from a third-floor window between twin brick chimneys reveals the simple yet dramatic design of this lovely garden. Liz Tedder, the garden's designer and owner, makes sure that its crisp lines and elegant borders endure throughout the seasons.

Formal mixed borders of perennials, shrubs, and seasonal annuals extend 100 feet out from a terrace on the house's south side. Between the flower borders, a rectangular lawn of tall fescue, a grass chosen for its green winter color and acceptance of sun or shade, serves as a stage. White picket fences and Yoshino flowering cherries flanking the borders direct the eye to the garden's striking focal point—a hexagonal gazebo directly in line with the same third-floor window.

The reverse view from the gazebo demonstrates Liz's eye for rhythm, continuity, and scale. The gazebo and fences echo the color of the house, while the brick landing and edging repeat the color of the chimneys.

A well-chosen palette of plants furnishes an abundance of cut flowers. It also keeps this garden blooming year-round except on winter's coldest days. Liz reworks the borders every four to five years to divide and thin overcrowded perennials and keep them in top bloom. Plantings include flowering cherries, pansies, tulips, irises, peonies, and roses in spring; daylilies, balloon flower, phlox, and coneflowers in summer; salvias and asters in autumn; and pansies in winter. Annuals that reseed themselves, such as love-in-a-mist and sweet rocket *(Hesperis matronalis),* fill gaps between plantings and extend the bloom.

LEFT *The upstairs view of this classic garden reveals a brick-edged formal lawn flanked by flower beds. Picket fences reinforce the symmetrical look and direct the viewer's eye to the gazebo, which serves as a focal point.*

BELOW *A comfortable wicker chair and cut flowers from the garden add to the cozy feel of the gazebo.*

DESIGN TIPS

❧ Keep the vista in mind when designing a garden. Both vista and garden should end with a focal point.

❧ Repeat plants, colors, and materials throughout the garden to establish a sense of rhythm and continuity.

❧ Use the strong lines of fences and edgings to bring order to relaxed and untamed plantings in borders.

FACING PAGE *Spectacular groupings of peonies highlight the spring garden, with the pink peony 'Sarah Bernhardt' leading the way. A succession of flowering perennials and annuals extends the show well after the peonies have finished blooming.*

ABOVE *The view from the gazebo to the house highlights the design's sense of rhythm and scale. The gazebo and fences echo the color of the house, while the brick landing and edging repeat the color of the chimneys.*

RIGHT *Lavender-pink sweet rocket reseeds itself and blends nicely with pansies and 'Pink Meidiland' shrub roses.*

STRUCTURE AND STYLE
Start with good "bones"

For landscape architect Ben Page, formality is the key to versatility. When he designed his backyard, he started with an architectural framework, or good "bones." Instead of limiting his choices, the framework gave him a lot more room for creativity.

"A structured design gives you the confidence to play with the garden," Ben explains. "It frees you to do more creative things than you would if you just relied on plants."

A mix of paving materials separates the garden into distinct areas. Just inside the gabled entry and louvered gate, a mosaic "welcome mat" made of stones greets visitors. A formal brick path leads to a flagstone terrace complete with fountain and fish pond. Neat gravel paths in the herb and perennial garden allow the plants to scramble over their borders, giving this formal area a more relaxed feel.

A second-floor balcony off the master bedroom provides an ideal vantage point for observing the design. So when Ben says he spends a lot of time looking down on his garden, he really isn't complaining.

FAR LEFT *A stylized entryway with louvered gate offers a sense of privacy without obstructing sunlight and shadows that filter through from both directions.*

LEFT *A balcony view reveals a design structure of patterned plantings and clear definition between garden areas.*

BOTTOM LEFT *A mosaic "welcome mat" greets visitors as they enter the garden gate.*

BELOW *The balcony also offers a glorious view of this garden's palette of yellows, peaches, lavenders, and pinks.*

DESIGN TIPS

❧ Start your garden with an architectural framework.

❧ Use different paving materials to separate the garden into distinct areas.

❧ Gravel paths allow plants to tumble over borders, relaxing the look of a formal garden.

PLANT LOVER'S DREAM
Weaving plants and colors

The owner of this garden just can't say no. When she sees a plant she likes, she simply can't resist owning it. Her garden contains hundreds of different trees, shrubs, perennials, ornamental grasses, wildflowers, and ground covers that happily coexist on a hillside among footpaths of native stone.

To bring order to what could become a mishmash of plants, the owner contacted nurseryman and garden designer Kurt Bluemel. He rearranged the collections of diverse plants and offered suggestions for dozens of new selections to fashion a cohesive garden and enhance the natural contours of the site.

The owner's favorite plants are needle-leafed conifers—dwarf Colorado blue spruce, blue atlas cedar, umbrella pine *(Sciadopitys verticillata),* and golden hinoki false cypress, to name just a few. "You can do spectacular things even in traditional borders by using conifers as backdrops and accents," she notes.

Today, this well-integrated collection of contrasting foliage colors, sizes, and textures is fascinating to wander through in any season. Outcroppings, paths, and walls made of native stone hold it all together—a design that allows the owner to add those new plants she just can't resist. "There's always a place for it if you love it," she says.

FACING PAGE *The rich green foliage of trees, shrubs, and wildflowers offers a perfect contrast to the foliage of golden hinoki false cypress and blue fescue, the chartreuse blooms of lady's-mantle, the needles of dwarf Colorado blue spruce, and the pink and red blooms of azaleas.*

ABOVE *Conifers, shrubs, perennials, ground covers, and native stone blanket a naturally contoured slope with a variety of textures.*

LEFT *The vibrant blue needles of 'Montgomery' dwarf Colorado blue spruce seem to glow against the surrounding green foliage.*

BELOW *A path of native stones offers sure footing on the hillside and weaves the plantings together.*

DESIGN TIPS

ॐ Conifers add structure, make good background plants for borders, and supply year-round interest and color.

ॐ A strong design keeps a collection of plants from looking unorganized and out of control.

DRAWING WITH NATURE
Through an artist's eyes

Design is all about variety and repetition," says art professor Bill Nance. And it was variety and repetition that allowed him to overcome the limitations of his small city lot. Bill transformed a narrow side yard on his property into an intriguing series of colorful, circular gardens that leads visitors from the front yard to the back. The shape and detail of these garden "rooms," together with the clever way in which they conceal a complete view of each garden beyond, make the side yard seem much bigger than it is.

Guests enter the side yard by walking through a lattice arbor into a foyer garden. A fish pond encircled by gravel paths serves as a focal point. Behind the pond, a vine-covered arbor marks the entrance to an herb garden. A few steps more and the corridor opens to an oval-shaped backyard bordered with shrubs and ornamental grasses with a circular lawn in its center.

Bill compares the design with creating a drawing. "First you create the lines, then you go back with an eraser and soften the edges," he says. "The flowers erase the visible lines, but the basic geometry of the design is still there."

DESIGN TIPS

❧ Create clean, strong design lines in the garden, then soften them with flowering plants.

❧ Repetition creates unity and rhythm. Repeat color and texture within a border in groups of at least three plants.

❧ The best planting schemes come from experimenting and experience. A good gardener is ready to move or replace plants.

FAR LEFT *The side yard entry includes a gate complete with copper sun and sun rays, a threshold made from a cracked marble tabletop, and a lattice arbor with a full moon in the peak.*

LEFT *Just beyond the entry, the foyer garden comes into view, resplendent with pond, gravel paths, and a variety of annuals and perennials. Behind the pond and through the vine-covered arbor with bench, a sunny herb garden awaits.*

ABOVE *A lattice summerhouse is the focal point of the backyard garden.*

RIGHT *Bordered by a neat brick path, clipped boxwoods contrast with the freer, richer textures of flowers and ornamental grasses.*

FAMILY CONNECTION
A kindred love of gardening

Even though this sloped backyard had no personality, no view, no shade, and no easy way to get to it, owner and garden designer Barbie Thomas saw its hidden beauty.

Barbie, her husband, Joe, and their children love to garden. Joe wanted a place to grow vegetables. Barbie wanted perennials and annuals for cutting, and they both wanted a water garden like their grandmothers had. With smart planning the Thomases fit everything they wanted into a yard the length of the house and extending out 25 feet.

Garden structures—paths, pond, fences, and walls—came first. The owners brought in soil to level the slope and form the flower beds that now flank the pond. Brick steps on either side of the pond lead down to the rest of the yard.

To create shade, Barbie planted several river birches in line with an existing dogwood up by the terrace. Because the trees were initially too small to provide much shade, Joe was able to grow vegetables in a bed right by the house. Later he moved his garden to a sunnier spot by the perennials. Irises and water lilies decorate a pond, whose fountain adds the refreshing sound of splashing water. Roses, peonies, and daylilies give Barbie plenty of garden flowers for cutting.

ABOVE *River birches give welcome shade from hot summer sun, while their handsome flaking bark takes center stage in winter.*

BELOW *Vines and potted ferns add interest and symmetry to an otherwise blank brick wall.*

FACING PAGE *The children lend a hand in planting and maintaining this beautiful backyard. Here, river birches arch gracefully over brick-walled beds of irises, peonies, and other plants that provide flowers for arranging.*

ABOVE *This tranquil pond is a replication of the water gardens the owners remember from their grandmothers' gardens. It's also an extension of the brick flower beds. The fountain spilling water into the pond drowns out unwanted noises.*

A PLACE OF THEIR OWN
Separating plants and pet

A dog may be man's best friend, but not so for flowers and plants. That's why the owners of this property asked landscape architect Warren Edwards to design a garden that their pooch and perennials could share.

Edwards divided the yard into two sections, creating a formal lawn and garden next to the house for entertaining and a lawn at the back of the house where the dog could run. Green lattice fencing that separates the areas allows breezes to flow through—a vital consideration in this region in the summertime. The lattice also supports roses, clematis, wisteria, and other climbers, adding privacy.

Two features serve as focal points: a custom-made arbor set in line with the back porch and a fountain, given to the owner by his father, that rests in the middle of a bright green lawn of tall fescue. Curving brick walls with flagstone caps frame two sides of the symmetrical lawn. Behind the walls, English-style perennial borders supply summerlong color.

LEFT *Raised perennial beds outline a lush lawn and enclose a formal garden. The perennials that cope best with the harsh and unforgiving weather in the region include Shasta daisies, daylilies, black-eyed Susans, pink and yellow yarrows, and blue and white balloon flowers.*

BELOW *A family heirloom fountain takes center stage in the garden. An arbor offers a welcome, shady retreat. Arches of galvanized pipe and wire mesh atop the arbor support grapevines and climbing roses, as well as other plants that provide shade.*

DESIGN TIPS

🌱 Protect plants and flower beds by creating a separate garden area for family pets.

🌱 Lattice fencing supports climbing plants and provides privacy without cutting off cooling breezes.

🌱 Choose the right types of plants for the climate conditions of your area.

GARDENING AT THE EDGE
Lattice tames the slope

When Molly Kiscaden and her husband, Scott, bought their home almost six years ago, she wasn't an avid gardener. Molly modestly insists that the garden designed itself, but her natural talents and enthusiasm deserve the credit for this blooming backyard.

The couple was faced with an expanse of lawn that was reasonably flat but eventually sloped away out of sight. "From the house, it looked as if it could be a sheer cliff," Molly says. Today, a lattice fence encloses the area and creates a sense of intimacy close to the house. Measuring 7½ feet at its lowest point, the lattice fence discourages deer from foraging the perennial beds, yet it also gives a feeling of openness. An arbor and a terrace at the far side of the garden provide a destination for casual strolls. Sweeping beds connect the structures.

Molly elevated the beds to give the perennials the deep soil they need to grow and a stage where they can be seen. Maiden grass *(Miscanthus),* tree-form wisteria, Siberian irises, blue star juniper, golden caryopteris, lamb's ears, and 'Montgomery' dwarf Colorado blue spruce grow in a rich tapestry of greens.

Molly and Scott spend many of their summer evenings on the screened porch enjoying the mingled fragrances of flowering tobacco *(Nicotiana sylvestris)* and lilies in the air.

DESIGN TIPS

❧ Panels of open lattice make a high fence seem less imposing.

❧ A destination such as an arbor or a terrace set away from the house invites you into the garden.

❧ Sweeping plant beds connect structures and create a feeling of unity.

ABOVE *A lattice fence at the edge of a steep slope encloses the garden and discourages foraging by deer.*

LEFT *An arbor and a terrace at the garden's far end are a destination point.*

ABOVE RIGHT *Sweeps of hostas add color and texture in the shade.*

RIGHT *Clusters of perennials and vines hug the lattice, creating a sense of intimacy.*

BEYOND THE GARDEN GATE
A bounty of bloom year-round

Guests are never confused about where to enter Karin Purvis's garden when they pull up in front of her 1920s bungalow. A stately arbor, inviting red gate, and tiny bells show the way.

"When I first set the arbor out there, it looked like I had built the Taj Mahal," Karin says. But now covered in vines, it provides just the right accent and sets the mood for the garden. Wrought-iron bells from her native Germany hang in an opening in the gate. To either side, a simple picket fence helps define the small front yard.

Sumptuous plantings of annuals, perennials, vines, herbs, grasses, ground covers, and shrubs occupy every square inch of the front and backyard not occupied by paths. For an enthusiastic gardener like Karin, deciding what to plant isn't as important as determining what *not* to. "I want everything," she says. "But, in a small garden [like this one], you would end up planting on top of things."

Containers help her make the most of tight quarters. She uses potted plants on broad steps or other flat surfaces. She also tucks them in planting beds. Pots of all shapes and sizes fill in whenever she needs a mass of green or a spot of seasonal color. They also allow her to rearrange beds without a lot of digging.

Conifers such as hemlock, spruce, and pine keep the garden looking good year-round. "You have to plant enough evergreens so that the garden isn't barren in winter," she says. A backyard terrace festooned with potted evergreens, succulents, and cool-weather annuals is a favorite place on mild winter days. Plants, garden ornaments, and a cozy lap robe magically transform the terrace into an outdoor "room."

LEFT *Square concrete pavers set in a diamond pattern lead guests through the garden to the front porch.*

ABOVE *A vine-draped arbor and red gate adorned with small wrought-iron bells welcome visitors to a magical garden. Tall clusters of yellow coneflowers (Rudbeckia nitida 'Herbstsonne') accent the entry.*

ABOVE *In the backyard, stepping-stones set in gravel define circular, formal planting beds that feature dwarf Alberta spruce (Picea glauca 'Conica'), verbenas, coneflowers, impatiens, and celosia. Variegated maiden grass flanks the back entrance.*

LEFT *This simple yet elegant arbor features a painted, adjustable shelf for outdoor buffets or displaying flower arrangements. It also functions as a potting bench.*

FACING PAGE, TOP *This cozy terrace offers warmth and cheer any time of year, but especially in winter when cool-weather annuals and evergreens in containers add interesting textures and color. The succulents may appear tender but are cold tolerant.*

FACING PAGE, BOTTOM *Inside the front gate, a small lawn continues to give way as new annuals, perennials, ground covers, and shrubs find new homes in the garden.*

DESIGN TIPS

∾ Container plants create versatility in a small garden by making it easy to change plantings without digging.

∾ Define garden entryways and structures with bold color.

∾ Use evergreens to give structure to the garden and keep it attractive in winter.

∾ Potted cool-weather plants can create a cheery outdoor space in winter.

OUT OF THE WOODS
A new, open view

At one time, this handsome home was in hiding. An unattractive wooded mound stood between the house and street. When the trees leafed out in spring, they completely screened the house and front door from view. The driveway made matters worse because it dropped guests off at the garage. Hiking to the front door meant negotiating a narrow, overgrown walk more than 100 feet long.

To open up the view from the house to the street and create a parking area out front, landscape architect Preston Dalrymple cleared the woods and installed an elegant parking court. Composed of interlocking pavers edged in cobblestones, the court provides sufficient turnaround space for three cars. A new brick walk and landing lead visitors right to the front door.

Garden designer Peggy Ford created a simple foundation planting of dogwoods and boxwoods underplanted with liriope. The composition complements the home's Williamsburg-style facade without screening it. The owners are not avid gardeners, so Ford and Dalrymple used massed plantings of 'Schipkaensis' cherry laurel, 'Edward Goucher' glossy abelia, 'Helleri' Japanese holly, and other easy-to-maintain shrubs and ground covers.

DESIGN TIPS

✎ Choose plants that highlight rather than hide your home and that are in scale with the structure.

✎ Give guests a clear path to your front door.

✎ Make sure the materials used in a new driveway or parking court complement your home's facade.

FAR LEFT *Simple plantings such as these 'Helleri' Japanese hollies are easy to maintain and complement the formality of the house and garden. Hand-molded bricks in the new walk and landing match those of the house.*

ABOVE *This home's new driveway and parking court open up the view of the house and provide turnaround space for cars. The base of the driveway and court is composed of interlocking pavers framed in cobblestones.*

PURE WEST TEXAS
Creating a sense of place

Making a garden fit into the skillet-bottom-flat, rock-strewn earth of West Texas has its challenges and its rewards. Landscape architect Rodney Fulcher started this garden with a blank slate. The backyard had no privacy, no shade, and no ornamental interest.

First he installed a privacy fence, softening it with vines and evergreen shrubs. Next he brought in soil to create low berms for relief from the flat landscape and give the illusion of extra room. "If you look across the bed, you think you're looking across 20 or 30 feet, when it's really 10," Fulcher explains.

He blanketed the berms with low-maintenance ground covers including liriope, Asian star jasmine, and juniper. The combination of different colors, textures, and heights adds a feeling of hidden depth.

A weathered cedar breezeway and arbor give respite from the sun. The breezeway acts as an open hallway from the house to the terrace with a lath-covered arbor. The arbor's pitched roof echoes the roof of the house.

As a finishing touch, Fulcher placed a few sandstone boulders in strategic spots among the berms. The porous rocks absorb water and provide a good surface for lichens and mosses. "The rocks make the garden look like West Texas," he says.

ABOVE *A brick-and-concrete terrace sheltered by a cedar breezeway and lath arbor extends the house into the garden, joining living and gardening areas.*

RIGHT *Rolling berms of lush liriope, Asian star jasmine, and juniper with their varying heights and textures make this small garden look much bigger.*

DESIGN TIPS

ꙮ Adding a berm provides relief in an otherwise flat landscape and creates the illusion of additional space.

ꙮ Plants of different colors, textures, and heights add a feeling of depth to garden beds.

ꙮ Even the simplest arbors can provide immediate shade for a young garden.

GLORIOUS GARDEN REBORN
A medley of old and new

Bursting forth in a symphony of bloom, this garden rewards its audience with spring-to-autumn color. But before orchestrating such showstopping compositions, the owners turned to landscape architect Dan Franklin to help revitalize the existing garden design.

The original garden, a legacy from the owners' grandparents, featured a circular pond that was cracked at the bottom and leaking, so the owners built a new pond over it. Because the new pond was 2 feet above ground level, yards of topsoil were brought in to raise the surrounding area.

To hold it all in place, Franklin designed stone retaining walls that stair-step down the backyard slope. The irregular granite face and caps look old-fashioned and complement the special history of the garden. Salvaged cobblestones that edge the beds also add a touch of the past.

The walls' geometric shape gives the garden a formal symmetry. But instead of planting in ordered rows, the owners have carefully cultivated a random-looking cottage garden. To determine where each plant belongs, they consider blossom and foliage color, plant size, texture, and season of bloom. Annuals tucked in among the perennials provide instant color in the foreground. Using a journal to log the garden's changes helps in their planning.

LEFT *The crepe paper–like blooms of Iceland poppies and 'Professor Blaauw' Dutch irises create a stunning duet.*

ABOVE *The view from an overlooking deck shows the geometric design of the garden. The original pond was built in the 1930s.*

TOP RIGHT *Plants are replaced from season to season for new combinations of color, texture, and fragrance.*

RIGHT *Curving stone walls, modeled after the ones in Atlanta's Chastain Park, divide tiers of flowers and repeat the pond's circular shape.*

DESIGN TIPS

~ Keep a garden journal to track what works and what doesn't from year to year.

~ Add stairs and retaining walls to help terrace a sloped lot.

~ Plant flowers in masses rather than straight rows for a cottage garden look.

~ Use salvaged materials, such as cobblestones, to link a new garden with the past.

OLD-WORLD BEAUTY
In a tropical setting

Joining a Mediterranean-style house and tropical plants with the European belief that a garden should be used and not simply admired is the foundation for this beautiful backyard.

Designed by St. Petersburg, Florida, landscape architect Phil Graham, the garden is a natural extension of the house. It supplies cut flowers and foliage for arrangements, and features inviting spaces for quiet dining, entertaining, and observing wildlife.

Both the steps and the terrace are paved with coquina, a native limestone made of crushed shells and coral. Carved coquina forms the balustrades as well. Step risers faced with hand-painted blue-and-white tiles from Italy highlight the stairs.

Tropical and semitropical plants, including ferns, palms, and peace lilies *(Spathiphyllum)*, flank a brick lower terrace. These dense plantings visually connect the house, which is higher on the lot, to ground level. They also supply plenty of niches for tucking in pots and whimsical ornaments. Attention to detail and surprises at every turn make lingering here a pleasure.

LEFT *An Italian porcelain pot set in among the foliage captures attention and adds striking detail in the garden.*

ABOVE *This tropical garden was designed to be both used and admired. Pentas, gingers, orchids, and other blooming plants attract butterflies and provide cut flowers.*

ABOVE RIGHT *Native limestone steps faced with Italian hand-painted tiles lead to the garden's upper terrace.*

RIGHT *An ornate wall fountain serves as a focal point, adds the cooling sound of splashing water, and attracts birds to the garden.*

KNOT PERFECT
An easy-care parterre

The owner of this property was tired of working on a temperamental rose garden and wanted something attractive that required little maintenance. Combining pretty with practical, garden designer Mary Zahl devised a plan that fits the formal architecture of the home.

Because the garden is viewed from upper terraces, it needs to look good from above. Sheared Japanese holly and abelia form a knot of hedges in the center of the 20-by-30-foot area, providing year-round interest with only occasional upkeep. Flower borders flank the sides of the garden with color that's easy to replace with changing seasons, while small boxwoods in elevated containers anchor the four corners. "It's a way of giving impact," Zahl says. "A small boxwood in a pot has a similar or greater impact than a large one in the ground, and is more economical."

To keep the new garden from looking out of place alongside the older home, Zahl repeated materials such as brick that were used elsewhere on the property. The new garden looks as if it has been there all along.

DESIGN TIPS

❧ Planting evergreens such as boxwoods in pots can be more effective than planting similar-size evergreens directly in the garden.

❧ Laying landscape fabric beneath gravel paths keeps them virtually weed-free.

LEFT *A row of 'Nellie R. Stevens' hollies at the edge of a steep slope keeps the viewer's eye in the garden and provides a nice evergreen backdrop. The holly shrubs help to make the garden feel roomy yet contained.*

ABOVE *Designed to be viewed from terraces above, this small garden features formal lines held in place by evergreens for year-round appeal. Blooms add bursts of color and change with the seasons.*

RIGHT *Small boxwoods in containers anchor the corners of the garden. Planting these shrubs in containers adds a formal touch and increases their impact.*

HEART OF STONE
A terrific terrace

Jodie Collins sees the world as one big potter's wheel. An accomplished ceramist who creates landscapes for a living, he views stone as just another type of clay. Small wonder, then, that native Texas limestone is the heart of his garden.

An arbor festooned with a tangle of wisteria and a rustic fence of red cedar poles guide guests into the backyard from the parking area. A curving terrace stretches into the center of the backyard, offering the perfect place to sit in the shade of pecan trees and escape the San Antonio sun.

The terrace is Jodie's solution to the sloped lot that used to drain toward the garage and caused water damage to the structure. He excavated the area to the same level as the garage to eliminate the slope, then created the terrace. Limestone walls edging the terrace retain the surrounding soil.

Jodie included a limestone fireplace in the garden. The idea evolved from days spent on the ranch burning bonfires of cedar brush. "Of course, you can't have a bonfire in the city," he says, "so this is how I bring a little of the ranch home with me."

FAR LEFT *A guest's first glimpse of the garden is through this cedar arbor covered with wisteria.*

CENTER *Excavating the terrace area eliminated the slope and solved the runoff problem that had rotted the foundation of the garage. Now excess water drains away from the structure.*

ABOVE *This limestone fireplace makes sitting outside a pleasure in late autumn and winter.*

BELOW LEFT *A curving limestone terrace stretches like a peninsula into the center of the yard. A strip of mondo grass separates it from the seating wall.*

DESIGN TIPS

∾ Using native materials is an excellent way to tie in a house with its surroundings.

∾ When designing a garden, check for drainage problems before tackling any other task.

∾ An outdoor fireplace lets you enjoy the garden on chilly days or nights.

FEAST FOR THE SENSES
A garden of touch, smell, and sound

Not only is this St. Louis garden beautiful to look at, it's also a feast for the rest of the senses. But when the owner, Doug McCarthy, first purchased the property, there was no garden to speak of, just a dozen pin oaks and a spacious, open lawn.

Doug, who is blind, planned the elements most important to him—the garden structure, walls, and walks. He worked with garden designer Charles Freeman to create a series of outdoor "rooms" that appeal to all the senses. They started with walls and hedges to carve

space out of wide-open nothingness. The gentle splash of water from a series of strategically placed fountains helps Doug navigate and draws guests through the garden. Wind chimes turn the breezes into music.

Lush tapestries of flowers, ground covers, trees, and shrubs create year-round interest and texture in the garden. Spring and summer announce their arrival with the honeyed perfume of lilac, sweetshrub, mock orange, and Korean spice viburnum, and then with the musky, sweet smell of roses, lilies, and hostas.

FACING PAGE *Handsome 18th-century wrought-iron gates define the entry to the garden beyond. A trim grass path, sheared hedge of European hornbeams (Carpinus betulus), alliums, and yellow flag irises greet visitors at the gate.*

ABOVE *The sound of splashing water from a series of carefully placed fountains guides the owner through the garden. Hostas and red tuberous begonias surround the small lead-basin pond that rests beneath the canopy of a crabapple tree.*

ABOVE *The varying textures of foliage in this garden appeal to the sense of touch. Here, the leaves of laceleaf Japanese maple* (Acer palmatum *'Dissectum'*), *climbing hydrangeas* (Hydrangea anomala petiolaris), *azaleas, and Virginia creeper add texture to the brick walls of the courtyard.*

TOP RIGHT *Dense rows of big-leaf hostas direct the owner along this brick path and screen its edges. Massed plantings such as this one also minimize maintenance by crowding out weeds and retaining moisture.*

RIGHT *Yellow flag irises, hostas, and other perennials form a rich composition of contrasting colors and leaf shapes in this mixed border.*

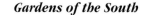
DESIGNED FOR COMFORT
A backyard for relaxing

Landscape architect Bill Smith had comfort in mind when he fashioned his own Atlanta backyard. "I get enough restless feelings during my day, so I want to feel calm when I see my own garden," he says.

His design combines both formal structure and a strong naturalistic element with a plan for easy maintenance. Sweeping perennial borders accent a backbone of evergreens, including aucuba, nandina, mountain laurel, holly, and hemlock. His reason for emphasizing evergreens is simple. "I want to look out on a winter day and see a garden, not a bare perennial bed," he says.

Bill uses color in the garden to command attention. In spring, the border features blue phlox, pansies, irises, sweet William, and tulips. In summer, ageratum, begonias, blue salvia, caladiums, sedum, and perennial phlox play a starring role.

After the flowers, the zoysia lawn edged in brick is the garden's most striking element. To accommodate the grade change between flower beds and lawn, Bill added brick steps instead of a wall to invite people into the border rather than keep them out. The small, tailored lawn sets off the nearby flowers, but takes only minutes to cut.

ABOVE *This garden is just right for savoring a quiet moment or gathering with friends. There are paths to stroll (left), places to sit, and flowers to enjoy. The lawn offers a smooth foreground to the rest of the garden, yet its size and shape make it easy to maintain.*

RIGHT *A flagstone terrace provides the perfect place for relaxing and enjoying the garden.*

DESIGN TIPS

❧ Never design more garden than you feel you can handle.

❧ If you want curves, don't use squiggles. Curves should be simple and bold, which makes them easier to maintain and easier on the eye.

❧ Color does not have to be complicated. Simplify your approach by planting annuals that will bloom all season long.

❧ Plant evergreens for garden structure and winter interest.

A WIDER PERSPECTIVE
For a long, narrow lot

Because this home sits at the end of a long, narrow lot, its front door seemed miles away from the street. But landscape architect Bob Hartwig found a way to help the house and property work together better.

By confining most trees and shrubs to the garden's periphery, Hartwig opened up the center of the front yard, made it appear wider, and focused attention on the house. Then, using paving and plants, he divided the lot into three rectangles—lawn area, parking court, and a welcoming courtyard. Each rectangle assumed its own separate space. Again, this helped the lot look wider.

Before, a border of shrubs separated the lawn from the drive. Hartwig removed them, then edged the turf on three sides with mondo grass, and ran the lawn up to the drive. Having the grass and paving together at the same level visually widened the entire area. At concrete joints in the driveway, brick rows bisect the drive, dividing it into shorter, wider-looking segments. Color in pots highlights the courtyard and entries and brightens the green landscape.

By creating a perception of width rather than depth, the garden and house move visually closer to the street. The front door no longer seems a cab ride away.

LEFT *Planting the lawn up to the drive makes this long, narrow lot look wider. Brick ribbons divide the drive into shorter segments that reinforce the wider view.*

ABOVE *A short openwork brick wall serves more to define space than to create a physical barrier. It establishes the courtyard as its own area, visually decreasing the length of the lot.*

RIGHT *A privet pruned as a small tree at the far end of the courtyard helps camouflage a large wall, adding intimacy to the space.*

GARDEN GETAWAY
A celebration of carefree plants

A contemporary interpretation of a cottage garden, Texas style—that's how the owners describe this garden medley of antique roses, perennials, herbs, and reseeding annuals that cluster around their weekend home. Populated by sturdy, easy-care plants, this garden serves as a testing ground for new plant discoveries and a haven for old favorites.

Many of the plants are hand-me-downs from the owners' families. They include pink wood sorrel *(Oxalis crassipes)*, 'Maggie' rose, crinum lilies, Louisiana irises, red carnations, and hardy gladiolus. The color combinations, quick-growing roses, and carefully considered structural details make this well-planned, young garden appear mature.

Horticulturist Bill Welch and landscape architect Nancy Volkman created this hard-working design. Gateways echo the gables of the house, while picket fences wrap the gardens in cottage style. "We wanted a lot of fence space to display flowering vines in addition to roses," Welch says. "So the fences and arbors serve not only to enclose the garden, but also act as trellises."

Because the owners visit only on weekends, plants here must fend for themselves. The carefree roses require little or no spraying, the lawn is drought-tolerant buffalo grass, and the old-fashioned petunias spring up from seeds that fell the previous year.

ABOVE LEFT *Open vistas and easy-care gardens make this 1906 Victorian cottage a welcome and relaxing weekend retreat.*

ABOVE *Gateway arbors repeat the framework of the house's gables. Plantings of pinks, petunias, and Texas bluebonnets cluster around a Victorian urn filled with yucca and Mexican sedum. Red carnations grow over the path.*

DESIGN TIPS

❧ Arbors and fences work double duty to define garden areas and serve as supports for climbing plants.

❧ Match the types of plants you choose with how much time you can spend in the garden.

❧ Design structures that complement the style of your home.

RIGHT *Cottage-style picket fences and trellises wrap the gardens on either side of the house and provide support for favorite climbing roses and vines. The buffalo grass lawn showcases roses and perennials that mingle in beds of harmonious color.*

A CAPITAL SURPRISE
Hideaway in the heart of D.C.

Walking from a noisy Washington, D.C., street, the owner of this house steps around to the backyard and in seconds is in the middle of quiet countryside.

At one time, explains garden designer Jane MacLeish, this backyard was little more than a few trees and a chain-link fence. Neighbors and busy streets bordered the yard on three sides. So one of her first tasks was planting a dense border of trees and shrubs to create privacy and buffer city noise.

The bowl-shaped backyard slopes away from the house. A winding network of paths leads through a potpourri of shrubs and perennials to the centerpiece of the garden, a beautiful, calming pool. With lawn grass nearly to its edge and water darkened by the addition of black coloring in the concrete form, the swimming pool looks more like a woodland pond.

Looking out over the peaceful landscape makes the city seem very far away.

LEFT *With its darkened concrete base and grass planted to its edge, the pool resembles a natural pond. Grass terraces offer comfortable areas for sitting or sunning.*

BELOW LEFT *A stepping-stone path flanked by impatiens, violets, and hostas trails down a slope.*

ABOVE *A thick border of trees and shrubs provides complete privacy from nearby neighbors.*

BELOW *In summer, these hostas and astilbes give an added burst of color to the shade-loving borders surrounding this gazebo.*

NEAT LITTLE RETREAT
A garden on the side

The owners of this brick home already had a large terrace that opened up to the backyard, but it didn't have the intimate feel they wanted. Landscape architect Brian Zimmerman gave them the solution they were looking for—an intimate garden "room" for two that still offers enough seating for small parties.

Zimmerman tucked this small courtyard into a side yard just outside the family room. For easy access from the house, he replaced the windows on both sides of the chimney with French doors. A 6-foot brick wall shields the area from the street and nearby neighbors. To soften the large expanses of brick wall, Zimmerman added plantings that blend with existing shrubs. He also added a small iris-shaped fountain that spills into a semicircular pond on the wall opposite the house. "The traffic noise from the street was louder than we realized, so the sound of splashing water combats it," he says.

For extra color and interest, a raised rectangular bed in the middle of the terrace brims with perennials and other favorite plants. Low-voltage lights directed upward were installed throughout the garden to add dramatic effects at night.

DESIGN TIPS

❧ Determine how courtyard space will be used (lively parties, relaxing, dining) and let function guide design.

❧ Don't make a courtyard so large that it loses its sense of intimacy.

❧ Courtyards for dining or entertaining should be easily reached from the house.

LEFT *A small brick courtyard added off the side of the house creates the perfect, intimate outdoor space.*

ABOVE *An iris-shaped fountain splashes water into a small pond, masking street noise beyond the garden walls.*

BELOW *French doors on both sides of the chimney provide easy indoor-outdoor access.*

CULINARY DELIGHT
Blending herbs and flowers

Herbs, with their various textures, colors, and scents, delight both cooks and gardeners. Mingling herbs, lettuces, and flowers in this small backyard creates a culinary patchwork that is as pleasing to the eye as it is to the palate.

When the owners were choosing a spot for the garden, they knew that area had to be well drained and receive at least four hours of sunlight each day. The soil here was less than ideal. So they tilled in lots of organic matter, such as compost, cow manure, and leaf mold, and added some sand to help improve drainage.

One advantage of growing your own herbs and vegetables is that you can experiment with ones that aren't usually available at the grocery store. This garden brims with several varieties of basil and leaf lettuce. Pots provide the drier soil that some herbs such as silver thyme and golden oregano prefer. The owners also use pots to elevate low-growing herbs so they don't get lost under their bushier brethren.

Narrow-leaf zinnia, cape plumbago, and Madagascar periwinkle *(Catharanthus roseus)* add bright color to the sea of green foliage. Stone edging keeps the garden in place and repeats the edging used in other parts of the yard.

FAR LEFT *An edging of native stone keeps the garden in place while allowing herbs to spill over the top and onto the path.*

CENTER *Dense plantings allow a lot of variety in a small space. The small dimensions of the garden areas and the proximity of the path make harvesting easy.*

ABOVE *Planting some herbs in pots highlights them in the beds and adds interest in the garden.*

ENTERTAINING CHANGE
Adding to a successful design

Over the years, gardens need to evolve with their own- ers' changing lifestyles. Landscape architect Wolfgang Oehme first designed this garden more than 15 years ago. Along with sweeps of ornamental grasses, perennials, and berry-producing shrubs that attract the birds, his original design included a stone terrace for the side yard. The owners decided against the terrace because they were concerned about losing the area's natural look and habitat for birds. But as years went by, they wanted a place to en- tertain and once again turned to Oehme for an answer.

Today, the L-shaped bluestone terrace, in the shade of Japanese zelkovas, blends well with its surroundings and nestles among ornamental grasses, perennials, and shrubs. A low stone wall along one side of the terrace encloses the area and provides casual seating.

A fountain placed nearby keeps the birds coming back. Created by designer Jim Birks, the fountain is made of river rock mounted above an underground basin that recircu- lates the water. The birds entertain themselves in the foun- tain while the owners entertain on the terrace.

FACING PAGE *Originally designed as a haven for birds, this garden now attracts people as well. The owners added a stone terrace with plenty of room for entertaining.*

BELOW *Surrounded by trees, shrubs, ornamental grasses, and perennials, the terrace becomes an intimate space for quiet conversation.*

INSET *The splashing sound made by this small recirculating fountain attracts many types of birds.*

DESIGN TIPS

- Plan for your garden to evolve with your lifestyle.
- Berry-producing shrubs and even the simplest water feature attract birds to the garden.
- Low walls are a great way to enclose a terrace and add extra seating.

A TOUCH OF THE MOUNTAINS
Down by the bayou

Walking into this backyard in the summertime was like stepping into a steam room. The heat and humidity had the homeowners dreaming of a favorite lakeside retreat high in the lush, airy mountains of North Carolina. With cool, refreshing water in mind, they turned to landscape architect Christopher Friedrichs for a design that would bring the mountains to the bayou.

Friedrichs looked to the garden's existing fish pond for inspiration. He used it to determine the classical proportions of the new swimming pool. "We just did a repeat of the oval but blew it up in scale," he explains. Using a dark color for the bottom of the pool also gives it the feeling of a lake.

To camouflage an unattractive wire fence, Friedrichs used "big sloppy rollers" to paint it charcoal gray. Masses of evergreens consisting mostly of viburnums were added to an existing screen of Japanese pittosporums for privacy. The loose character of the planting gives the garden a natural look and makes it easy to care for. Evergreens offer a pleasant contrast to the bright lawn of St. Augustine grass.

The new stone terrace provides plenty of room for relaxing or entertaining. The terrace and wide coping that border the pool are a dark gray, repeating the dark color used in the bottom of the pool. White caladiums add to the garden's cool feel in summer.

FACING PAGE *The oval swimming pool mimics the shape of an older fish pond on the property. Dark gray stone coping repeats the coloring of the bottom of the pool. Mass plantings of evergreens mask a wire fence and give the garden a lush, natural look.*

LEFT *An old lead urn in the center of the fish pond provides the cool sound of trickling water. The urn, fish pond, and swimming pool are on an axis with the rear of the house, adding formal lines to the garden.*

BELOW *The terrace is next to the swimming pool, offering a comfortable spot to sit and visit. The same dark gray stone selected for the pool coping was also used for the terrace.*

DESIGN TIPS

 Mirroring the style of an existing water feature helps a new pool blend with the rest of the landscape.

 Dark paint is an inexpensive camouflage for an unattractive wire or chain-link fence.

 Plants in a cool palette of colors make a sultry garden seem cooler.

LARGER THAN LIFE
Garden "rooms" add a feeling of space

Orene and Tate Horton's backyard may be small—60 by 60 feet including the driveway and garage—but its garden "rooms" make it feel spacious rather than cramped.

A picket fence and vine-covered arbor separate the driveway from the garden. Walking under the arbor and down the brick walk, you reach a garden where attention to every detail makes it feel private and quite secluded.

Instead of devoting a separate space to outdoor dining, Orene designed an area along the walk that is wide enough to accommodate a table and chairs. Down the walk that borders the manicured lawn, a rose-laden arbor

announces the entry to a second garden room. An evergreen screen of viburnums on either side of the arbor's brick columns completes the partition.

A Lutyens bench beyond the arbor invites you into this smaller "secret" garden. Orene placed the bench directly in line with her back porch to act as a focal point. A view from the bench to the back porch reveals an exuberant collection of potted plants on the back steps. Containers of 'Evergreen Giant' liriope and cape plumbago reside there year-round, while sedums, pansies, and petunias paint the setting in seasonal colors.

FACING PAGE *Framing a birdhouse, an arbor covered with gold flame honeysuckle marks the entryway from the driveway to the garden. When you step under the arbor and onto the brick paths, you feel as if you have entered a more secluded space.*

ABOVE *A 'Sombreuil' tea rose drapes an arbor, softening the look of the structure. Potted boxwoods at the base of each brick column and an urn framed by the arbor add a formal touch to the garden "rooms."*

LEFT *A wide brick walkway separates a small, tidy lawn from the diverse and rambunctious plantings that fill the flower beds.*

DESIGN TIPS

☙ Using shrubs and garden structures to create a series of outdoor "rooms" can make a small yard seem large.

☙ Plants in containers of different shapes and sizes create interesting settings and can be easily moved around.

☙ Planting vines on walls and arbors maximizes planting space in a small garden and visually adds depth to narrow beds.

HILLSIDE PARADISE
Making the grade

It takes dedication and a true love of plants to carve a garden from the side of a mountain. Carter Giltinan's leafy paradise clings to a 40-degree slope where she reclaimed the garden "from woodland brush and a sea of English ivy." She started almost 50 years ago with a treasure trove of native stone buried under a rotten porch. Those stones later

formed the retaining walls for her beds. Over the years, the first hillside plantings have grown from modest borders to lush sweeps of perennials that clamber up the slope and cling to the ridges of the yard. Carter happily sacrificed large expanses of lawn in favor of grass paths that wind gracefully through the perennials.

Summer beds bloom with hostas, astilbes, bee balm, daylilies, smooth hydrangea, primroses, and Queen Anne's lace, bringing splashes of color throughout the garden. But the garden's richest treasure is its sea of green foliage. "Green is a great teacher," Carter says. "I look out and see 35 shades of green in my hosta bed. It teaches you to consider plant form and foliage texture. Once you get green under your belt, you can master flowers."

CENTER *Years of dedication and hard work turned a steep slope into a luxuriant garden. Though astilbes, bee balm, hydrangeas, and primroses add seasonal colors, the garden's primary color is green.*

ABOVE *Walls made of salvaged stone retain the hillside garden. Below them, a medley of vines and perennials grow against the house.*

RIGHT *Astilbes, primroses, and ferns, like most moisture-loving plants, flourish from generous applications of compost each year.*

BACKYARD BEAUTY
Unifying the elements of pool, house, and garden

Sprucing up this small backyard and pool involved both home remodeling and the clever use of color. Before, the pool deck was exposed aggregate and the entire back wall of the living room consisted of sliding glass doors, giving the garden a dated look.

Architect Dale Selzer updated the house by replacing the sliding doors with a series of French doors in heavy frames. Existing arborlike structures over the doors and windows were painted gray to match the new doors and harmonize with the rest of the house.

Landscape architect Naud Burnett chose flagstone for the pool deck. Individual stones in a blend of gray, green, and brown complement the mottled tones of the brick walls. Burnett selected a light green plaster for the base of the pool and light green slate for the pool's coping.

"The area is so small, you need neutral colors to make it seem as big as possible," he explains. The colors also help structures to recede into the background, making plants the center of attention.

Flowering dogwoods, 'Savannah' holly, live oaks, yaupons, and Japanese maples furnish both shade and privacy. Hibiscus and caladiums add splashes of seasonal color to the rest of the garden.

LEFT *French doors and sidelights make this lovely walled garden an extension of the living room. Muted colors ease structures into the background, allowing the garden to take center stage.*

ABOVE *A wood and brick fence, trees, and plantings of dogwoods offer afternoon shade and provide privacy from nearby neighbors.*

TOP RIGHT *Hidden by gray river stones, a drain between the house and pool deck keeps runoff out of the pool.*

RIGHT *French doors and a flagstone pool deck helped to update this backyard. The gray, green, and brown colors of the flagstone complement the mottled tones of existing brick walls.*

A WELCOME CHANGE
Dressing up the driveway

Creating parking space in front of a house does not always mean sacrificing the front yard to sterile concrete. Design contractor William Leathers and landscape architect Steve Harrell show how to do it right.

This new driveway greets family and friends with a brick herringbone-pattern "welcome mat." "We call it a rumble strip, because you feel it when you drive over it," Harrell says. "You know you've arrived."

Although parking in front of the house is logical, it can often detract from a home and its curb appeal. Here, a handsome brick wall solves the problem by screening the parking area from the street. It also blocks the house from the glaring headlights of approaching street traffic.

Large trees by the street also screen the house. "We had to take extra care when building the wall to save the two existing oaks," Leathers says. "All the trenching for the wall footing was done by hand." Setting the brick welcome mat into a bed of sand without mortar allows water and air to reach the tree roots.

The landscape design also includes a brick landing and walkway leading to the front door. Beside the walkway, a crepe myrtle surrounded by low, easy-care plantings helps to balance the proportions of the home's high-pitched roof.

ABOVE *A 'Natchez' crepe myrtle highlights the entry and tones down the steeply pitched roof. Entry plantings include liriope, juniper, and wintercreeper euonymus.*

LEFT *A brick "welcome mat" at the front of the driveway greets guests and, with its sound, announces their arrival as they drive over the mat.*

ABOVE RIGHT *This brick wall helps screen the parking area from the street. By design, the wall jogs around a large oak shade tree to avoid damaging the roots.*

RIGHT *A bubble awning brightens the entry and protects the front door from rain.*

FLOWER AND WATER
A natural fusion

It's hard to imagine a prettier place for a pool and garden than this one, which rests along the banks of San Domingo Creek on Maryland's Eastern Shore. The credits go to landscape designer Jan Kirsh of Bozeman, Maryland, and building designer Clint Wadsworth of Royal Oak, Maryland.

Environmental rules prohibited placing the pool at the most logical spot, between the house and the creek. This forced Kirsh to locate it in the front yard in full view of the drive. She created privacy by extending a hedgerow of native eastern red cedars and adding bayberries behind the pool. Then she surrounded the pool with flowers, grasses, shrubs, and vines to tie it in with the rest of the landscape. The plantings frame the creek view, while bluestone pavers at the pool's far end form a point that draws your eye through an opening in the trees out to the creek beyond.

The cottage-style pool house was Wadsworth's design. "I tried to capture the relaxed, comfortable, and unassuming flavor of the Eastern Shore," he says. Wadsworth added a small pavilion to unify the pool house and garden, leaving an open section of pressure-treated pine rafters as a trellis. A lush trumpet honeysuckle now makes its home there.

LEFT *The combination of butterfly bush, Russian sage (Perovskia), purple heart, and crepe myrtle reflects the owner's preference for the cool shades of blue, purple, and pink.*

ABOVE *Thanks to its cottage-style pool house, shimmering water, and colorful plants, this garden has a calm and refreshing look. A hedgerow of eastern red cedars behind the pool house provides privacy.*

RIGHT *Ornamental grasses mulched with gravel and river stones add an oriental touch. Contrasting textures create a handsome effect year-round.*

DESIGN TIPS

❧ Native trees and shrubs tie a garden to the land, giving it a sense of belonging.

❧ Arrange sitting areas where afternoon shade and breezes cool the garden in summer. Vines often provide shade more quickly than trees.

❧ If your site has a terrific natural feature such as a creek, use the garden to enhance rather than compete with it.

RUSTIC CHARM
A glade in the shade

Tucked into a grove of hardwoods, Hilda Bolin's cabin provides respite from the summer heat and sun. The garden that sweeps in front of the house brims with shade-

loving plants, as well as special touches that reflect the gardener's personality. When Hilda is expecting company, she cuts flowers from the garden and sets the arrangements outside. An open gate adorned with a container of freshly cut hydrangea blossoms is an irresistible invitation for guests to step into the garden.

Chip-bark paths, peppered by rocks and moss-covered logs gathered from elsewhere on the property, weave through the front yard. Ferns among the wood and rock make the area look like a lush glade.

"Plants are a lot like people," Hilda says. "Some are real fussy, while others are easy and just take care of them-

selves." She keeps her design simple by relying on plants that are at home in this site. Big sweeps of impatiens planted in stacked-stone beds offer bright, sunny color in dense shade, and hostas and ferns make the garden seem cool even on the hottest summer days. Hydrangeas, mahonias, and nandinas create a handsome backdrop for colorful annuals and perennials.

FAR LEFT *Surrounded by impatiens, this rustic chair made from bent willow branches offers a comfortable place to sit and relax.*

ABOVE *This cabin and garden are perfect examples of a landscape that incorporates its natural surroundings. Mulched paths pass by ferns and flowers, moss-covered logs, and native plants before converging at the front door of the cabin.*

LEFT *Above a stacked-stone wall, leatherleaf mahonias and a sweep of red impatiens thrive in the shade of native hardwoods.*

TOP RIGHT *An open gate festooned with cut blossoms of oakleaf hydrangea invites visitors in for a stroll in the garden.*

RIGHT *A galvanized watering can springs to life with cut daylilies, Queen Anne's lace, and the handsome veiny foliage of hardy begonias.*

LOUISIANA LEGACY
No longer raising cane

Carved from cane fields and bordered by a rustic picket fence, this south Louisiana garden bursts with a lavish mix of color and texture.

Garden designer Michael Hopping makes his home here on the banks of the Mississippi in an overseer's cottage just downriver from Homestead plantation. Michael designed his garden with order and abandon. An underestimation of how much work was involved got him started, but a streak of perfectionism kept him going.

Perpendicular gravel pathways edged in brick give structure to the profusion of flowers that spill from the beds. Clipped boxwoods anchor the corners and add formal contrast, an idea borrowed from the English. Hollyhocks stand at attention, while poppies, society garlic, and lilies scamper through the beds like children playing tag.

A tin-roofed toolshed, which was converted from an 1850s privy, provides a focal point in the garden. "It's so flat here, especially this close to the river," Michael explains, "[that] the toolshed adds something tall to the garden."

ABOVE *Just behind a levee on the Mississippi River grows a wondrous garden. Lush in both plantings and design detail, the garden seems much larger than it really is.*

RIGHT *Lilies-of-the-Nile surround a sugar-kettle fountain. At one time, kettles like this one were used to boil sugarcane juice into syrup.*

RIGHT *Pathways and views align on an axis with one another, maintaining structure in this casual garden. An arch of bent iron tubing, designed by the owner, frames the view into the garden from the front gate.*

BELOW *A metal rooster watches over a garden bordered by a boxwood hedge.*

DESIGN TIPS

❧ Use structures, such as arbors and outbuildings, to add height to a flat landscape.

❧ Strong bed lines and edged paths keep a garden that's overflowing from looking unruly.

❧ Use garden ornaments that reflect your region's culture and history.

RIGHT *Potted boxwoods and the peaked gateposts of a cedar fence frame a French olive jar and hollyhocks. The jar's porous surface adds earthy tones to the cool pinks and mauves of the garden. A toolshed, once a mid-19th-century privy, adds height and serves as the garden's focal point.*

Alice Williams garden
Atlanta, Georgia

PLANNING YOUR GARDEN

As you look out at a barren or unruly yard, the prospect of transforming it into something beautiful may seem utterly daunting. But before you start, close your eyes and picture your ideal garden. Does it contain a gazebo, terrace, and pool for lively outdoor entertaining? Or is it secluded and serene, with a hammock swinging beneath a wisteria-covered arbor? Is it untamed and exuberant, with flowers jockeying for space and roses rambling at will? Or tailored and refined, with a white picket fence framing a manicured lawn?

Whatever your ideal garden may be, the following pages will help you turn it into reality. You'll learn to see the world through the eyes of a garden designer as you analyze your site, settle on a style, implement basic design principles, and build your plan. With these fundamentals behind you, you're well on your way to the garden of your dreams.

PLANNING WITH A PURPOSE

When designing or renovating a home garden, your first task should be to consider the kinds of activities you hope to enjoy there. Do you like to eat and entertain outdoors? Do you prefer to swim or to play basketball? Do your children need a spacious lawn on which to play? Or are you more interested in relaxing in peace and quiet?

Be realistic about the potential of your site to accommodate your favorite pastimes. A steep slope, for example, isn't suited to soccer. Raising ostriches in suburbia isn't practical or legal. And few neighbors will appreciate looking out on a concrete pad that's a permanent home to your collection of old cars.

Family demands

Your family's needs, now and in the future, will dictate many aspects of your design. If your family includes small children or elderly or disabled persons, you'll need to plan for safety and ease of movement. Secure walls, fences, and railings can safeguard people against danger posed by swimming pools, driveways, busy streets, and elevated decks. Ramps and graded paths with smooth, firm surfaces will ease the passage for the disabled and infirm. Night lighting will enhance safe movement, as well as discourage intruders.

To make the garden more comfortable you may have to modify the climate. Well-placed shade trees, tall screens, and arbors can offer respite from the summer heat. Fences, walls, and hedges can buffer cold or salt-laden winds.

Gardening goals

Like most gardeners, you probably have both aesthetic and practical aims. You might wish to beautify your yard with luxuriant shrub borders and flower beds. You might long for a vegetable and herb garden or even a backyard orchard. Or you may need a home for special collections of roses, hostas, or daylilies.

Beauty and functionality can also be incorporated into your garden structures, some of which can serve dual purposes, such as elevated decks with storage underneath. Well-designed work areas, terraces, fences, and walks will ultimately increase the value of your home.

But before doing anything, think hard about how much upkeep you're willing to undertake. Spacious lawns, swimming pools, clipped hedges, and rose and vegetable gardens all need considerable maintenance. An automatic irrigation system can save many hours of hand-watering. But there's no way to automate raking, mowing, fertilizing, pruning, and spraying.

A WELL-DESIGNED LANDSCAPE

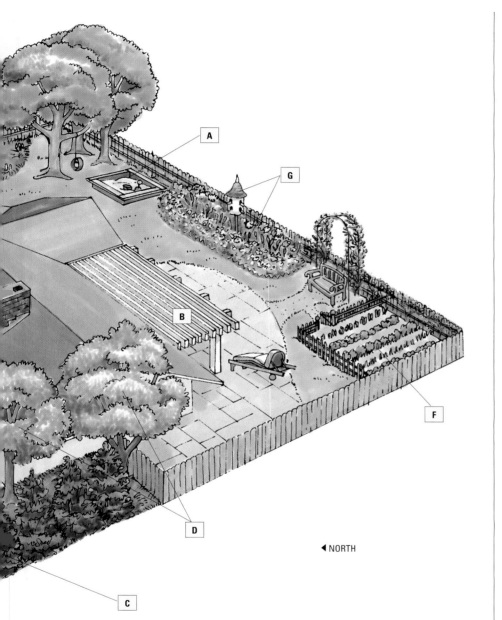

◄ NORTH

LANDSCAPING GOALS

A. Provide recreation. A children's play area is sited under cooling shade trees. The spot is in clear sight of the kitchen and the deck.

B. Invite entertaining. A covered arbor is really an extension of the living room. It creates a shaded, sheltered space to dine with friends or just relax and look out on the garden.

C. Create privacy. A row of screening shrubs shields the driveway and front entrance from the neighbor's property. Low fences serve as boundaries without blocking desirable views.

D. Modify the climate. Large deciduous trees block the southern sun in summer but allow the winter sun to warm the interior after leaves have dropped. The arbor also provides cooling shade.

E. Beautify the property. Specimen trees and flower beds by the front entryway create an attractive view from the street, soften the lines of the house and wall, and add color.

F. Grow a kitchen garden. A small vegetable plot along the south side of the rear yard offers an ideal spot for raising herbs and vegetables, and is convenient to the kitchen.

G. Attract wildlife. Plantings, native and otherwise, and a birdhouse lure birds and butterflies. The bench supplies a secluded place for viewing.

H. Reduce maintenance. A smaller lawn saves work and water. Low-care ground covers and and liberal mulch throughout the garden are good replacements.

UNDERSTANDING YOUR SITE

Every property presents unique opportunities. But along with them come unique challenges. You'll need to realistically assess these, then find a way to balance them with the features you want in your garden. The following pages on soils and microclimates will help you identify the important natural features of your property.

You'll also need to evaluate any manmade structures and existing plantings, especially trees and shrubs. Sketching out these features on paper gives you a "base plan," which forms the foundation of your design.

You'll save yourself many hours with your tape measure by locating any of the following:

∾ a deed map that gives actual dimensions and the orientation of your property

∾ a topographical plan, with contour lines showing the exact shape and elevation of your site

∾ architectural plans giving the locations of all buildings

If you can't find these, you'll need to measure your property and transfer the dimensions to your base plan, preferably on graph paper. Use a scale of ¼ inch for 1 foot.

After you finish, slip the base plan under a sheet of tracing paper and sketch designs to your heart's content. This lets you try out a variety of ideas before actually committing yourself to those things you really want in your garden.

Don't dig yet

If you've just moved into a new home, don't reach for your pick and shovel right away. Try to live with your yard for a full year. You'll get to know your garden throughout the seasons and can experiment with various plants. Thorough knowledge of your site will produce a better plan.

Of course, sometimes it pays to be ruthless. There's no need to design your garden around a scraggly tree or an ugly fountain, just because it's already there.

A final point—if you decide to develop just one area of the yard at a time, think about how the changes will affect the rest of your garden. For example, a row of tall hollies might supply immediate privacy. But they might also shade out your newly planted flower bed.

Base Plan Basics

Mark the following on your base plan:

∾ Compass directions to help you determine the patterns of sun and shade (see page 113).

∾ Boundaries and dimensions of the lot.

∾ Outlines of the house and other existing structures.

∾ Locations of all doors and windows of the house.

∾ Eaves, overhangs, downspouts, and drains.

∾ Existing paved areas.

∾ Locations of easements and setback boundaries.

∾ Existing plants, noting size, shape, and general condition.

∾ Direction of slopes, including high and low points.

∾ Direction of prevailing winds throughout the year.

A BASE PLAN

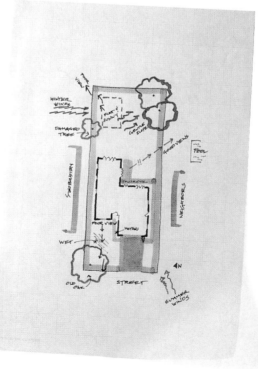

ANALYZING YOUR GARDEN

Here are some of the problems and opportunities presented by this site.

A. The front view from the living room is of noisy street traffic, passersby, and parked cars.

B. Damp pockets of soil can limit plant choices.

C–D. Warm air blows in summer from the southwest **(C)**; winter winds blow from the north **(D)**.

E. Concrete terraces reflect excessive heat into the home; they are too small for entertaining.

F. Neighbors' homes are very close to the property line, thus limiting privacy.

G. Gently sloping land and existing trees could be incorporated into the garden design.

H. Open, sunny areas in the rear and on the south side yard offer space for a swimming pool or for sun-loving plantings.

I–J. Rear views from the patio are pleasant in one direction **(I)** but unpleasant in another **(J)**.

NORTH ▶

Other Considerations

Local zoning or other laws may restrict or prohibit your planned construction. Consult the following documents, agencies, or individuals before proceeding with your design and note any relevant restrictions on your base plan.

YOUR PROPERTY DEED:

Exact location of property lines.

Easements or rights-of-way.

Building restrictions.

Tree removal restrictions.

YOUR LOCAL BUILDING OR PLANNING DEPARTMENT:

Setback requirements.

Height limitations for fences, buildings, or other structures.

Lot coverage guidelines.

Safety codes for pools and spas.

Requirements for firewalls between adjacent buildings.

Open burning restrictions for firepits.

Building codes for construction.

Tree or historic preservation ordinances.

Building permits for fences, retaining walls above 30 inches in height, other garden structures, and electrical or plumbing work.

YOUR LOCAL UTILITY COMPANY:

Location and depth of underground utility lines.

Building or planting limitations under power lines.

YOUR WATER COMPANY:

Restrictions on water use for irrigation, pools, and water features.

YOUR NEIGHBORS:

Their views into your property (and your view into theirs) and your mutual need for privacy and quiet, sunlight and air flow.

Their concerns about existing trees and other plants, structures, and shared walks or driveways.

Homeowners' association restrictions.

SOILS OF THE SOUTH

Nothing determines which plants you can grow more than your soil. Fortunately, soil isn't like the weather—if you don't like it, you can change it.

Soil is classified according to the particles that comprise it. Sandy soil has large particles, contains lots of air, and doesn't compact. Water and nutrients run right through it. Clay soil, on the other hand, has tiny particles. It holds water so tightly it forces out air, compacts easily, and dries hard as a brick. Silty soil has intermediate-size particles and properties.

For most garden plants, the perfect soil is loam—a light, crumbly mixture of nearly equal amounts of sand, clay, and silt with a good bit of organic matter added. Organic matter loosens heavy clay soil, allowing penetration of water and air. It also improves the water- and nutrient-holding capacity of sandy soil.

But soil texture isn't the whole story. The map at right, prepared with help from USDA's Natural Resources Conservation Service, shows the regions where more than 25 percent of the land is likely to have problems with soil chemistry (excess acidity or alkalinity) or soil structure (hardpan, caliche, or bedrock close to the surface).

Soil pH

One of the most important measurements of the soil is its pH. The pH measures acidity or alkalinity on a scale of 0 to 14. A pH of 7 is neutral; everything below that is acid and everything above it is alkaline. Each plant prefers a certain pH, but most adapt to a range of between 5.5 to 7.5. Soils with a pH below 5 or above 8 seriously restrict the availability of soil nutrients and make things tough for plants.

Soils east of the Mississippi tend to be acid, while those west tend to be alkaline. One reason for this is that it rains more in the Southeast, which washes sodium and other alkaline minerals out of the soil. Another is that huge deposits of limestone exist in the Southwest, and limestone is alkaline.

Each region has its surprises, though. Eastern Texas around Tyler has acid soil. Pockets of Alabama, Tennessee, Kentucky, Georgia, Florida, and Missouri are alkaline. So the surest way to determine the pH of your soil is to test it.

Just because your soil has an undesirable pH doesn't mean you're stuck with it. You can add lime to overly acid soil and sulfur to overly alkaline soil. But adding amendments isn't a permanent cure; you'll have to repeat this periodically. Therefore, the best low-maintenance solution is to choose plants that enjoy your existing soil.

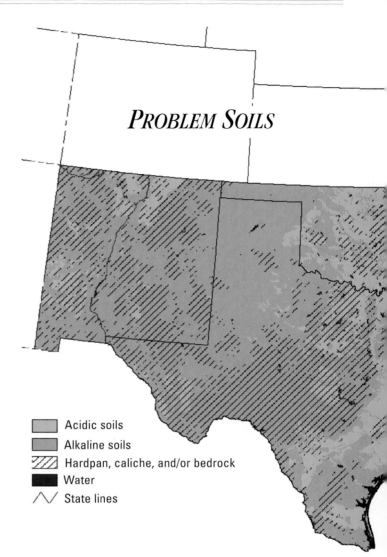

PROBLEM SOILS

- ▨ Acidic soils
- ▨ Alkaline soils
- ▨ Hardpan, caliche, and/or bedrock
- ■ Water
- ∧ State lines

That awful clay

Also known as adobe or gumbo, clay is many a gardener's curse. Ranging in color from red to black to gray to brown, it produces a heavy, poorly draining soil that's hard to work and even harder for plants to grow in. When it's wet, plants rot. When it's dry, plants shrivel. But there are proven ways to greatly improve clay soil over time.

First, work in plenty of organic matter—chopped leaves, shredded bark, composted manure, grass clippings, garden compost—every year. Organic matter binds clay particles together into larger particles, allowing air, water, nutrients, and plant roots to penetrate between them. Second, till in lots of coarse builder's sand or gravel. If you can't amend your soil each year, build raised beds above the clay to which you add good soil.

The colored areas on this map indicate regions where more than 25 percent of the land has certain soil characteristics.

Areas designated as acidic soils are dominated by soils that have an average pH of less than 7.0 in the upper 20 inches of soil. Areas designated as alkaline soils are dominated by soils having average pH above 7.0 in the upper 20 inches.

Areas symbolized as hardpan, caliche, and/or bedrock occur where more than 25 percent of the soils have a root-restricting layer, such as hardpan or bedrock, in the upper 40 inches of soil.

Hardpan

Hardpan, known as caliche to Southwestern gardeners, is an impermeable layer of earth that can be up to several yards thick. It usually forms in areas that get just enough rain to dissolve minerals and carry them just below the surface, but not enough to wash them out altogether. These minerals then cement the soil together. A hardpan can also be formed by repeatedly tilling clay soil while it's wet.

The closer a hardpan is to the surface, the more trouble it causes. It prevents roots from reaching nutrients and water, resulting in stunted growth or even death. Areas with hardpan within 40 inches of the soil surface are shown on the map.

Areas that may have impermeable bedrock within 40 inches of the soil surface are also shown on the map. Although you can loosen hardpan with a lot of work, it's impossible to break up bedrock. The addition of plenty of topsoil may be the solution. As with clay soil, you may also want to build raised beds for favored garden plants.

MASTERING MICROCLIMATES

Almost every gardener knows the frustration of having a favorite plant freeze or fry, while the same plant thrives in the neighbor's garden across the street. This sorry event is proof of the effect of microclimates.

Microclimates result from a combination of factors, including the path and angle of the sun, season of the year, proximity of water, topography, and wind patterns. Most gardens produce several microclimates—areas that stay a little warmer or cooler, wetter or drier, more or less windy than others. Because these areas determine what you can grow and how and when you can enjoy the garden, understanding how they work should be a vital part of your planning.

Air movement

Warm air rises and cool air sinks. Thus, cool air tends to pool in low spots and back up behind obstacles such as hedges and walls, creating frost pockets. Slopes are the last places in a garden to freeze, because cold air constantly drains away and mixes with warmer air as it goes. Flat areas, by contrast, cool quickly as heat radiates upward, especially during clear, still nights. Overhead structures, such as arbors and overhangs, reduce this heat loss and often protect the plants beneath them from frost.

Soil moisture

Soil moisture has a profound effect on the local climate and growing conditions. Moist soil in winter helps insulate tender plants, because as water freezes, it gives off heat. Also, cold doesn't penetrate moist soil as deeply as dry soil. Moreover, moist soil cools its surroundings in summer as water evaporates. That's why summer heat records frequently occur during extended droughts. The lesson here is that sufficient soil moisture reduces temperature extremes.

Garden structures and paving

As gardeners with courtyards can tell you, what grows inside the garden wall is usually a lot different than what grows outside. This is because in addition to blocking cold winds, walls store heat during the day (especially if they're made from dark-colored material) and release it at night, keeping the enclosed garden warmer. Dark-colored paving stores heat too. As a result, plants growing near walls or paving tend to survive the winter better than those in exposed spots.

Sun and shade

In summer, the morning sun rises in the northeast, arcs high across the southern sky, and sets to the northwest. This long passage means extra hours of daylight, which benefits many vegetables, annuals, perennials, and flowering trees and shrubs. By contrast, the winter sun rises in the southeast, passes low across the southern sky, and sets to the southwest. Days are much shorter, which triggers the blooming of short-day plants, such as Christmas cactus and bougainvillea.

That shifting sun angle means longer shadows in winter and shorter ones in summer. Thus, plants hidden in shade in winter often step into the sun in summer. The pattern of sun and shade also varies according to the time of day. At noon, when the sun is highest, shade is harder to find than good barbecue in Brooklyn. So you need to plan for these changes, lest one day you find a prized, shade-loving plant just stewing in the sun.

Exposure

Slopes that drop toward the south or southwest get more heat and light during the day than those that drop toward the north or northeast. Similarly, walls that run east and west reflect extra heat and sunlight onto plants growing on their south side and less on plants growing on the north side. Heat-lovers, such as crepe myrtle and lantana, flourish in full sun. But the soil dries much faster there, so provide a little extra water.

COLD-AIR POCKETS

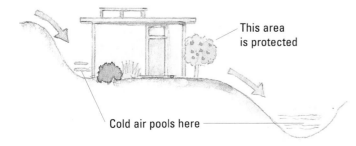

This area is protected

Cold air pools here

Cold air flows downhill like water, and "puddles" in basins. It can be dammed by a barrier such as a house, wall, or fence. So if you build a sunken patio or planting area, you may find yourself shivering, even when higher or more protected surroundings are balmy.

SUN ANGLES

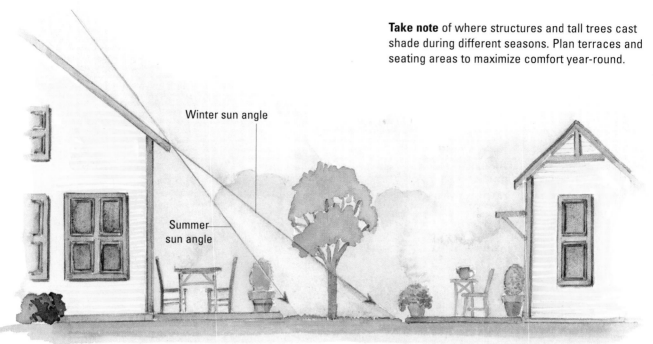

Take note of where structures and tall trees cast shade during different seasons. Plan terraces and seating areas to maximize comfort year-round.

Winter sun angle

Summer sun angle

NORTH ▶

SUMMER AND WINTER SHADOWS

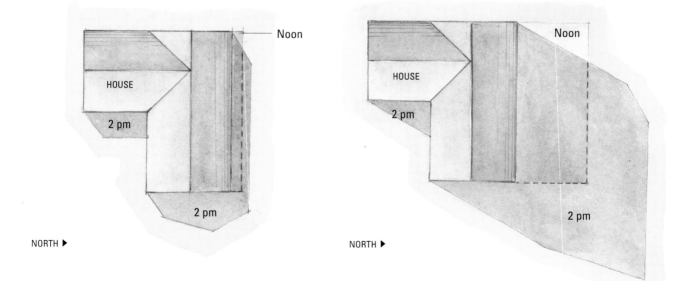

NORTH ▶

NORTH ▶

In summer, only those areas immediately beside the house are shaded. Note how features of the house, such as the roof, affect the shadows below.

Winter shadows are much longer and can shift dramatically within the space of a few hours. Compare the shadow cast at noon to that cast at 2 pm.

SOUTHERN GARDEN STYLES

Okay, you've evaluated your site. Now it's time to determine your garden's overall style. Southern gardeners have long been inspired by cultural influences from Britain, France, Italy, Africa, and Asia, as well as the South's own agrarian past. Combined with the variety of climates and natural landscapes found in the South, the result is a series of garden styles unique to our region.

Your chosen style will affect every aspect of your garden's design—the plants and how they're combined; any structures and special features you add; and the materials you use to build fences, walls, gates, walks, and paving. So when considering which style to adopt, resist the urge to mix and match. Although blending elements of different styles can sometimes be effective, for most of us it's better to develop a clear, unifying theme.

Also, select a style that is appropriate to your climate and compatible with the architecture of your house. Certain home designs suggest a particular garden style. For example, formal gardens may suit a large Georgian home, but look out of place around a simple Craftsman bungalow. Other architectural styles are more accommodating: a contemporary house can look just fine surrounded by a garden based on a tropical, cottage, or drought-tolerant theme.

Sometimes the materials from which the house is built dictate the garden's style. A home built from logs or native stone, for instance, may call for a rustic, naturalistic garden rather than a regimented, formal plan.

Formal gardens relate strongly to the architecture of the house, usually Georgian, Mediterranean, French, or Victorian. The symmetry of the plantings reflects a similar symmetry in the house design. Here, the precise placement of the gate, fountain, and statue emphasizes an axial line with obvious focal points. Sheared evergreens line formal parterres, creating a strong, regular pattern.

A. Naturalistic gardens exemplify the authentic look of their region without strictly adhering to a palette of native plants. Exotic (non-native) plants are included, as long as they blend with the native flora that reflects the colors of the season and the casualness of the wild. In the Alabama garden at left, native Piedmont azaleas and flowering dogwoods mingle with non-native daffodils, mondo grass, and lenten rose.

B. Rustic gardens recall simpler, less pretentious times, when people gardened for enjoyment or for homegrown produce, rather than to impress the neighbors. The overall mood is casual and relaxed with colorful, untamed plantings. Natural materials, such as unpainted wood and local stone, provide structure. Found objects, such as old tools, lanterns, and watering cans, add personality.

C. Drought-tolerant gardens feature trees, shrubs, grasses, perennials, and other plants that thrive with very little water. Although these gardens are most common in Texas, the vast array of drought-tolerant plants makes them possible just about anywhere. Mass plantings, mulched beds, and small lawns help minimize water use. Using plants indigenous to the region often creates a more pleasing effect.

A. Woodland gardens take advantage of the shade and feeling of solidity provided by existing trees. The understory may consist of a variety of shade-tolerant shrubs or simply be a blanket of wild-flowers or bulbs. Maintenance is minimal, consisting of occasional raking or pruning and watering during droughts. Paths are unpaved and structures are usually wood or stone.

B. Traditional gardens take their cue from the restraint, order, and simplicity of colonial landscape architecture. Notable examples are the gardens of Colonial Williamsburg, such as the one shown here. Flowers are restricted to the back yard and flower beds and lawns are formal. Foundation plantings are minimal and symmetrical, designed to show off the house. A white picket fence is common.

C. Tropical gardens teem with exotic plants flaunting bold, lush foliage and striking, colorful flowers. They're found in areas with very mild winters, high humidity, and ample rainfall. Dense plantings mimic the rain forest—vines might snake up palm trees, while orchids and bromeliads clutch tightly to towering trunks. A water feature is typically found in the garden. This style suits both contemporary and Victorian homes.

D. Cottage gardens abound with colors, shapes, sizes, and textures. Formal lines and symmetry give way to beds overflowing with dozens of plants, seedlings sprouting in pathways, and vines clambering over fences and trellises. Vibrant, long-lasting color is the goal, rather than "acceptable" color combinations. This style emphasizes individual tastes.

E. Coastal gardens must endure challenging conditions, such as constant wind, salt air, and sandy soil. Together, these can desiccate tender specimens, so coastal plants must be tough. Many sport leathery or waxy leaves and stems to reduce water loss. Natives such as century plant, live oak, cabbage palm, yaupon, and wax myrtle are good choices.

LANGUAGE OF LANDSCAPE DESIGN

Every discipline employs its own jargon, and the field of garden design is no different. To understand the principles underlying a well-planned garden, it helps to familiarize yourself with some of the basic design terms used by landscape architects, garden designers, and garden writers. Some terms are used throughout the broad field of design. "Focal point" and "symmetry," for example, are often bandied about by architects, interior designers, and graphic artists alike. Other terms, such as "borrowed scenery," are specific to landscape architecture. As you read this book, you will understand these terms as they are used to describe various garden features. When you create your own garden, you'll find it easier to communicate with professionals if you use their lingo. (You can also use it to impress your friends.)

Symmetry exists when matching elements are balanced on either side of a central axis, most commonly seen in formal gardens like this one. Asymmetry occurs when those elements are different, which may be found in both formal and informal gardens.

A. A focal point is an object, such as this fountain, which draws the eye due to its placement in the garden. In formal gardens, a focal point is usually placed in the center or at the end of an axis. In less formal gardens, a focal point may appear anywhere, but its distinctiveness attracts attention and draws you closer.

B. An axis is the centerline of a view or walk. Here, it runs through the archway and reflecting pond to the distant vista. Elements often align on either side of an axis. In informal gardens, the axis may be a visual line between two significant elements.

C. An accent draws attention to itself by contrasting boldly with its surroundings, as this 'Crimson Queen' Japanese maple stands out from its neighbors. Accents add variety and depth to a composition and emphasize a particular spot in the garden.

D. The texture of plants refers to the relative shapes and sizes of their leaves, branches, and flowers. Textures may be fine or coarse, delicate or bold. Using plants with contrasting textures, such as these caladiums underplanted with Asian star jasmine, creates interest and impact.

PRINCIPLES OF LANDSCAPE DESIGN

Every good garden owes its success to the following basic design principles. These "rules" have proven themselves again and again, and they apply to all areas and levels of garden design, from the most elaborately detailed arbor to the simplest of borders.

You can learn a lot by studying gardens that you visit or see in magazines, as well as those illustrated on these pages and throughout this book. Try to relate the elements that make these gardens work to the design principles illustrated here. Then keep them in mind as you plan your own garden.

In a well-designed garden, no one plant, structure, or feature is completely dominant. Rather, all the parts work together to establish a sense of unity. Make sure that all elements—structures, beds, borders, and water features—are in proportion to the rest of the garden and in scale with the size of the house and property. By repeating

certain plants, colors, and materials, you can bring rhythm and emphasis to the design. And you can create a feeling of harmony in the garden by balancing simple lines and forms with a variety of different plants and materials.

A. Repetition and rhythm carry your eye throughout a garden. They are especially important when a garden contains several distinct areas and a wide variety of plants. In this garden, repeating the upright conifers amid a complex mixed border establishes a unifying theme. In addition, these multiple vertical accents draw your attention from place to place.

B. Simplicity is the art of restraint. It keeps an elegant, understated scene from becoming cluttered and unfocused. Here a simple vine-covered arbor beckons visitors into the garden beyond. Flowers at its base add a welcome touch of color, but don't detract from the arbor's overriding purpose.

C. Unity of design is the essence of this garden. Serpentine sweeps of annuals, hydrangeas, ground covers, and brick edging tie together the various plantings and areas of this front yard. Without such unity, the garden could easily look jumbled, chaotic, and unplanned. With it, the design is immediately discernible and pleasing to the eye.

D. Scale refers to the balance between sizes of various landscape elements, including the house, walk, fence, containers, and plantings. No one of these features should overpower the others. In this garden, the modest-size house calls for low plantings, a small lawn, and a single, medium-size shade tree out front.

E. Balance doesn't necessarily depend on symmetry. Rather, it results when adjoining areas of the design carry equal visual weight. Here, the addition of a two-story covered porch created an asymmetrical front with the original house dominating. But adding three large yaupons in front of the covered porch helped to balance both sides of the house.

TRICKS AND TECHNIQUES

Hand-in-hand with sound design principles go an array of techniques used by professionals to create specific effects. Some make the garden a more comfortable and livable space. Others fool the eye into perceiving the garden in a certain way.

Many of these ideas are quite basic, such as taking into account the size of the human body when designing garden structures. For example, building comfortable steps means considering the average human stride when sizing the treads and risers (see page 179). Similarly, pathways need to be at least 4 feet wide, to accommodate two people walking side-by-side, and built-in seating for decks must be 16 or 17 inches deep in order to be comfortable.

Other techniques achieve their purpose by altering our sense of space. They do this by manipulating materials, colors, and textures; taking advantage of a change in elevation; blocking views and opening vistas; and dividing a large space into a series of smaller ones.

Help your garden realize its full potential by employing some of these tricks. You'll find them especially helpful if you're renovating or upgrading an existing garden or if a particular part of your garden has never really made you happy.

A. Frame a view. There's no question where your eyes are drawn in this South Carolina garden. The arbor in the foreground acts as a picture frame, focusing attention on the distant chairs, birdhouse, and flowers. In fact, the framed view becomes its own composition.

B. Define space. Most people instinctively feel uncomfortable in boundless, open space. They need borders to shape and limit the view, reducing the space to a human scale. In this garden, sweeps of azaleas divide a large lawn into smaller sections. Each section feels cozier and supports its own range of activities.

122

C. Create a little mystery. One of the joys of exploring a garden is wondering what surprise lies just around the corner. By not revealing all the garden's secrets at once, you can create a sense of anticipation. Here, an inviting bench awaits at the top of the steps. Is there a pot of flowers at its foot or a water feature beyond? You must ascend the steps to find out.

D–E. Change the elevation. This is a marvelous tool for both creating depth and producing different viewpoints in smaller (D) and larger (E) spaces. A garden design that is concealed from below may reveal itself in a surprising way when viewed from above. Narrow or shallow spaces can suddenly seem larger, as each level assumes its own identity.

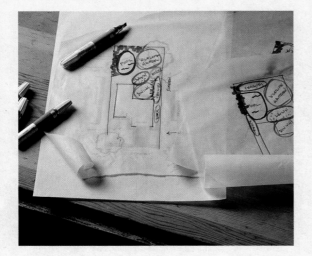

Bubble Diagrams

To experiment with various arrangements of space in your garden, try the designer's trick of using simple "bubble diagrams." These quick studies can be drawn on tracing paper over the base plan you have made of your property (see page 108). Each bubble (which can be a rough circle, square, or oval) should represent a particular activity or garden space that you hope to incorporate into the design, and each should be approximately the size and shape needed. Make the bubbles different colors to distinguish them from each other (use green for planting areas, blue for a pool, and brown for decks and terraces, for instance).

Let the bubbles overlap where activity spaces will merge with each other. Where spaces need to be separated, draw a line to suggest a screen or barrier. Simple cross-hatching can designate areas that need overhead protection from the sun. Show steps as sets of parallel lines and roughly indicate entrances to the house or front yard.

Sketch several versions, considering with each one the microclimates, potential views, and existing features identified on your base plan. Note how well the placement of activities in each diagram takes advantage of the warm spots and shady areas in your garden. Look for smooth transitions from one space to the next and address practical issues by including spaces for work, storage, and service areas.

After you have done several diagrams, lay them out and compare the different arrangement of spaces, then settle on the one that will form the basis for your final design.

DESIGNING YOUR GARDEN

Now that you've identified the basic features and found a garden style you like, you are ready to put your creativity to work. The first step is site planning—creating and arranging the activity spaces in your garden. Study carefully how all these spaces relate to the rooms inside your home and try to locate the outdoor activity spaces near their indoor counterparts. For example, if young children are a part of the family, place their outdoor play space near a room in the house where you spend a lot of time, so that you can easily keep an eye on them. Organize vegetable and herb gardens near the kitchen, if possible, to make it easy to bring the harvest to the table. Decide whether some areas of the garden should serve multiple functions—whether a sheltered walkway could also house a storage area, for example.

Look at the entire garden and lay out spaces that will flow logically and easily from one to the other. Plan a circulation path that won't require walking through a work area or past the trash cans to get from the terrace to the swimming pool. Settle on an arrangement of planted areas that will permit grouping plants according to their watering needs. As you sketch, you'll begin to make general decisions about the plants and structures you'll need and where they should go. Bubble planning (left) can help you mock up some designs. You'll need to refer frequently to your base plan to remind yourself of site features and conditions.

Odd-shaped lots

Don't worry if your lot isn't a simple rectangle like the one shown previously on page 109. Most homes don't have rectangular lots. In fact, topography and street patterns mean that most lots have somewhat irregular shapes. For example, a cul-de-sac subdivision results in pie-shaped lots with little street frontage and plenty of privacy toward the rear. And steeply sloped lots frequently have unusual boundaries, because some of the land is unbuildable and the house may be built on uneven terrain. However, whatever the size and shape of your lot, the tips and techniques described here will help you make the most of it.

But before you get carried away with the excitement of creating a whole new garden, carefully consider how much time, effort, and money you're willing to pour into it. If the commitment looks daunting, don't despair. Just break the project into stages—most important ones first, less important ones later—and complete them as time and money allow.

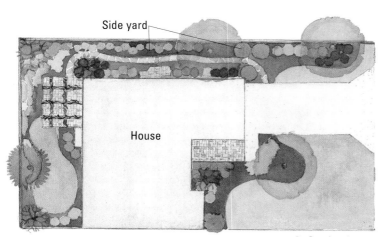

Side yard

House

A. Garden home

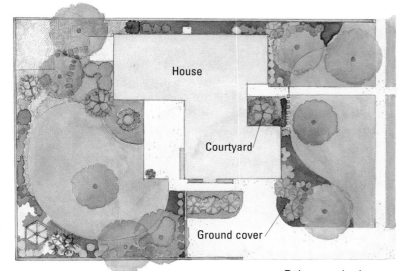

House

Courtyard

Ground cover

B. Large suburban

Fruit trees

C. Cul-de-sac

Work space

Play area

Terrace

House

Shrubs

THREE LOTS, THREE SOLUTIONS

A. Garden home lots typically lack privacy, and, because of their length and narrowness, they can look like bowling alleys. Here, a side yard planting anchored by evergreens adds privacy. Broadleaf evergreens flanking the path at the front corner of the house also block views of the side yard from the front, giving the front yard its own space. Segmenting the lot like this makes the narrow property seem wider. Note, too, that the backyard is more wide than long.

B. Large suburban lots often feature huge, shapeless lawns that merge into those of the neighbors. Here, curving beds of evergreen ground cover border lawns in both front and back, transforming mundane grass areas into dynamic design elements. Ground cover beds in front also guide visitors to an elegant iron gate that marks the entry to a secluded courtyard. Downsizing the lawn in back simplifies maintenance, while still leaving plenty of room for family recreation.

C. Cul-de-sac lots are often shaped like slices of pizza, with narrow street frontage and wide backyards. Dividing such lots into a series of garden rooms, each one hidden from the other, diverts attention from the odd shape. Here, densely planted shrub beds in the front yard border a gracefully curving lawn, stopping your eye. In back, an undulating lawn disguises the property's angular lines. The backyard affords ample room for a variety of needs, including a terrace, children's play area, perennial beds, small fruit orchard, and a work area.

TOOLS OF

A. Square plan

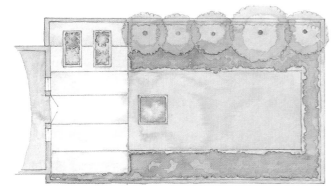

B. Rectangular plan

C. Circular plan

Once your experiments with bubble diagrams result in a preliminary sketch, lay a clean sheet of tracing paper on top of it. On this sheet, begin drawing the various elements of your final design—paved areas, walls or fences, arbors, lawns, pools, flower and shrub beds, and even dog runs. This schematic drawing will look rough at first, but will gradually take shape as you continue.

Working with shapes

At this point, keep in mind two tricks of the garden designer. First, work with clear, simple shapes. Second, relate those shapes to the lines of your house. A design consisting of such familiar shapes as rectangles, squares, circles, and curves is a lot easier to make sense of than one dominated by trapezoids, hexagons, and abstract lines. Repeating a familiar shape brings simplicity and order to your design, unifying beds, borders, paving, and other features. To add interest, you can vary the sizes of shapes you work with or let them overlap. But don't use too many different shapes or you'll end up with a very busy design.

ONE GARDEN, THREE WAYS

A–C. These simple plans were created for the same basic lot using one of three different geometric shapes (square, rectangle, or circle) to guide the design. Each design presents a similar arrangement of paved terrace, small lawn area, and planting beds with a mix of ground covers, shrubs, and trees. But the repetition of a different geometric shape gives each design a distinct character.

To follow this approach in your own garden, select a shape that appeals to you. If you choose a square or rectangle, use that shape as a grid module; you can form modules with convenient dimensions such as 3 by 3 feet or 3 by 6 feet, or you can use different sizes for various elements. No grid is needed for circular elements; simply use circles of different diameters, allowing some to overlap and others to stand alone. Whatever shape you use, play with the alignment and position of elements in a symmetrical or asymmetrical arrangement. Eventually you'll settle on one that pleases you.

DESIGN

Using grids

As you gain experience and confidence in drawing a design, you'll find it easier to come up with a finished plan by making use of a grid. A grid consists of squares or rectangles repeated over and over, like the squares on a checkerboard or the bricks in a wall. Graph paper provides a ready-made grid on which you can draw.

Transferring your design to a grid can help you crystallize your thoughts and expedite your decisions. A grid allows you to easily determine the dimensions of planned features, see how they relate to other features, and decide whether they're the right size, the right shape, and in the right spot. With a grid, you can connect elements of the garden to the major architectural features of your house. It also helps you quickly calculate quantities of materials needed for paving, decking, mulching, and sodding.

D. Visualizing a grid

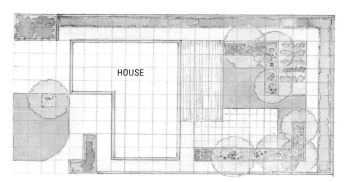

E. Large trellis

VISUALIZING A GRID

D. Connect the garden to the architecture of your house with gridlines that run out to the garden from major features of the house. Here, lines marking the doorways, windows, and corners of wings have been drawn on the plan of the garden. Elements such as flower beds, paved terraces, and pools can then be placed within this irregular grid pattern.

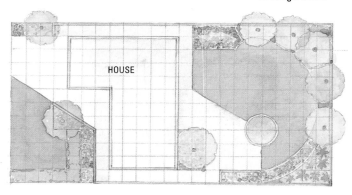

F. Spacious lawn

THREE PLANS FOR A RECTANGULAR LOT

E–G. The gardens at right use the same simple 5-by-5-foot grid to show very different design solutions for a rectangular property. Garden **E** incorporates a large overhead trellis or arbor to shade a portion of the paved terrace, while an L-shaped fence and planting bed screen a vegetable garden, compost area, and work area from view. Garden **F** allows more space for a sweeping lawn, backed up by a curving line of trees to enclose the garden; a round pond echoes the curve of the lawn. Garden **G** places a bold, circular lawn just off center, almost surrounded by a paved surface of varying width.

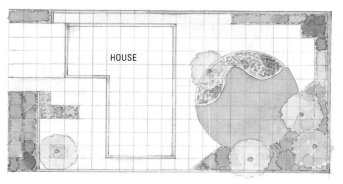

G. Circular lawn

CREATING PRIVACY

Fences can form backdrops, control access, and provide instant privacy.

Movie stars may long for exposure, but we average homeowners need a certain amount of privacy, a time that we can be alone with our thoughts, family, and garden. This privacy can be hard to come by, though, especially in small gardens in neighborhoods devoid of hills and woods. Fortunately, you can provide the privacy that nature didn't.

∾ Planted screens may be formal sheared hedges of boxwood or informal, such as an unclipped screen of hemlock, Leyland cypress, or holly. These all offer a natural means of concealment. For more information on specific plant choices to help create privacy, see page 224.

∾ Berms are artificially created, low mounds that provide grade changes to flat lots. Often planted with ground cover, perennials, or shrubs, they serve to deflect the wind, control runoff, screen unwanted views, and furnish privacy. It's best to have them professionally created. Otherwise you can end up with a poorly sited berm that resembles a pile of soil dumped out by the street.

∾ Fences and walls can be stunning elements that define space, complement the house architecture, direct the eye, block views, and more. Although similar in function, fences are generally less formal than walls (see pages 180–185).

A. Made of brick or stone, walls are solid barriers. But building large ones can be expensive. The homeowner here surmounts the problem by screening the neighbor's house with a combination of a low brick wall with tall Leyland cypresses behind.

B. Planted screens don't have to be evergreen. Densely branched trees and shrubs can provide the necessary separation even after they lose their leaves. The single row of pink crepe myrtles at right effectively partitions one driveway from the other.

PRIVACY MATTERS

A. Screen of clipped hedge blocks wind and neighbor's view; prune up trunks to add height yet allow room for beds below.

B. An arbor covered with vines provides overhead protection and enclosure.

C. Single tree placed at front corner of driveway blocks view of the entrance.

D. Fence with gate offers security.

E. Shrubs and hedges at waist or chest height form partial screen for pool.

F. Bare trunks of mature trees can be concealed with low-level shrubs.

G. Plantings soften the appearance of a solid but plain barrier.

H. Berm in front of house is covered with low-growing shrubs, specimen trees, and ground cover.

BEATING THE HEAT

Heat and humidity are inescapable facts of life for most Southerners. The combination can make the prospect of sitting in the garden about as alluring as spreading hot tar on the highway. You can't change your climate, but with some careful planning, you can change how it makes you feel.

During summer, the sun's force is almost audible and escaping it is the prime task for both man and beast. For many people, the most pressing need for shade is on the south and west sides of the house, because this is where the hot afternoon sun strikes. If you have no existing shade trees, you can cool down the garden by planting trees or adding structures such as arbors or awnings.

Trees are a good choice, providing you can wait a few years for them to grow. For large areas, choose tall, fast-growing trees with ascending branches, such as Japanese zelkova, Chinese pistache, tulip poplar, and red maple. For smaller areas such as patios, choose shorter, less messy trees (see page 210).

But sometimes you just can't wait for relief. In that case, consider building an arbor over a seating area; the rafters will cast broken shade right away. Increase the shade by training vines up the structure.

You feel much more comfortable in a warm, sticky room when there's a fan blowing on you. The same principle of cooling your skin by using moving air to evaporate moisture applies outdoors. So determine the direction of prevailing summer breezes, then orient your garden or sitting area to take advantage of them.

Solid fences, walls, and hedges block air movement. But lattice fences and openwork brick walls allow breezes to pass through. You can also increase air movement by building an elevated deck instead of one at ground level, and installing fans in arbors and gazebos.

During summer hot spells, temperatures downtown often exceed those in the countryside by 5 or 6 degrees—all of that asphalt and concrete in the city radiates heat. The same principle applies in your garden. The more paving or bare soil it contains, the hotter it will be. The more lawn, ground cover, and planting beds it has, the cooler it will be. Light-colored paving doesn't feel as hot underfoot, but it often produces uncomfortable glare. One solution—tint concrete gray or choose gray- or tan-colored gravel and stone.

C

D

A. Spray misters mounted in the roof of this gazebo cool the air during hot summer days.

B. Splashing water from a fountain and water jets makes the pool area seem cooler. Surrounding vegetation also provides welcome shade for non-bathers.

C. Lattice fencing gives needed screening and separation without blocking cooling breezes.

D. Shaded paving, such as this driveway, parking area, and walk, cools the entire area by stopping concrete or asphalt from absorbing as much heat.

DEALING WITH DROUGHT

With the exceptions of west Texas and the Texas and Oklahoma panhandles, the South gets plenty of rain. In fact, Mobile, Alabama, can boast the highest average rainfall (67 inches) of any big continental U.S. city.

But Southern rainstorms tend to be what Andy Griffith calls "frog stranglers"—furious downpours that come every 6 weeks and drop 4 to 5 inches of rain in a single hour. So it pays to make a plan for dry periods.

∾ Downsize the lawn. There's no doubt the lawn guzzles water. Convert some of it to ground cover, mulched beds, natural areas, or meadows. Or, choose an unthirsty lawn grass (see page 236). During droughts, cut the grass ½-inch higher than normal. Water deeply, but not often; set your irrigation system to water once a week for 1½ hours.

Denizens of the desert, cacti and succulents thrive through droughts.

∾ Choose drought-tolerant plants. You'll find a comprehensive list in the *Southern Living Garden Book*.

∾ Mulch, mulch, mulch. Cover bare soil with a 2- to 3-inch layer of mulch to retain moisture.

∾ Concentrate color. Make an impact by placing colorful plants, such as annuals, roses, and potted tropicals, into one area you can water easily. Group thirsty and drought-tolerant plants in separate areas, so you don't have to drag a hose all over the yard.

∾ Buffer drying winds. Group plants on the leeward side of structures and berms. Choose plants with succulent, leathery, scaly, or waxy leaves that lose little moisture; you'll find a complete list in the *Southern Living Garden Problem Solver.*

Winding lane. This combination of unthirsty grasses and stone is carefully constructed, despite its casual air. The blue and tan tones of rosemary and Mexican feather grass *(Stipa tenuissima)* echo those of the stones used in the walkway.

A smaller lawn can mean big water savings. You'll also have to water less if you plant a drought-tolerant grass, such as this buffalo grass lawn in San Antonio. An automatic irrigation system will deliver water in the most efficient way.

A. Succulents, cacti, and pink-flowered verbena provide beautiful shapes and textures in dry-climate gardens. A planting mound raised above the pathway assists drainage. Most of the variety in this arrangement of succulents comes from the different forms and colors of the foliage.

B. Lush entryway. This combination of unthirsty plants and shrubs frames a doorway. The varied colors and textures of the plants belie the planting's easy-care nature.

C. Plants with silvery, gray, or woolly leaves generally need little water. But good drainage is a must. Here, a mound of licorice plant *(Helichrysum petiolare)* repeats the color of a stacked stone wall.

LOW MAINTENANCE

L et's be honest. Most of us enjoy looking at gardens a whole lot more than maintaining them. And why not? The fact is, summers in the South are long, hot, sticky, and buggy. So when faced with the choice of weeding, watering, and being bitten by fire ants or relaxing on the sofa in air-conditioned bliss, most of us choose the latter.

But reducing garden maintenance isn't just a question of comfort. For many of us, it's also an issue of time. Free time is precious in households where both spouses work. Devoting hours to hand-watering and deadheading isn't always time well spent.

This wildflower meadow in Georgia needs little upkeep beyond annual mowing and seeding.

Fortunately, you can create the garden you want without burying yourself in upkeep. Just consider these suggestions.

ᗏ Don't plant more garden than you can easily care for. This is the most common mistake beginning gardeners make. If you find yourself getting up an hour before dawn to water the hydrangeas or neglecting family duties to keep the roses sprayed, your garden is probably too big.

ᗏ Choose plants that are well-adapted to your climate, especially native plants. You'll have less watering, fertilizing, and spraying to do. See the extensive lists of carefree plants and Southern native plants in the *Southern Living Garden Book*. You'll also find a list of trouble-free roses in the *Southern Living Garden Problem Solver.*

❧ Reduce variety. The more different kinds of plants you have in your garden, the more individual needs you'll have to meet. So if time is limited, limit your palette. Also, group together plants that require similar growing conditions. Planting a sun-loving plant next to a shade-loving plant means one of them won't be happy.

❧ Plant in masses. This simplifies maintenance by reducing variety and allowing you to treat large areas the same. Mass plantings also discourage weeds.

❧ Avoid invasive plants that spread by seed, bulblets, or roots. Examples include running bamboo, mint, mimosa, most violets, horsetail *(Equisetum hyemale)*, and star of Bethlehem *(Ornithogalum umbellatum)*. Set them loose in your garden and you'll have to spend forever and a day getting rid of them.

❧ Install an irrigation system, if you can afford it. Then you won't have to drag hoses all over the yard (see pages 358–361).

❧ Reduce the size of your lawn. People spend more time on lawn care than on any other garden activity. Instead, devote more space to ground covers, mulch, and natural or paved areas. Plant ground cover beneath groupings of trees, so you won't have to worm the lawn mower in between trunks.

❧ Forget about large beds of roses or vegetables and long, clipped hedges. They're always begging for attention.

❧ Mulch planting beds. Mulch conserves soil moisture, so you won't have to water as often. It also discourages weeds.

A. No mow worries. Rather than devote his front yard to a high-maintenance lawn, the owner of this Florida garden covered it with paving and ground cover. Little work is required to keep the garden looking good besides occasionally sweeping the pavers or trimming the ivy.

B. Lush but low-care. This planting has variety, but a careful choice of plants keeps maintenance to a minimum. Undemanding shrubs like barberry, ground-hugging junipers, ferns, *Sedum telephium* 'Autumn Joy', and rudbeckia can be left in place for years. Mulch and drip irrigation ensure a constant amount of adequate water.

WINTER INTEREST

Gardeners in the Tropical South are lucky. They don't have to worry about dead-looking gardens in winter. Everything looks pretty much the same as in summer.

Not so elsewhere. When trees drop leaves and flowers die, it can be a challenge to keep the yard worth looking at—unless you've put some careful thought into planning your garden.

Review the gardens you most admire in the pages of this book. Although they represent different areas and feature a variety of plants, they all share a common feature—a strong, underlying structure that gives them form and impact in any season.

This structure consists of apparent lines, curves, and focal points that define space and shape the design. It's like the pencil sketch an artist does before adding the colors.

Winter blooms—lenten rose, camellias, forsythia, and early daffodils.

You can use both plants and nonliving elements to provide structure. But evergreen plants add more structure than deciduous ones, because their appearance remains consistent year-round. A classic example is boxwoods anchoring the corners of a formal garden.

Nonliving "hardscape" elements include walls, fences, paved walks, pools, rocks, and edging. They also include structures such as gazebos, arbors, and tool houses, as well as fountains, sculpture, and various garden ornaments.

If you live where most trees and shrubs drop their leaves in winter, don't overlook the dramatic impact that a sweep of green can have. For example, a bright green winter lawn bordered by deciduous woods can become your garden's premier attraction in January. The same can be said for dark green English ivy framing a beige zoysia lawn.

Of course, the winter doesn't mean the death of all flowers. Pansies and violas will bloom in all but the coldest weather. And a surprising number of trees and shrubs bloom in mid-to late winter, including 'Okame' flowering cherry, cornelian cherry *(Cornus mas)*, flowering quince, Japanese flowering apricot *(Prunus mume)*, wintersweet *(Chimonanthus praecox)*, common camellia, and winter jasmine. For a more extensive list of winter bloomers, see pages 286–287.

A. **Well-designed.** An ornate well provides year-round structure, while the arching branches of crabapple laden with bright red berries illuminate the winter garden.

B. **No longer in hiding.** Evergreens come to the fore when deciduous plants drop their leaves. This majestic Norway spruce dominates the surrounding winter scene.

C. **Cold outside, cozy within.** In Virginia, a glass garden room attached to the house becomes a tropical oasis in winter, offering soothing views of the snow-covered hills outside.

D. **Pooling resources.** Even a pool can be the focus of a winter garden. The key is lots of structure and the choice of appropriate plants. Here, a stacked stone wall, waterfall, bench, and river birches give the pool a vibrant presence when the snow has settled in for the season.

BRINGING IN THE GARDEN

A garden needn't be solely an outdoor experience. In fact, if you live in a place that suffers punishing heat in summer, the only comfortable place to enjoy your garden may be from within an air-conditioned room. Careful planning can blur the distinction between indoors and outdoors, bringing the garden into the home and letting it function as almost another room.

There are a number of ways to accomplish this. Sunrooms equipped with glass doors and large windows can let you admire the entire garden from the comfort of a rocking chair. Paving a walk with the same tile or stone used for the floor of a kitchen or hallway can unite indoors and outdoors. Courtyards and terraces that adjoin the house can also repeat details from house walls or doorways, visually linking the different spaces. Houses themselves can be skillfully designed to accentuate special views of the gardens from the living room, dining room, kitchen, and bedroom. And as demonstrated here, you can even capture an outdoor garden inside a screened frame, so you can enjoy the plants without the bugs.

If your home features large windows, it's especially important to enhance the view. This may involve pruning or removing trees to open up vistas, or planting specimen trees and shrubs that draw the eye. You can also install plants close to your house perimeter in creative ways. Train a climbing rose or sweet-smelling vine around your window casement and you can enjoy the fragrance and pick bouquets without stepping out the door. Or plant a window box with flowering plants or herbs that can be easily cared for and harvested from inside (see pages 296–297).

Tender plants that can't survive outdoor winters can be turned into house plants for the winter; examples include citrus, bougainvillea, ferns, bird-of-paradise, and many succulents. Given sufficient but not too much water and a sunny spot, many outdoor plants will thrive during these indoor retreats.

Of course, one of the time-honored ways to bring your garden indoors is to keep vases filled with fresh flowers from your cutting garden. Don't forget that branches, cones, berries, and foliage are all good materials for creative indoor displays too, especially during the winter months.

A. Through the looking glass. Replacing opaque walls with glass doors allows the garden to function as an extension of the house. Trees, shrubs, flowers, lawn, and garden furniture become part of a room's decor. Even with the door shut on hot or cold days, you still feel you're "out in the garden."

B. Clothed with greenery, this intimate walled courtyard lies just beyond a master bath suite. Creeping fig coats the wall's surface year-round. Wisteria flexes its way around a wire trellis bolted into the top of the wall. A waterfall of river birches growing behind the wall ensures total privacy.

C. Pretty as a picture. This garden was designed to be viewed from the breakfast room, where the occupants spend a good deal of time. Together, the waterfall, arbor, stones, and pond appear almost like a painting mounted on the wall.

D. View from on high. Sitting high above a salt marsh, this elevated deck places its owners smack dab in the tree canopy. Screened walls keep out bugs. It's hard to imagine a more delightful place to watch sunrises and sunsets or listen to the sounds of nature at night.

E. Indoor-outdoor garden. Lanais, or screened-in garden rooms, have become popular in Florida and the Coastal South. Made of screen attached to aluminum frames, they allow sunlight, rainfall, and air to penetrate, while excluding flying insects.

SLOPES

There's a good reason why real estate agents are eager to point out a "flat lot" when selling a home. It's because the more steeply sloped a lot is, the less usable space it has. But that doesn't mean you can't turn a potentially negative situation into one that's very positive.

As the illustrations at far right demonstrate, how you go about dealing with a slope depends on how much slope you have. A slightly sloped lot is actually advantageous, because it's easy to direct rainwater away from the house and usable space is almost the same as with a flat lot. Plus, you can put a garage in the basement.

Steeply sloped lots present a challenge. Creating level, usable spaces, such as lawns, play areas, pool, and garden beds, requires liberal use of retaining walls. Construction costs can be considerable. An easier and less expensive alternative is to dedicate steep slopes to native vegetation that controls erosion, maintains privacy, and needs little maintenance (see illustration, lower right).

If we could leave you with one thought about steep slopes, it would be to forget about growing grass on them. Mowing on an angle is the easiest way to lose one or two of your favorite body parts.

A. Don't grow grass on a steep slope. It's difficult to mow and also dangerous. Two better solutions are planting the slope with ground cover or treating it as a natural area. Here, at Dumbarton Oaks in Washington, D.C., thousands of naturalized daffodils decorate a slope.

B. Happy landings. A slope in front of the house often means climbing a lot of steps to get to the front door. One way to make the ascent less daunting is to break up the steps with a series of landings. Changing the direction of the walk at each landing also makes the climb seem less steep.

THREE DEGREES OF SLOPE

Shallow slope. To create a level lawn area in front, the grade has been raised at the street and lowered in front of the house. Ground cover has been planted on the slopes edging the driveway and entrance walk. In the backyard, terraces with steps between create level areas for a lawn, play yard, and planting beds.

Streetside retaining wall

HOUSE

Entrance walk and driveway are ramps

Medium slope. Low retaining walls in front create five different levels; four levels solved the slope problem in the backyard. Lawn is a gentle slope, so that the mower need not be lifted or pulled up and down steps.

HOUSE

Retaining wall serves as seat

Landing interrupts flight of stairs

Terraced retaining walls with low ground cover

Steep slope. The simplest and least expensive way to create level space on a steep lot is to build a deck. Tree planting that brings foliage to deck height lessens the feeling of being perched above ground level.

Tree roots prevent erosion

Containers permit gardening on deck

HOUSE

Steps need frequent landings

FROM PLAN TO REALITY

Before drawing up your final plan, you may wish to consult a landscape professional to assist with the design or its implementation. Although many homeowners feel confident tackling the entire design and construction of their garden themselves, others rely on various professionals to help with some of the steps along the way.

The role of landscape architect

Creating a garden can call for the addition of patios, decks, dining areas, play yards, shade structures, drainage systems, and perhaps a pool or spa. Designing such structures and relating them to a unified plan for your garden is where a landscape architect comes in.

In addition to determining the most effective use of paving, planting, and lighting, landscape architects are licensed to design exterior structures, solve site problems such as ungainly slopes and poor drainage, and give advice on siting a house and locating service lines, entries, driveways, and parking areas. A landscape architect is familiar with landscape and building materials and services, and can suggest cost-saving options.

For individual services or for simple consultation, landscape architects usually work at an hourly rate. More commonly, however, a landscape architect provides a complete package, from conceptual plans to construction drawings and supervision of an installation; fees will depend upon the complexity of the project, its length, and the amount of time spent actually supervising the installation.

Other professionals

Landscape architects are not the only professionals involved in the creation of fine gardens. The terms landscape designer and garden designer apply to professionals who may be self-taught or may have the same academic credentials as landscape architects, but may lack a state license. The focus of their work is more likely to be residential gardens, and if you are not in need of a complex deck construction or high retaining wall, they may well serve your needs, as their fees may be lower than a landscape architect. A landscape designer usually works in conjunction with a licensed landscape contractor, an important professional, especially when construction beyond the limits of do-it-yourself projects is involved. A licensed contractor is trained in earthmoving, construction, and planting.

You may work directly with a contractor, or your landscape architect or designer may select and supervise the contractor. In either scenario, the contractor will submit a bid, either as a lump sum or as a figure based on the estimated time and materials. The latter approach allows more modifications during construction.

Finally, there are professionals who work primarily with plants. Horticulturists are trained in the selection and care of garden plants; many have some design training as well. If you are merely looking for plants to complete a design, you can work with a horticulturist. Arborists are trained in the care of trees and other woody plants; although not usually able to prepare a design for your garden, they can guide you in the handling of existing trees on your site, identifying healthy ones and those needing pruning, shaping, or removal. Local nurseries may also offer design services and may have talented designers on their staffs; but beware of free design services, as the designer may be obligated to work only with plants and other materials offered by the nursery employer.

Finding the right professional

Begin by identifying the professional services you need. Be realistic in assessing the amount of work you want to do yourself. Collect names from friends and neighbors—even if it means knocking on doors when you spot a good design. Then call each of the designers or contractors whose work you like to set up an interview either at your home (there may be an hourly fee for this) or at their offices (often free). Inquire about the nature of their work, their workload, and their fees. Most important, ask for references—other residential clients whose gardens may give you an idea of the range and quality of the designer's work or the caliber of the contractor's construction. Above all, you must feel a rapport between yourself and the professional; you will be working closely on the design and installation of your garden and need someone with whom you feel comfortable.

When the designer of your choice makes the first visit to your site, use the time wisely. Prepare in advance a list of wishes, needs, and problems that must be dealt with in the design, making sure everyone in the household has had a chance to participate in this step. Give serious consideration to your budget and your time schedule. When a design is complete, meet with the contractor and the designer to make certain that the contractor understands the design and is comfortable working with the materials proposed.

To protect yourself from any surprises, be sure to request a contract from any professionals you hire. This legal agreement should spell out the services to be provided, the schedule to be followed, and the fees to be charged.

Southern Living Custom Landscape Plans

You want to create a new garden or update an existing one. But hiring a landscape architect sounds expensive and time-consuming. Wouldn't it be great if you could get an expert plan quickly and affordably?

You can. With the help of Southern Living's *Custom Landscape Plans, an ordinary yard can become something beautiful.*

Here's how it works. After contacting our Plans Service, you'll receive a detailed questionnaire and a single-use camera. You'll also receive specific instructions on how to photograph your home and property to give us a good idea of what it looks like from every angle. Then you'll send the camera and completed questionnaire back to us.

Our design professionals will develop a plan just for you. You'll receive three copies of the master planting plan, each with a complete plant list, and a binder with fact sheets on most of the plants. You'll also receive a computer-enhanced photo of the front of your home, showing how it will look when the plan has been implemented. You can do the work yourself or hire a contractor. For more information about Southern Living's *Custom Landscape Plans, call 1-800-755-1122.*

THE DESIGN MOCK-UP

Whether you have completed the design of your garden yourself or have in hand a professionally rendered landscape plan, the next step is to translate the design to your property. If you are having difficulty visualizing the finished garden or can't quite decide on the specifics of certain elements, you may wish to mock up the design on your property. Seeing an approximation of the layout on site in the form of stakes, strings, and markings will help you to determine the exact dimensions necessary for some features, such as decks, terraces, and walks. Even if you feel your paper plan is final, be prepared to make some adjustments as you lay out the design on site until the arrangement of spaces and elements feels just right.

There are a variety of methods for staking out your design. Choose the one that works best for your situation; the choice

A flexible boundary. Where your design is mostly curving lines and free-form shapes, snake a garden hose to lay out the lines to your liking. The hose can be curled at nearly any radius, especially if it is warm. As an alternative, use PVC pipe that you will later use for your irrigation work; the pipe can be softened in the warm sun and gently bent to mark your design.

Colored powder. Limestone or gypsum, common soil amendments, can be used to lay out free-form designs such as the outlines of beds and borders. Powdered chalk of various colors is useful if you have overlapping elements. Measure corner or end points, then dribble a line of powder along the outlines. To make changes, simply turn the powder into the soil and start again.

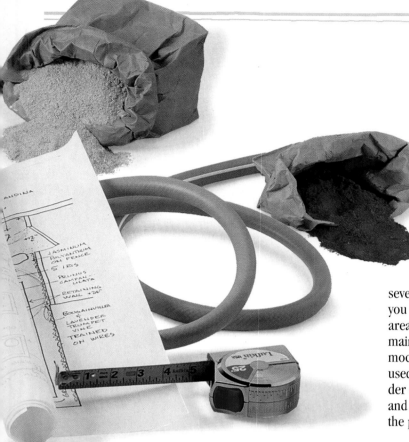

will be likely to depend on which features predominate—straight lines or curving lines, geometric forms or free forms. Use materials that you have on hand or that can be found at your local hardware store or garden center, such as bamboo or wooden stakes, kite string, clothesline or garden hose, powdered gypsum, lime, or even flour.

Live with your design layout for a few days before making any final decisions or beginning construction. Walk through or sit in your "mock garden" several times to be sure that it provides you with the spaces you need, circulation paths that are comfortable, and garden areas that suit your interests and the time you have to spend maintaining them. When you are ready to begin construction, mock-up techniques will also come in handy. Staking is often used to mark an area of concrete to be poured; colored powder can show the true boundaries of planting areas in borders and beds; and a hose snaked along a pathway can help guide the placement of pavers or bricks.

Strings and stakes. For straight or gently curved lines, mark each corner with a short stake and connect them with strings to outline paving areas, deck construction, pathways, hedges, and planting beds; use taller stakes to mark fences and walls. Then test how they affect traffic circulation through the garden and whether they block any important access points or views.

A mock garden. Tall stakes can stand in for trees or elements like fountains, sculpture, or posts for overhead construction. Large pieces of cardboard on the ground can indicate paving or decks; cardboard can represent fences and walls. Note any shadows cast by planned vertical barriers. The neighbors may stare, but you'll get a better sense of how your design is shaping up.

PUTTING IT ALL TOGETHER

You don't need a big house or budget to make a big difference. As the owner of this modest older home discovered, all you need are an honest assessment of your property's weaknesses and a game plan for achieving your goals.

In this case, the backyard suffered from some glaring problems:

∾ The empty yard was devoid of interest and bordered by unattractive fences.

∾ A sunken flagstone terrace by the door was too small and drained poorly.

∾ To get to the back door, guests had to leave their cars on a narrow flagstone driveway between the owner's house and the house next door.

The first order of business was tearing up the old driveway and terrace and stockpiling the stones for later use. Next, contractors tore off the flimsy back steps and replaced them with a deck made of pressure-treated pine. Built-in benches

Before. *The backyard was barren and uninviting.* **After.** *A new parking area welcomes guests to a terrace and deck surrounded by lush plantings.*

on the edges of the deck supply ample seating. A PVC pipe running from a corner downspout under the deck to the side of the house improves drainage. Beside the deck, a service area surrounded by fencing provides hidden storage for trash cans and equipment.

The second phase involved extending the old driveway around a large, existing oak, so that it ends with a spacious parking court. Compacted limestone gravel provides a firm surface. Salvaged flagstones from the old driveway and terrace supplied sturdy edging for the parking court and garden beds, new stone steps leading down from the parking area to the deck, and a new stone terrace in front of the rear bedroom. Beds of shrubs hide existing unattractive fences. Improvements to the house—fresh paint, new roof and gutters, and shutters for the bedroom window—add the finishing touches.

BEFORE

Before. Exposed trash cans, flimsy back steps, and a small, sunken terrace were dreary afterthoughts.

After. A new service area hides the trash cans, while the deck replaces the old steps and terrace.

AFTER

Top right. Built of pressure-treated pine, a sturdy deck greatly increases space for outdoor entertaining.

Above. Flagstones salvaged from the old driveway and terrace were used to edge the parking court and garden beds.

Rosamund garden
Columbus, Mississippi

DESIGNING WITH STRUCTURES

Walls, walks, pools, and other structures give your garden shape and dimension. Like plants, they can enrich the outdoors with form, texture, and color.

Garden structures often play dual roles, satisfying both aesthetic and functional needs. For example, fences and trellises can create separate spaces, while supporting beautiful and fragrant roses and vines. Low, wide walls can enclose a terrace and provide extra seating too. Gazebos and arbors can serve as both focal points and shelters. And paths can establish formal sight lines, as well as guiding visitors on the way.

Structures are the costliest part of the garden. So plan them carefully, and check local building codes prior to construction. Make sure their design complements both the overall setting and the architecture of your house. Finally, select the most durable materials you can afford. This will ensure your structures pass the test of time.

ARBORS AND GAZEBOS

There's nothing quite like an arbor or gazebo to enhance your enjoyment of the garden. Both structures furnish shade during the day and shelter during cool evenings, yet are always open to breezes and the enticing scent of flowers. Both give you a place to sit and relax, host a party, or simply to mingle with family and friends. And these structures play other, more practical roles as well: They can link your house to the garden, define different areas of the garden, direct foot traffic through the landscape, mask an unattractive feature, or frame a spectacular view.

Gazebos come in a variety of styles, from old-fashioned Victorian designs to contemporary or rustic motifs. Though typically built with open, airy framing, a gazebo lends a feeling of enclosure to those sitting inside, due to a solid roof overhead. By contrast, arbors frame the walls and ceiling of

an outdoor room and can be embellished with fragrant or colorful vines (see page 240). You can build an arbor in almost any style, from simple archways to elaborate neoclassical pavilions.

As you think about where to put a new arbor or gazebo, take a walking tour of your property under different weather conditions. Glance back at the house often. Look for a vantage point that marries a good view of the house with the property as a whole. Avoid unsightly areas unless the structure will conceal them. Also consider exposure—if your main deck or patio is in full sun, you may prefer to locate an arbor or gazebo in a shady corner. Lastly, don't give up on a garden structure just because your yard is small. Tiny spaces often profit from the focal point created by a small arbor or gazebo (or even a covered barbecue or cooking area).

Sinuous smokewood vine brings style to substance on this 12 × 12-foot pavilion. The structure sits on a latticed deck and is topped by a low-pitched, V-crimp metal roof.

A. Framing a pathway, this cedar arbor unites the main house with an adjacent shade house. Widely spaced rafters allow sunlight for plants to thrive.

B. Nighttime delight can be found in this lighted garden pavilion at woodland's edge. The brick steps and flooring blend nicely into the garden walls.

C. Attached to the house, this arbor makes a graceful transition from interior to exterior space. White-painted columns and lattice complement the house walls and window framing.

A. **From boardwalk to beach,** matching shingles and crisp white trim and railings tie this gazebo to the beach house beyond.

B. **Simple arches** give height to a colorful planting bed and frame a view of the pool beyond.

C. **This gated metal arbor** marks the garden entry, while supporting the luxuriant growth of evergreen crossvine.

D. **With a sturdy roof** to provide shelter from rain and falling leaves, this poolside gazebo nevertheless looks open and airy.

E. **Shading a terrace** of Pennsylvania blue-green stone, this red cedar arbor is of a simple, classic design. Suspended fans keep bugs at bay.

F. **Placed deckside,** the scale and style of this gazebo match that of the surrounding palms, background fence, and decking design.

A. The long "legs" and pitched roof on this structure give it a somewhat gangly, informal look, perfect for a casual entryway.

B. This wisteria-topped pergola is a formal retreat, its hefty classical columns calling to mind a Grecian temple.

A BASIC ARBOR

Beams bridge posts; local codes specify sizes and spans

Lattice screen adds privacy and shade; it doubles as a trellis

Piers of cast concrete are embedded in poured concrete footings

Designing an arbor

Your first step in designing an arbor is taking a good, long look at your house. Repeating interesting architectural details you find there—such as a railing pattern, the pitch of a gable, or even a paint color—will visually tie together house and arbor and unify the garden.

Arbors vary in height, but 8 to 10 feet is about right for most. This provides plenty of headroom, but also makes it easy to prune any vines growing on the arbor. When deciding upon your arbor's length and width, remember that a roof overhead always makes the floor space below seem smaller than it is.

The key to arbor construction is to think of a crisscross of materials, with each new layer placed perpendicular to the one below it. Whether freestanding or attached to a building, the structure is

Rafters sit atop beams and are spaced for plant support or shade. Orientation determines the extent of shade cast below

Posts are 4 × 4 lumber or larger; post-to-beam connections may need bracing. Metal anchors secure posts to piers or to a concrete slab

Concrete footings support the weight of the posts, arbor, and plants; they should extend below the frost line in colder areas

supported by posts or columns, which in turn support horizontal beams and rafters. (With an arbor attached to a house, a ledger takes the place of an end beam and the rafters are laid directly on the ledger.) Although you build an arbor from the bottom up, you should design it from the top down. Decide first on the spacing and size of rafters, because this will dictate that of the support members below. Wooden rafters can be as plain or as fancy as you like, ending in curves, notches, or elaborate scrollwork. You can leave them uncovered or cover them with shadecloth, plants, lath, or lattice.

Arbors are typically built from standard dimension lumber; use only pressure-treated pine or naturally decay-resistant cedar. Make sure the arbor can support the weight of any vining plants; for added strength, add crossbraces where the posts meet the beams.

Lattice Panels Fill the Gap

Instead of building a full-size arbor in a small space, consider installing a trellis for climbers directly onto an existing wall. In this compact garden, a garage wall and the lattice trellis mounted on it are painted in contrasting colors. The inset window and the wall fountain provide a focal point, with the arched window echoing other arches elsewhere in the garden.

Rather than being mounted directly on the wall, the custom lattice panels are fastened on top of 2-by-4 spacers, giving the panels more depth, shadow, and room for vines to climb. A 1-by-4 facing board conceals the junction of two panels. Lush plantings surround the base of the lattice, so it is impossible to see that the panels are not actually sunk into the ground. Even though pressure-treated pine was used, keeping the wood above the soil line minimizes the likelihood of rot and extends the life of the trellis.

An Elegant Gazebo

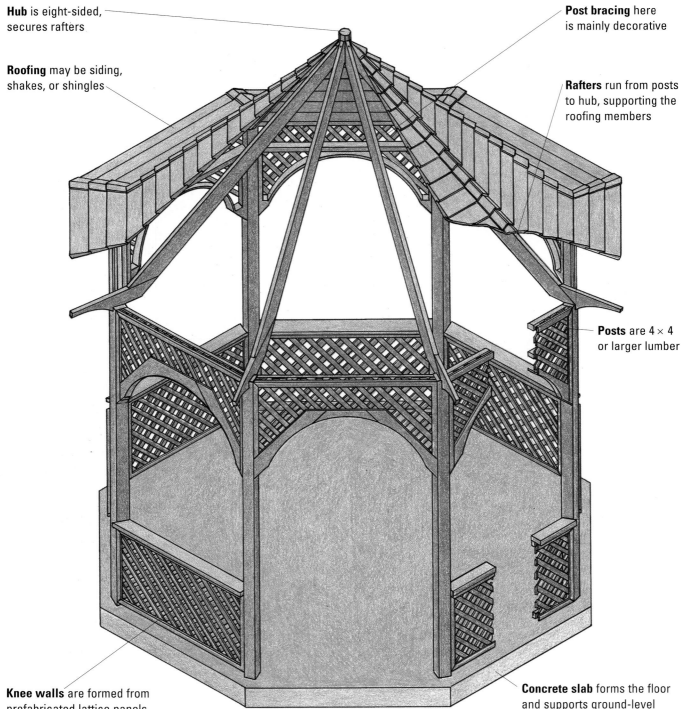

Hub is eight-sided, secures rafters

Roofing may be siding, shakes, or shingles

Post bracing here is mainly decorative

Rafters run from posts to hub, supporting the roofing members

Posts are 4 × 4 or larger lumber

Knee walls are formed from prefabricated lattice panels

Concrete slab forms the floor and supports ground-level gazebo. Other options include wooden deck framing, piers, and concrete footings

Planning a gazebo

Although there are many designs for gazebos (also called belvederes or summerhouses), most adhere to the same basics. All require a foundation, posts or walls, beams, rafters, and some type of roofing (left). Cramped quarters are no fun, so make your gazebo at least 8 feet tall with sufficient floor space to easily accommodate several pieces of furniture—at least 8 feet wide and deep.

With few exceptions, support for a gazebo comes from a simple post-and-beam frame built of sturdy, pressure-treated lumber. A gazebo roof may take a variety of forms. By far the trickiest one to lay out is the most traditional one—a six- or eight-hub style; a roof with four sides is much simpler. Remember that if the roof is made of solid materials (and most are), it must be pitched to allow water to run off. Framing connections are most easily made by means of readily available prefabricated metal fasteners (see page 324).

If building an entire gazebo from scratch seems overwhelming, look into ordering a set of plans with complete instructions (right) or building one from a kit. The kit will usually contain everything but the foundation: You must set a gazebo on a concrete slab, a deck, concrete piers, or a bed of crushed stone. For most gazebos, assembly will take a weekend or two and require only basic tools and skills—but it's a job for at least two people.

Southern Living Plans

The design team at Southern Living *has put together a series of gazebo plans from which you can choose to build your own garden retreat. The one shown above was inspired by Gothic style. It's an eight-sided structure measuring 12 feet in diameter. The steeply pitched roof of cedar shake shingles soars 30 feet. Chippendale railings combine with white wicker furniture for a classic, airy design.*

All of the Southern Living *gazebo and other building plans contain detailed construction information offering options for you to customize the project (the gazebo above features a handcrafted cupola and a copper weather vane as a decorative crowning touch). If you have good woodworking ability and a fair knowledge of construction techniques, you should be able to understand these plans and construct your own gazebo with some help from a friend or the assistance of a hired carpenter.*

To order this plan or to find out about other plans for garden structures, including playhouses, toolhouses, and storage buildings, call 1-800-755-1122.

Tempting retreat. This classically styled gazebo offers shade, shelter, and enticing views of the surrounding gardens. Interior details include lattice walls, arched roof rafters, and a floor of painted concrete.

DECKS

A deck expands your home's living area and sets the stage for outdoor activity. A properly planned deck becomes a focal point in the garden, redefines the grade of the yard, and provides new views of the garden and its surroundings. Built to accommodate seating, tables, and grilling equipment, a deck essentially functions as an outdoor room.

Decks can abut the house or tuck into a remote corner of the garden, but most are reached from the house through French or sliding doors from a living room, kitchen, or master bedroom—or all three. So when planning your deck, keep in mind interior traffic patterns as well as outdoor ones.

Why build a deck rather than a patio? Your site or the style of your house can be the determining factors. A deck can bridge an uneven site or "float" over swampy low spots that might sink a brick patio. Decking lumber is resilient underfoot, and it doesn't store heat the way masonry can, making a deck cooler in hot areas.

A low-level deck can link house and garden at flower height, offering a new perspective on garden beds. Such a deck makes a good replacement for an existing concrete slab—you can often use the slab as a base for the deck. A low wraparound deck links interior spaces with a series of boardwalks or landings. You can follow your home's shape or play off it with angular extensions or soft curves.

Detached decks form quiet retreats, whether tucked behind lush plantings or elevated to catch afternoon sun or shade. The route to such a deck can be direct or roundabout. You can enhance the feeling of a hideaway with the addition of an arbor, gazebo, or nearby water feature.

The ultimate feel of a deck is determined by the details, and safety is the only limiting factor. Decking patterns, railings, lighting, and other touches offer an opportunity to be truly creative. Just make sure that the style of your details reflects—or at least complements—the detailing of the house or nearby structures.

Though they are more expensive than pressure-treated pine (the most popular lumber for outdoor projects), consider more refined-looking cedar or cypress. Other options include recycled or man-made products (see page 340).

Coat any deck periodically with a wood preservative, stain, or finish to reduce the sun or water damage that can eventually lead to cracking, splintering, and warping. Also check regularly for signs of insect damage or rot, which can easily travel from the deck into house siding or framing.

A. Nestled in the woods is the perfect spot for a deck—cool, shady, and in keeping with its surroundings. This deck is dressed up with bright containers that can be changed with the season.

B. A deck with a view and several seating areas overlooks the surrounding marsh and a terrace and pool below. Special features include white painted benches, natural decking, and dark green handrails that don't show dirt.

C. Space savers. A handsome roof offers shade and shelter to this elevated deck. The space below has been cleverly converted to a children's play area.

Deck-building guidelines

Lumber grades vary greatly in appearance and price, so start by determining the least expensive lumber for decking and trim that's acceptable to you. Whatever the species and grade of exposed wood, use pressure-treated lumber for the under-structure—it stands up to insects, weather, and in-ground conditions.

A deck can be freestanding or, as shown here, attached to the house with a horizontal ledger strip. Concrete footings secure precast piers or poured tubular pads, which in turn support vertical wooden posts. One or more horizontal beams span the posts; smaller joists then bridge the ledger and the beams. The decking itself, typically 2-by-4 or 2-by-6 lumber, is nailed or screwed to the joists. The standard pattern of planking shown is but one of many options; remember that the more complicated the design, the harder the decking is to install.

Roofs, benches, railings, and steps are often integral to a deck's framing. While it may be possible to add these extras later, it's simplest to design and build the whole structure at once. While you're planning, think about whether you'll need to install plumbing pipes for running water or wiring for electrical outlets and outdoor light fix-tures. And if you need extra storage space or planters, why not build them into the deck as per-manent features?

One advantage of building a deck as a do-it-yourself project is that much of the engineering work has been done for you. Standard span tables (listing safe working spans by dimension for each common lumber species) are widely available at lumberyards. Remember that these are mini-mum guidelines; for a firmer footing, choose beefier members or reduce the spacing between them.

Posts taller than 3 feet may require brac-ing; elevated decks must be surrounded with railings with slats no more than 4 to 6 inches apart (check your local building code). Fascia boards, skirts, and other trim details can dress up the basic structure.

A low deck is easiest to build. But a simple raised deck like the one shown at right can also be built by a homeowner with some con-struction skills (see pages 326–327). Generally, decks that are cantilevered out from an upper story or over water must be designed by a qualified structural engineer and installed by a professional. Likewise, decks on steep hillsides or unstable soil, or those more than a story high, should receive professional attention.

A BASIC DECK

Decking boards are nailed or screwed perpendicular to joists; they are typically 2 × 4 or 2 × 6 lumber

Storage bin can be concealed under built-in bench

Railings (maximum openings specified by local code)

Fascia (trim)

Rim joist secures joist ends

Planters on deck require adequate drainage; deck must support weight of soil and plants

Access to deck leads from dining or living room, kitchen, or bedrooms. French or sliding doors are best choices

Electrical lighting and outlets may be 120 volt or 12 volt and may require permit to install

Ledger secures deck to house framing. Flashing guards against moisture

Beams bridge posts; they may be single timbers or twin 2-by members that "sandwich" posts as shown

Joists are typically spaced 16 or 24 inches center-to-center, and secured to ledger with joist hangers

Posts are secured to piers with post anchors. Minimum post sizes and spacings are set by local codes

Piers are made of precast concrete and embedded in poured footings

Poured concrete footings extend below the frost line

A. **This deck light** automatically turns on at dusk, illuminating steps and other deck surfaces for safety.

B. **Low bench seating** with spaces between boards allows water to run off more easily, preventing rot.

C. **Don't get fenced in** by an unattractive railing. This Chippendale pattern looks rustic unpainted; painted white, it could suit a more formal design.

A. **This small sideyard deck** has been spruced up with an arbor, lattice panels, a storage compartment, and old green cypress shutters from a salvage shop.

B. **Built at grade level,** this deck was designed to preserve existing tree roots. Varying the decking pattern made the structure more interesting.

C. **A low-level deck** can be beautifully integrated into the garden with well-placed plants, boulders, artwork, and even a koi pond.

D. **Curving gracefully,** this wooden deck extends over a hillside and connects seamlessly with the gray concrete pool coping.

C

D

PATIOS AND TERRACES

A secluded, comfortable spot in which to sit is an essential part of the Southern garden. Classic square or rectangular brick terraces have graced Southern homes for generations, but there are many options available. You can give your terrace a different look by incorporating an arbor, fountain, or pond. You can also raise or recess a terrace if your site is flat. (But because sunken or raised terraces can create drainage problems, consult a landscape professional.)

Most terraces consist of paving material resting atop a poured concrete slab or a bed of clean, packed sand (see pages 342–345). Your choice of materials depends mainly on the style you're seeking and price you can afford. Brick, trimmed stone, and cobblestone look formal if mortared atop a slab in a symmetrical pattern. Irregular flagstones, concrete pavers, and bricks set on a sand bed give a terrace a casual appearance. Plain poured concrete tends to

Symmetrical plantings, elegant furnishings, and traditional materials (plaster walls, iron railings, and stone paving) lend formality to this semi-enclosed terrace.

impart a commercial rather than a residential feel to a garden—textured, exposed-aggregate, formed, and stamped concrete are all more garden-friendly (see page 338). For economy and a comfortable, casual look, use such loose materials as gravel, river rock, or wood chips to accent and expand your terrace borders. These filler materials will help improve surface drainage too.

Terraces are typically constructed adjacent to the house, where they serve as a good transition between the indoors and outdoors—the terrace becomes an extension of the house, a natural place to entertain, take meals, or just relax. Still, a detached terrace has much to offer in terms of providing a quiet, private retreat, especially if connected to the house by a path of similar material. If shade is lacking where you build your terrace, consider planting shade trees. Choose types without invasive roots or excessive litter (see page 210).

A. Filled with perennials, this island bed helps the terrace flow into the garden. The mixed flagstone-and-brick paving pattern contributes to the feeling of movement.

B. This patio serves as both an entry and a pleasant seating area. The tightly fitted bluestone and central water feature lend a formal air.

C. Curves and naturalistic ground covers integrate this patio with the landscape. It's easy to sweep fallen leaves and acorns from the poured-concrete surface.

A. Simple materials can still lend a patio a traditional air, as this gravel-on-sand seating area shows. Simple plantings and stepping-stones complement the design.

B. Expansive, multi-level patios offer the utmost versatility. This bluestone patio provides access from several rooms of the house and leads to different areas of the yard.

C. Recycled brick lines this 40 × 10-foot terrace, which extends the length of the house. Sturdy wooden columns and potted plants give the terrace a relaxed, back-porch feel.

D. A raised terrace of earth-tone tile edged with blue glass weaves through a colorful court-yard laid with tumbled marble. Palms enhance the tropical, contemporary look.

COURTYARDS

Although you can define a courtyard as simply an enclosed space adjoining a house, that does little to evoke the unique atmosphere you feel when you're inside one. Because they're separated from the rest of the property, courtyards have an intimate, romantic feeling, unlike a simple patio or deck. Water features—especially fountains—are particularly at home in a courtyard. Decorate the walls with vines and add subtle night lighting, and your courtyard becomes a haven.

But a courtyard is not all romance. It may join together wings or sections of a house, or perhaps link the front yard and backyard. Although courtyards are often accented with entry gates, these are not a necessity unless required for security or privacy.

Courtyard floors are typically constructed from the same types of material as terraces and patios. Brick, pavers, concrete, stone, and even gravel all may be used to good effect. Just make sure the material—and the pattern in which it is set—complements the house.

Keep scale in mind when designing a courtyard. A huge courtyard tacked onto a small house looks out of place. Likewise, a tiny courtyard fronting a regal entryway looks ludicrous. And remember scale when designing plantings. A huge Southern magnolia is not the right choice for a 20-by-20-foot courtyard. Entry courtyards are viewed throughout the year, so try to provide for more than single-season interest. Again, match the look of the plantings to the courtyard and house, perhaps choosing paired plantings for formal homes and asymmetrical arrangements for more contemporary designs.

A. **Brightly colored walls** and bold tropical plants bring a sense of fun and adventure into this brick-paved courtyard.

B. **Entry gates** provide security and privacy, but can also frame a view or issue an invitation to come inside and visit.

FIREPLACES

Congregating around a warm fire adds comfort and intimacy to garden gatherings. After sundown, flickering firelight enhances your surroundings. As a practical bonus, the warmth of a fire can be welcome on cool evenings, allowing you to enjoy the garden in late fall and even winter.

The most attractive fireplaces are designed to fit in with the homes and gardens they accompany. Some fireplaces are attached to the main house or outbuildings; others stand alone in secluded corners.

Except for open firepits, outdoor fireplaces contain the basic elements of indoor ones: a center firebox, with a back wall that reflects the radiant energy of the fire outward; and a chimney, which improves the draw and lifts any smoke above roof height. Chimney height becomes especially important when the fireplace is close to the house—your local building department will have details. You'll probably have to check with the building department in any case, as a freestanding fireplace may be considered a separate structure that requires a building permit.

Try to locate your fireplace so that you can see it from the house as well as the garden. Not only will this double your enjoyment of the fire, it will let you keep an eye on the structure to make sure it's being used safely. An open firepit must be located away from the house, to avoid problems with sparks and smoke.

A. This subtle blend of European and Southwestern influences is enhanced with pots, decorative objects, and a tracery of creeping fig.

B. Fending off the chill, a fireplace marks a cozy refuge. This stucco-over-block example features an arched firebox, a decorative tile inset, and a raised hearth.

DRIVEWAYS AND ENTRYWAYS

Of all the points where home and garden meet, the entryway draws the most attention. It sets the tone for your garden—if the parking is accessible, the walk to the house pleasant, and the wait enjoyable, then your home extends a gracious welcome to your guests before you have even opened the door.

The entryway and driveway work hand in hand to make the approach to your door convenient and pleasant. The end of the drive should be visible from the street. The driveway should be wide enough for both parking and walking. The front door—and the path to the front door—should be clearly recognizable, and stairs easy to navigate. The steps should also be wide enough to accommodate at least two people walking side by side. An awning or a roof overhead will offer protection from the elements. Finally, the area should have adequate lighting for security and safety.

Plants can go a long way toward making the entryway inviting. Select those that will draw attention to, or accent, the doorway. Small trees and large shrubs are popular choices for entryway plantings. But make sure to allow them enough room to reach their full, mature shape. Vines twining around a trellis or lamppost make good accents, especially when in bloom. Small flower beds—perhaps with a seating bench—work well as entryway plantings too.

A parking court can provide plenty of space and still enhance the entryway. This one features a stone grid that gives the surface an attractive pattern while holding compacted gravel in place.

PARKING OPTIONS AND DIMENSIONS

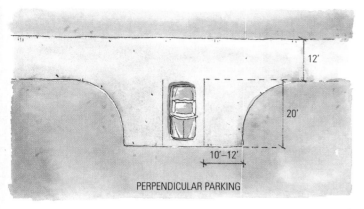

PERPENDICULAR PARKING

12'
20'
10'–12'

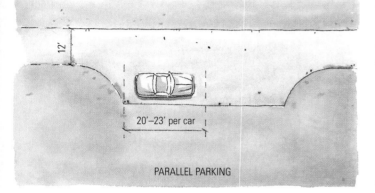

PARALLEL PARKING

12'
20'–23' per car

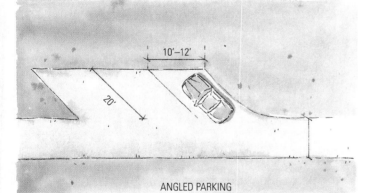

ANGLED PARKING

10'–12'
20'

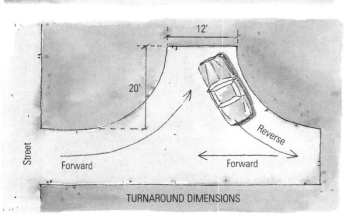

TURNAROUND DIMENSIONS

12'
20'
Street
Forward
Forward
Reverse

Parking Matters

It's important to strike the right balance when designing parking. Not enough space means constant shuffling; too much and your yard may resemble a valet lot. If you need more parking, look at the options. Auxiliary parking areas may be designed in shapes and dimensions to suit most properties, but each design has its own advantages and disadvantages.

If you have enough room in your yard, build your parking area larger rather than smaller, but make sure the paving won't dominate the landscape. Each parking space should be at least 10 to 12 feet wide and 20 feet long.

Asphalt is a bit cheaper than concrete, but concrete is more durable and can be dyed if you don't want the usual white color. Brick can be set in a variety of patterns but, while there's nothing like it to enhance a formal setting, it's costly to use.

Perpendicular parking *requires more space than parallel parking but can accommodate several cars. It works well where the driveway dead-ends near the house—drivers can back up, turn around, and head straight down the driveway when exiting.*

Parallel parking *intrudes the least on the yard and is most useful on narrow lots. If designing space for more than one car, make sure to allow adequate room for each car to maneuver back onto the driveway.*

Angled parking *takes up the greatest amount of space but is the easiest to pull into or back out from. In addition, the width of most driveways makes turning around after backing out fairly difficult.*

A turnaround *allows cars to exit the driveway front first—an important feature for properties facing a busy street.*

Circular driveways *must be at least 10 feet wide—16 feet wide to allow cars to pass each other. The distance from the center point of the half-circle to the inner curve of the drive should be at least 15 feet.*

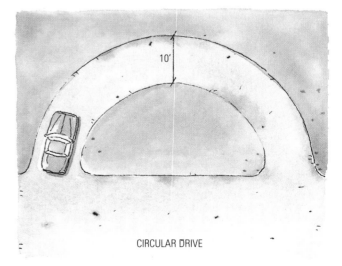

10'

CIRCULAR DRIVE

A. This narrow parking area feels less confined due to a clever combination of colored walls, espaliered plants, and neat hedges.

B. Placing parking spots between tall trees helps to hide the paving. These palms also shade the cars.

C. A sweeping drive gives a home a luxurious feeling; this one is perfectly in scale with the house and outbuildings. Symmetrical entryway plantings add to the overall formality.

D. A large swath of driveway can easily dominate a landscape. Bands of brick divide this drive into sections, making the paved area look smaller.

E. **Gravel paving** has many virtues. It gives an appealing natural look and costs less than brick or concrete.

F. **This compact front yard** integrates a gravel-over-asphalt parking court, privacy plantings, a handsome flagstone walk, and a terrace for welcoming visitors.

PATHS AND STEPS

Man probably invented the garden path about the same time he invented the garden. After all, it couldn't have taken long to discover the value of a few strategically placed stepping-stones. In the modern garden, a walkway beckons visitors to enter, leads them on a guided tour, tempts them to follow it around the bend to see what lies beyond.

Tailor your choice of materials to how the path will be used. Major access walks should be made of formed or stamped concrete, brick, pavers, or stone slabs for easy traffic flow and an even, nonskid surface. Brick, pavers, and stones can be set in concrete or in a bed of sand (see pages 342–345). Another good choice for a major pathway is cedar or cypress decking atop a pressure-treated base, or pressure-treated timbers laid at regular intervals side by side.

By contrast, a rustic path of gravel or bark chips can meander through the garden, its uneven texture and natural colors blending into the surroundings. Such a path encourages leisurely strolling, giving visitors more time to admire the surrounding garden. Rough cobbles, salvaged bricks, and other casual stepping-stones also make appealing paths, especially when embedded in a less expensive, contrasting filler material, such as gravel, sand, or wood chips.

If you prefer a natural look, also consider grass paths. Grass can be quite elegant when bordered by sweeps of ground cover or mulched planting beds. And no surface is easier on the feet.

A. Tricycle-friendly, an exposed-aggregate pathway provides a safe and even surface for wheeled and foot traffic alike. The brick edging that softens the utilitarian look won't impede a mower.

B. Rustic flagstones weave through this side yard, helping to preserve the natural feeling of a woodland garden. Mulch stops weeds from sprouting between the stones.

C. Its paving pattern makes this small, straight walkway distinctive. One-foot squares of lilac Pennsylvania stone, laid diagonally, are bordered by rectangular stones. A single step down is preferable to a sloping walk.

D. Four-by-four timbers serve a dual purpose. Their height allows the beds on either side to be slightly raised, and they do a great job of keeping gravel in place.

A. Grassy paths are easy to install, cushion the feet, and look tidy if edged in brick.

B. Wooden boardwalks offer clean, secure footing even in wet weather. Varying the direction of the boards adds to the design.

C. Bricks are extremely versatile. They can be mortared in or laid on sand, and arranged in a number of patterns.

D. Mixing stone and gravel in a pattern made this pathway a decorative focal point.

Safe Stepping

Safety is a primary concern for paths. Materials that grow slick when wet are obviously poor choices for entry walks, as they will inevitably be used in rainy conditions by guests in dress shoes. Stepping-stones should be placed a comfortable distance apart—6 to 9 inches is best. Make sure to provide adequate lighting, especially on steep steps.

How wide should your path be? It depends on how you'll use it. If it will wind discreetly through a garden and serve only as a walking surface, 2 feet is adequate. To allow room for lawn mowers and wheelbarrows, make it 3 feet wide. For two people to walk abreast, as on an entry path, make it at least 4 feet but preferably 5 feet wide.

Steps

A good set of steps helps you traverse your garden's ups and downs. Even if you have a relatively flat piece of land, you may want to create a change in elevation, such as a sunken garden or raised terrace. Generally, the best way to bridge these grade changes is with steps.

Steps usually mark transitions in the garden, but can also serve as accents. Most dramatic are wide, deep steps that lead the eye to a focal point. A set of steps can also double as retaining walls, planters, or garden seating.

Materials influence the styles of steps. Poured concrete, masonry block, and concrete pavers usually present a substantial, somewhat formal, look. Natural materials such as stone and wood are more informal and fit into less structured gardens. Informal steps are also easier to build (see pages 354–355).

Matching the material with that of terrace paving or garden walls helps unite a garden's overall design. On the other hand, contrasting materials draw attention to the steps and can create a transition between unlike surfaces. For example, you can link a brick patio to a concrete walk with steps made of concrete treads and brick risers.

Steps needn't attack a steep slope head-on. Sometimes the most appealing solution is an L- or U-shaped series of multiple flights with wide landings in between.

A

B

C

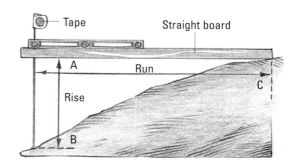

Steps by the Numbers

Ideally, the depth of the tread (the surface you step on) plus twice the height of the riser (the vertical surface) should equal 25 to 27 inches. Though riser and tread dimensions can vary, their relationship remains the same. Risers should be no lower than 4 inches and no higher than 8 inches. Treads should never be less than 11 inches deep. And all the risers and treads in any one flight of steps should be uniform in size.

Rarely will the steps fit exactly into a slope as it is. You may need to cut and fill the slope to accommodate the steps. To calculate the number of steps you need, divide the desired riser height into the total rise of the slope (see below). Drop any fraction and divide that whole number into the rise; the resulting figure is the exact measurement for each of the risers. Check the chart to see if the corresponding minimum tread will fit the slope's run.

A. Wide steps gracefully terrace this hill. Stacked sandstone retaining walls keep planting beds at eye level.

B. Alternating materials, in this case wooden decking and tiles, makes the way up more interesting.

C. These bluestone steps set amid the oaks are kept well lit at night, thanks to carefully placed low-voltage lights.

D. Solid stone steps curve casually up to this front entryway. A simple handrail helps prevent slips by the door.

E. Vigorous mazus fills the cracks between stone steps, adding a softening touch.

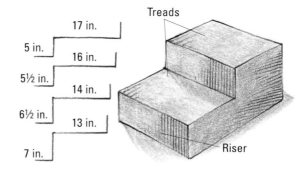

FENCES AND WALLS

Walls and fences do a good job of closing things in—or out, depending on what side you're on. As partitions, they can divide the yard into separate areas for recreation, relaxation, gardening, and storage. As decorative elements, they can introduce a bit of elegance, intrigue, and romance into the garden. While fences may serve many of the same purposes as walls, they're generally less formal in appearance, easier to build, and less expensive. But stone walls bring an unparalleled sense of permanence to a garden. In fact, some of the oldest structures in the world are stone walls—still standing after centuries.

Begin by choosing the size and style of a fence or wall according to its function. For example, a tall board fence may be the best choice for a privacy screen but not for a garden focal point. Then double-check that the style and materials used coordinate with your house, existing garden structures, and yard. While a casual stacked-stone wall might pique your fancy, it would probably be less attractive fronting a traditional-style brick house than a rectilinear brick wall.

fences are readily available, easily maintained, and simple to install—plus the darker varieties blend better with the landscape than silver chain link. If you don't like the look of wire or mesh fencing, plant annual vines such as morning glories or nasturtiums for quick cover. Or install perennial plantings for permanent concealment.

Most wooden fences have three parts: vertical posts, horizontal rails, and siding. Posts are usually 4-by-4 timbers; rails are usually 2-by-4s. Fence siding can range from weathered boards to ready-cut pickets. Posts should be made of pressure-treated wood.

Most communities have regulations restricting fence height, so be sure to check

Building a fence

Fences commonly come in one of three basic types: post-and-rail, picket, and solid board. You can include louvers, slats, lattice, or trellises if you want to frame a particular view. Most fences are wood. Alternatives to wood include vinyl, galvanized wire, plastic mesh, or ornamental iron. Vinyl mesh

before you build. (Remember that you can add more height by training a plant to grow along the top of the fence.) If your fence will be on or near a boundary line, make certain you have the property line clearly established. Typically a boundary fence is commonly owned and maintained by both neighbors. Make every effort to come to a friendly agreement with your neighbor on the location, design, and construction of the fence. (One option is a "good neighbor" fence with crosspieces mounted in alternating directions so the fence is attractive from both sides.)

Few lots are perfectly flat. If your fence line runs up a hill, you can build the fence so that it follows the contours of the land. Or construct stepped panels that maintain horizontal lines (see pages 328–329).

A. Wisteria adorns the top of this white picket fence. The thick posts and alternating short pickets add substance to the structure.

B. This open-work brick wall was angled to avoid the roots of the red oak. Its "perforations" let in cooling breezes.

C. Rustic split-rail fences offer little privacy, but are perfect boundary markers for open spaces.

D. Wooden balustrades mimic stone for a timeless look. This fence is well suited to the aged brick pathway.

GATES

Think of gates as doors to the garden. A low picket gate or one made of airy lath invites you in with its open, friendly appearance. A gate tucked into an out-of-the-way corner seems mysterious. A high, solid gate guards the privacy and safety of those within.

Although sometimes used with hedges, gates are typically associated with fences or walls. It's usual to match the gate's style and materials to those of the fence or wall. But you can also choose contrasting materials, such as a wooden or wrought-iron gate within flanking brick pilasters.

A basic gate consists of a rectangular frame with a diagonal brace running from the bottom corner of the hinge side to the top corner of the latch side. Use pressure-treated or other rot-resistant wood. Siding fastened to the frame completes the gate.

Choose strong hinges and latches; it's better to select hardware that's too hefty than too flimsy. Attach both hinges and latches with long galvanized screws, and be sure to use galvanized hardware.

The minimum width for a gate is about 3 feet, but an extra foot creates a more comfortable entry. If you anticipate moving gardening or other equipment through the gate, make the opening wider. For access for cars, consider a two-part gate or even a gate on rollers.

A. Rusted metal pickets are framed by wooden posts. Cross bracing adds strength.

B. Graceful but solid, this gate is set in an ivy-covered wall that arches overhead.

C. Crisp white, stacked panels give a contemporary look to a traditional picket fence and are a perfect foil for the blue door beyond.

A CLASSIC GATE

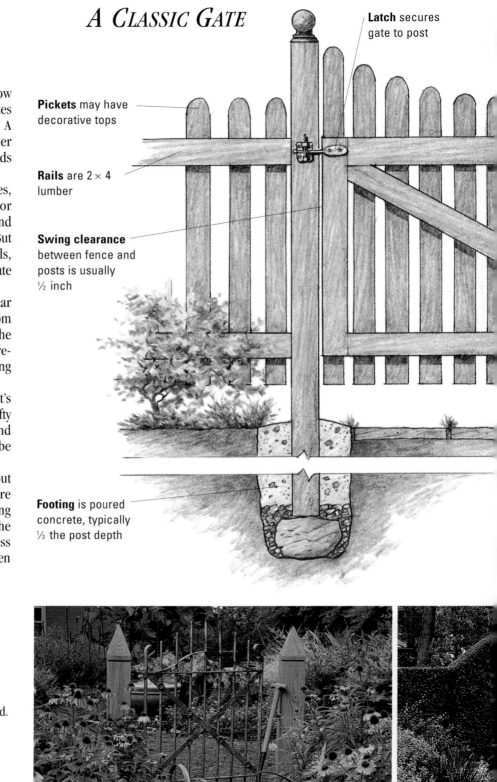

Latch secures gate to post

Pickets may have decorative tops

Rails are 2 × 4 lumber

Swing clearance between fence and posts is usually ½ inch

Footing is poured concrete, typically ⅓ the post depth

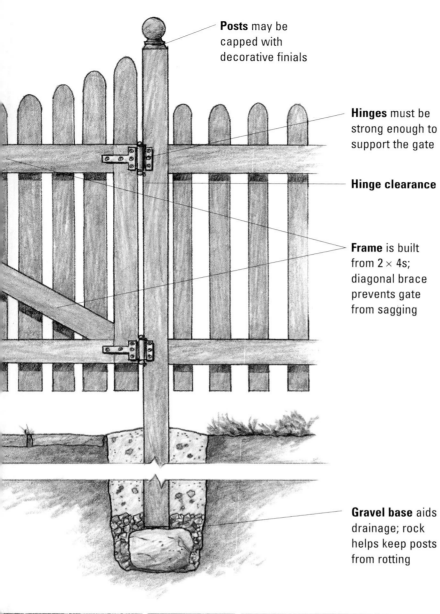

Posts may be capped with decorative finials

Hinges must be strong enough to support the gate

Hinge clearance

Frame is built from 2 × 4s; diagonal brace prevents gate from sagging

Gravel base aids drainage; rock helps keep posts from rotting

D. An attractive half-gate serves as an entry; a vine-covered trellis frames the view beyond.

E. Simple sticks make a lightweight gate hung between a wooden pole and a substantial stone column. This type of gate is more a visual than a physical barrier.

Building walls

Among typical materials for garden walls are uncut stone, brick, concrete block, and poured concrete. Brick and concrete block are the easiest to work with—their uniformity makes them easy to assemble piece by piece. You can choose a decorative pattern for laying the courses, incorporate a solid or open-work face, vary the thickness, and employ a combination of materials.

In the hands of a skilled mason, stone creates walls that seem to be integral to the landscape. Stone native to your region will look the most natural. However, poured concrete offers more design possibilities because surface texture and shape are established by wooden forms.

Regardless of the type of wall you plan to build, you need to support it with a solid foundation or footing (see page 349). Poured concrete is best, because it can be smoothed and leveled better than other materials. Usually, footings are twice the width of the wall and at least as deep as the wall is wide. But consult local codes for exceptions. For very low walls (no more than 12 inches high) or for low raised beds, you can lay the base of the wall directly on tamped soil or in a leveled trench.

In most cases, a freestanding wall more than 2 or 3 feet high should have some kind of reinforcement to tie portions of the wall together and prevent it from collapsing. Steel reinforcing bars, laid with the mortar along the length of a wall, provide horizontal stiffening. Placed upright (for example, between double rows of brick or within the hollow cores of concrete blocks), reinforcing adds vertical strength that can keep a wall from toppling due to its own weight. Special steel ties in various patterns are made for reinforcing masonry or attaching a stone veneer to a poured-concrete or concrete-block substructure.

Vertical columns of masonry, called pilasters, can be tied into a wall to provide additional vertical support. Many building departments require that they be used at least every 12 feet. Also consider placing pilasters on either side of an entrance gate and at the end of freestanding walls.

A BRICK WALL

Header course spans front to back, helps lock the wall together

Corners overlap with 3/4- and 1/4-inch "closure" bricks

Common-bond wall has staggered joints from course to course. Double-thickness ("double wythe") wall is much stronger than a single row of bricks

Reinforcing bars strengthen structure (check local codes)

Poured footing is typically twice wall's width and 12 inches deep (or as deep as frost line)

Gravel base ensures good drainage

Retaining walls

A gentle slope may be tamed with a single low retaining wall or a series of garden steps that hold the surface soil in place. And though a long or steep slope may seem a liability, dividing it into terraces with two or three substantial walls can provide new, usable space.

Because retaining walls act like dams, they must resist pressure from the soil they contain. For maximum stability, a retaining wall should rest on cut or undisturbed ground, never on landfill. Hire a professional contractor if extensive grading is required. If space permits, the simplest approach is not to disturb the slope at all, but to build the wall on the level ground near the foot of the slope and fill in behind it. In all cases, planning for the build-up of water, known as hydrostatic pressure, is critical and may also call for the advice of a professional.

Engineering aside, you can build a retaining wall from dry-stacked or mortared stone, stuccoed or painted concrete block, or brick. New systems for building concrete retaining walls consist of precast modules that stack or lock together via lips, pins, or friction. These modules are easy to install by homeowners and ideal for building 3- or 4-foot retaining walls (see page 351). Wood is another good option for retaining walls, whether various-size boards or railroad ties or wood timbers set vertically or horizontally.

Where engineering is critical, poured concrete may be the only solution. But the labor required can make a concrete wall a costly project. You can make concrete more interesting by using rough boards to texture the finish or by applying a surface veneer.

A. Topped with cedar fencing, this stone retaining wall divides the garden into two level terraces. The fence looks good in its own right, and helps extend the height of the wall without blocking the view from either side.

B. Timeless stacked stone walls add character to the garden and make a sturdy base for a tumble of beautiful flowers. In this case 'Bath's Pink' dianthus fits the bill.

C. A sweeping curve of retaining wall distinctly separates the lawn from the ground cover and other plantings. Vertical 6 × 6 posts are buried up to half of their total length for stability.

GARDEN STORAGE

It's amazing how quickly gardening supplies pile up. Sooner or later every homeowner has to face the challenge of where they can all be stored. While the garage is often the answer, a gardening shed can be both a practical and handsome solution. If you make it big enough to include a counter surface for potting plants and other tasks, the space will be even more functional.

Place a shed where you can get to it—you don't want to traipse across the yard to retrieve a trowel. But if the shed is purely utilitarian, try to nestle it away from outdoor entertainment areas. Fenced yards can often accommodate a small storage space in a corner.

This clever design accommodates a work area, tool storage, and space for trash cans just below the deck. Fence panels conceal the area; mulch keeps it neat.

Repeating the fence pattern on the surface of the shed minimizes the impact the shed has on the view.

The easiest route to storage is a prefabricated shed. Plastic and metal structures are readily available at home centers. More expensive—but also more attractive—are wood sheds, either those you build yourself or from a kit. Although a concrete foundation is preferable for a wood shed, you can cut costs by placing the shed on concrete blocks and building a wooden ramp down to ground level. Check with your local building department before adding a shed—if the structure is considered "permanent" you may need a permit.

A. **An array** of antique tools on the wall of this tin-roofed shed is a reminder of its function in the garden.

B. **Built-in storage** is cleverly concealed behind the lattice-covered door on this arbor. When closed, the compartment is completely invisible.

C. **A variety of uses** suit this covered cabana— storage, shelter, or even a quiet getaway.

D. **The double French** doors of this shed open wide to give easy access for bikes; custom lattice and climbing roses dress up the exterior.

KID STUFF

Children love the outdoors and need a place to expend their energy. But young children have little sense of danger, so play areas must be safe as well as fun.

Preschoolers feel more secure—and can be more easily watched—if the play area is close to the house. You may prefer to site an area for older, noisier children within view

but farther away. Because most children fall in love with wheels at an early age, a good addition to the garden plan is a smooth concrete or asphalt path at least 24 inches wide.

Many public playgrounds feature metal play structures rather than timber, because wood may rot and splinter. Still, wood is a warmer and more versatile material. Use rot-resistant woods such as pressure-treated pine, red cedar, or cypress, and regularly inspect the structure for rough edges and splinters. Plastic slides are comfortable, durable, and won't overheat in the sun. Whatever the material, well-designed structures offer activities for children of different ages.

Sandboxes are another popular feature. Add a wide rim around the top for a convenient seat. You should also consider adding a lid to keep out pets, leaves, and rain.

Perhaps the ultimate embellishment to a play yard is a playhouse—designs range from small-scale Victorian mansions to fairy-tale cottages. If you plan properly, the playhouse can have a second life as a potting shed or a storage area when the kids grow up. Before you begin construction, though, check with your local building department—you may need a building permit.

A. This charming cottage is built with pressure-treated lumber and brightly painted. It can be converted later into a potting shed.

B. Design play structures, such as this one, to blend in with the surroundings and other outdoor buildings.

C. A touch of whimsy can be a delight for children. This comical scarecrow figure is humorous to young and old.

A

Playing It Safe

Site a play area on level ground, far enough from the street to prevent balls from escaping into busy traffic, and away from plantings that can't stand up to rough-and-tumble activity. Look for a spot with dappled shade, as the sun can make metal slides or bars burning hot. But avoid placing play structures near trees with low branches—these present climbing opportunities you may prefer your kids not to have. In a treeless yard, position the play space on the north side of the house. Construct a simple lath or canvas canopy over the area, or build cover from the sun into the play structure itself.

In addition to being sturdy, play structures should be firmly anchored into the ground. To avoid accidents, make sure to allow adequate clearances for swings and around the ends of slides. Plan a "fall zone" of at least 6 feet of space around all sides of play structures, then cushion the area well. A 3-inch layer of wood chips or shredded bark is one choice; increase depth to 6 inches under swings. Sand also provides a good cushion—the deeper the better, even up to 12 inches. Edge the play yard to contain loose materials and keep the cushion thick. Grass also makes a good play surface, but avoid seed mixtures containing clover, because its flowers attract bees. Likewise, ensure that any other plantings immediately around the structure are free of thorns, poisonous berries, or seeds, and are not attractive to stinging insects. Keep grass to 2 inches high for sufficient cushioning.

Ensure that railings are spaced closely together and that wooden surfaces are free of splinters, rough edges, and protruding nails or screws. Regularly inspect fasteners and joints to make sure they are holding fast. Likewise verify that any climbing or swinging ropes are unfrayed and securely attached.

A. This fun playhouse features scaled-down shutters and siding, brightly painted surfaces, and a sandbox with a fitted lid.

B. Ship ahoy! Climbing ropes, a pirate ship, and a soft surface suit these sailors just fine.

C. Framed with cut mimosa branches, this unpretentious playhouse uses runner beans for walls.

SWIMMING POOLS

Once reserved as a luxury, swimming pools are becoming common. With such a wide range of styles—and price ranges—it's easier than ever to add a pool to your garden.

A swimming pool dominates the landscape year-round, so it's important to design it well. First figure out how you plan to use the pool, then let your purpose influence its features. If diving is your passion, you'll need depth; by contrast, lap-swimming requires a long pool, but it need be only 4 to 5 feet deep. Usage by small children dictates a wide shal-

low area for nonswimmers (for more on pool safety, see page 195). A pool just for cooling off or floating a raft or two can be much smaller than one that routinely accommodates groups of boisterous teens. If cost or space are issues, consider an above-ground pool—they are less of an investment than in-ground pools, are often easier to install on sloped sites, and can be landscaped with decking and plantings to be nearly as attractive as an in-ground structure.

Pools typically come in rectangular, oval, L, square,

Curving like a woodland pond, this Maryland pool hugs the hillside. Stone retaining walls hold back the surrounding slope. A dark gray tinting in the pool's finish mimics the quiet waters of a lake.

kidney, angular, free-form, and round shapes. Depending on how the pool is constructed, it's also possible to create your own design, although this will add expense. Try to match the shape of the pool to the style of your house and garden. If you have a Colonial-style home surrounded by formal plantings, for example, a rectangular or L-shaped pool will fit in better than a curvilinear shape.

It's also possible to integrate your pool into the surroundings for year-round interest. Native stone paving, a dark liner or dark-colored plaster that gives the water the look of a lagoon, a natural curving shape, a built-in stream or water-

fall, and planting pockets at the water's edge will help make the pool both an aesthetic and recreational pleasure.

Another factor to consider when adding a pool is the paved area or deck that will surround the water. If you'll be entertaining often, try to incorporate a space that's at least equal to the area of the pool itself. Not only will this give you plenty of room for guests, tables, and chairs, it will help isolate lawns and flower beds from the pool; otherwise, swimmers will inevitably drag plants and soil into the water.

The most common repair for older pools is replastering, which fixes minor cracks, hides stains, or changes the pool's color. You can also install new trim tile or replace the coping to dramatically improve the look of an outdated pool.

A. Screened from the neighbors by a pergola, this pool area is enhanced with bluestone paving and brick bullnose coping.

B. Spraying fountains add the soothing sound of falling water to this graceful setting and turn the pool into a decorative feature.

C. Seeming to vanish into the salt marsh beyond, the pool water spills over the edge into a narrow trough and is recirculated.

Building a Pool

Before building a swimming pool, check into the legal requirements set forth in deed restrictions, zoning laws, and building, health, and safety codes. Also familiarize yourself with the building codes that apply to related structures, such as decks and fences.

In-ground pools are constructed either from sprayed concrete on a steel-reinforced frame or from thick vinyl suspended on a sturdy frame. Concrete pools offer the advantages of durability and design flexibility; in addition, you can choose an interior finish of paint, plaster, or tile (in ascending order of cost). With a vinyl pool, shape is limited to what the manufacturer offers, and your choice of interior finish boils down to the color of the liner. The advantages of vinyl pools are that they're less expensive than concrete and more quickly installed. While it's less durable, you can expect a high-quality vinyl liner to last at least 10 years, and rips and tears can usually be repaired without draining the water.

Above-ground pools cost substantially less than in-ground types. They are made from a steel or aluminum structure and a vinyl liner in a fairly limited number of shapes: circle, oval, square, or rectangle. Above-ground pools are most successfully integrated into a garden's design when recessed at least partially below grade and built with a surrounding deck or raised platform.

A. Natural by design. Tucked into a landscape of predominantly native plants, a spa spills over a stone weir to the pool below. Positioned close to an outdoor fireplace, the spa extends the bathing season through most of the year.

B. On an axis with the house's screened-in porch, a fountain by this L-shaped pool serves as a focal point. The pool looks surprisingly like a pond thanks to fieldstone decking and darkened concrete. A lush mix of trees, shrubs, and flowers borders the pool.

Pool Safety

For pool owners with children—or with young visitors or neighbors—water accidents remain a constant threat. That's why all swimming pools require protective barriers.

Although height requirements vary, most communities insist that properties with pools have a fence to completely enclose the pool area. The fence should have self-closing gates with self-latching mechanisms beyond the reach of young children. If the fence has vertical bars, they should be no more than 4 inches apart; the fence should also have no horizontal pieces that could provide toeholds for climbing. Areas immediately outside the fence should be kept clear of chairs or other objects that could be used to help climb over. If the pool is above ground, you must be able to remove or block the ladder or steps that lead up to the pool, and then remember to always do so. If your entire yard is already fenced, you may not have to add another fence right around the pool, but check with your building inspector to make sure. Most municipalities have a minimum distance from the water's edge to the yard fence, and the yard fencing must also fulfill safety requirements.

Doors and windows that lead from the house directly to the pool can be made more secure with additional locking mechanisms installed at least 5 feet high. Options for sliding glass doors include locks for the top of the moving panel and its frame, automatic sliding door closers, or removable bars that mount to the frame.

Another safety factor to consider is the decking material that surrounds the pool. Because the majority of pool-related accidents involve slips and falls, the decking must have a slip-resistant textured surface. It must also drain properly, to avoid puddles of standing water.

WATER FEATURES

Most people consider water one of the most delightful elements in the garden. For many homeowners, the question is not whether to incorporate water into their gardens, but merely how. Remember that it doesn't take much water to create a cooling, relaxing effect—even the smallest feature will bring refreshing sights and sounds into the garden. If you wish to start small, consider the portable decorative pools and wall-mounted fountains available at garden centers and statuary stores. Spill fountains are another choice—water flows from the outlet into a pool or series of tiered pans.

The obvious spot to place a pond is where everybody can enjoy it. But if you're planning to raise aquatic plants and fish, there are other considerations. The pond must be protected from wind and situated away from deciduous trees that shed leaves and twigs into the water. Proper drainage is also important: Don't choose a low-lying area that will be inundated in wet weather. And remember that the backyard needn't be the only place for a pond. The addition of moving water to a front patio or entryway both cools the air and masks the noise of passing traffic.

The elements bordering a water feature tie it to its surroundings. The choices are many: a grass lawn; an adjoining bog garden or rock garden (often piled against a partially raised pond or used at one end of a sloping site); native stones and boulders; flagstones laid in mortar; a wide concrete lip (especially useful as a mowing strip); brick laid in sand or mortar; or terra-cotta tiles.

Ponds can be built using either a thick, flexible pool liner or a rigid preformed shell. A liner-built pond gives you more design latitude, as shells are available in only limited sizes and shapes (see page 356). Large ponds were traditionally made of concrete but today have been almost entirely replaced by liner-built pools.

A spray fountain or waterfall can be incorporated into any type of pond. Spray fountains suit formal ponds. Assorted fountain heads can shoot water in massive columns or lacy mists. Waterfalls send a cascade toward the pond from a simple outlet pipe. Both features use a recirculating submersible pump. Check with an electrician or your local building department before bringing electricity out to the pond. Water and electricity can be a deadly mix, and safety codes give precise specifications. Because children find ponds irresistible, also check with your local building department about safety and other requirements. Generally, ponds less than 24 inches deep do not need a building permit. (Bear in mind that the minimum depth for raising plants and fish in a pond is about 18 inches.)

A. An old millstone finds new purpose as the centerpiece of this small spraying fountain.

B. Another recycled item is this broken-handled urn, which spills recirculated water into a small pond.

C. **Flea-market finds** such as this battered brass horn make inexpensive eye- and ear-catching fountains.

D. **Native stones and plants** help this cascading waterfall blend into a hillside.

E. **A classical feature** such as this cherub fountain is a simple way to dress up an elegant swimming pool.

A Simple Pond

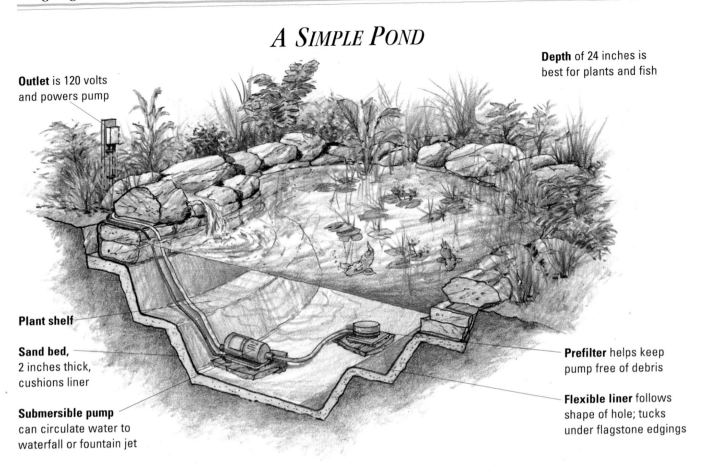

Outlet is 120 volts and powers pump

Depth of 24 inches is best for plants and fish

Plant shelf

Sand bed, 2 inches thick, cushions liner

Submersible pump can circulate water to waterfall or fountain jet

Prefilter helps keep pump free of debris

Flexible liner follows shape of hole; tucks under flagstone edgings

Pond in a Pot

Water features don't have to be expensive. The simple one shown here cost under $400 and took a weekend to make.

Start by purchasing a concrete planter with a drain hole in the bottom. Then coat the inside of the planter with water sealer to keep the concrete from absorbing water. This will prevent cracking during a freeze.

Purchase a small submersible pump—consult your local garden center about what size to buy. Set the pump in the planter, and run the cord through the drain hole (if the hole is too small for the plug, either enlarge the hole with a drill fitted with a ⅝-in. drill bit, or remove and then reattach the plug after the cord has been threaded through the hole). You can conceal and protect the cord by running it through ¾-inch plastic conduit (top left) to a grounded electrical outlet.

Set the pump at the desired height, then use a cork to plug the drain hole and hold the cord in place. Seal both sides of the hole with silicone sealant (available at hardware stores).

Let the silicone set overnight. Make sure the container is level (top right) before filling it with water and plugging in the cord. Surround the fountain with flowers and sit back to enjoy the wonderful sound of water.

C. Flea-market finds such as this battered brass horn make inexpensive eye- and ear-catching fountains.

D. Native stones and plants help this cascading waterfall blend into a hillside.

E. A classical feature such as this cherub fountain is a simple way to dress up an elegant swimming pool.

A SIMPLE POND

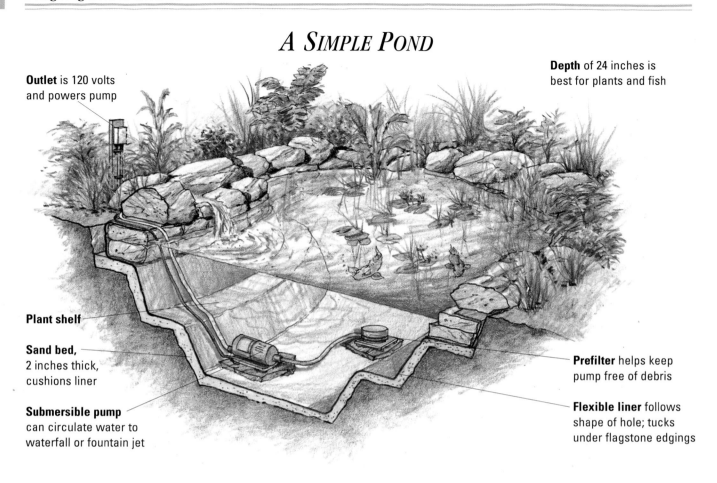

Outlet is 120 volts and powers pump

Depth of 24 inches is best for plants and fish

Plant shelf

Sand bed, 2 inches thick, cushions liner

Submersible pump can circulate water to waterfall or fountain jet

Prefilter helps keep pump free of debris

Flexible liner follows shape of hole; tucks under flagstone edgings

Pond in a Pot

Water features don't have to be expensive. The simple one shown here cost under $400 and took a weekend to make.

Start by purchasing a concrete planter with a drain hole in the bottom. Then coat the inside of the planter with water sealer to keep the concrete from absorbing water. This will prevent cracking during a freeze.

Purchase a small submersible pump—consult your local garden center about what size to buy. Set the pump in the planter, and run the cord through the drain hole (if the hole is too small for the plug, either enlarge the hole with a drill fitted with a ⅝-in. drill bit, or remove and then reattach the plug after the cord has been threaded through the hole). You can conceal and protect the cord by running it through ¾-inch plastic conduit (top left) to a grounded electrical outlet.

Set the pump at the desired height, then use a cork to plug the drain hole and hold the cord in place. Seal both sides of the hole with silicone sealant (available at hardware stores).

Let the silicone set overnight. Make sure the container is level (top right) before filling it with water and plugging in the cord. Surround the fountain with flowers and sit back to enjoy the wonderful sound of water.

A. **Viewed from garden's end**, this brick-edged circular pond and gravel path form a strong central axis in the yard.

B. **Stone edging** and a natural shape help this pond blend seamlessly with the fountain and surrounding garden.

C. **Flowing down a rocky bank**, this stream splashes into a koi pond. Lacy Japanese maples, ferns, and mosses add texture.

D. **This sunken garden** has as its centerpiece a small concrete-rimmed pond. The setting is formal, yet relaxed.

A. **This well-worn** stone trough, nearly overflowing with ivy, contributes to the atmosphere of seclusion in this garden.

B. **Vivid colors** and a strong geometric form create a dynamic and striking centerpiece within a narrow, contemporary space.

C. **The epitome of elegance,** this beautiful fountain is the focus of a formal parterre garden.

D. **Brick edging** and an ornate fountain are classic features for a raised pool. Even a small water feature such as this can house a water lily or two.

DRAINAGE

Water inexorably runs downhill and, in so doing, cuts the earth, often leaving gullies in its wake. It also pools in low-lying spots, causing problems such as dying plants, soggy areas, rotting wood, a wet basement, and mosquitoes. So it's worth making sure your garden drains well.

Cutting a swale into the ground is a common way to channel water. A swale is nothing more than a small gully—if you already have water washing its way through your backyard, then you probably have a natural swale carved through your yard. Muddy and messy, these miniature ravines alternately flood and dry, depending on the season.

A far better alternative is to guide excess water over the ground in a dry creek (a man-made stream bed of river rocks). Unlike wet creeks, which have a constant stream of water flowing through them, dry creeks handle only occasional runoff. The stones slow the flow of water, as well as anchor the banks and prevent the swale from widening. And, when azaleas, mondo grass, ajuga, irises, hostas, daylilies, and other plants are planted alongside, a dry creek can look pretty and natural year-round. Just make sure not to divert water onto adjoining properties—doing so not only is unneighborly, but may also be illegal.

Create a dry creek by lining the bottom and sides of the creek with any kind of rocks. Smooth river rocks will give your dry creek a natural look. Large stones work just as well, including ones dug from your own property. In more formal settings, consider lining the bottom of the dry creek with bricks.

Although it is possible to divert runoff by regrading a site or channeling water through underground pipes to a sewer, retention pond, or dry well, you run the risk of losing existing trees whenever you excavate. These alternatives

---

Lined with gravel and bordered by a stone retaining wall, this drainage channel directs water away from the base of the trees.

are expensive and tear up the yard. Consider instead planting trees and shrubs that absorb lots of water, such as bald cypress, bayberry, red maple, river birch, weeping willow, and sweet pepperbush. Perennials such as canna, cardinal flower, elephant's ear, forget-me-not, Japanese iris, yellow-flag iris, and ferns also thrive in wet conditions.

A. This formerly soggy slope is now a waterfall surrounded by river stones and skillful plantings.

B. A simple brick drain captures excess runoff and channels it away.

C. Up a creek. This dry creek is planted with ferns to resemble a woodland stream—and to prevent erosion.

'Constance Spry' rose

DESIGNING WITH PLANTS

If a garden's structures provide its "bones," plants flesh it out. With endless variation, plants add color, texture, movement, and fragrance. Placed correctly, they can focus views or dazzle with an eye-catching show. They cool down summer days and buffer frigid winds, affording us both comfort and shelter. Some plants attract wildlife, while others supply cut flowers and foliage to bring the garden indoors.

The best-laid gardens are not simply a collection of individual plants, chosen for their unique properties, but a woven tapestry of flower, form, and foliage. Each plant adds a vital thread.

As you create your garden, remember that it will never be static. Unlike building materials, plants are ever-changing. They bloom, change color, grow, and mature. Helping—and watching—this happen is the greatest reward of a well-designed garden.

TREES

No matter where you live or what garden style you prefer, the first questions you should ask when developing your garden's design are, "Where are my existing trees?" and "What new trees would I like to add and where do I want them to go?"

As your garden's largest living element, trees have an enormous impact, both practical and aesthetic. On the practical side, they offer shade and shelter from the wind, enhancing your comfort and often considerably reducing your home's energy consumption. As design elements, trees can frame the house, establish scale, sport colorful blooms and foliage, conceal unsightly features, or draw the eye toward attractive vistas.

Among the most important contributions trees make to a garden is to lend an air of permanence. While a hollyhock may give up the ghost after a year or two, an oak can live for centuries. A stately tree that forms the centerpiece of your garden may well have been the legacy of a farsighted gardener from many years earlier.

For stunning fall color, sugar maple in shades of gold, orange, and red, and scarlet 'October Glory' red maple are excellent choices for the South.

TREE SILHOUETTES

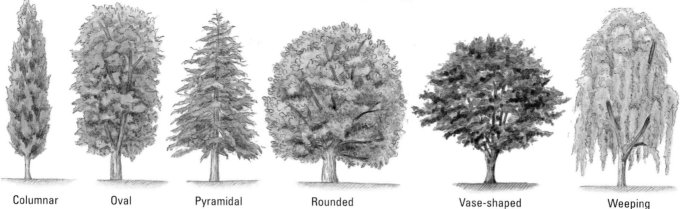

Columnar   Oval   Pyramidal   Rounded   Vase-shaped   Weeping

Choosing the right tree

When selecting trees for your garden, ask first what you want the tree to do. Should it shade the yard? Pick a tall-growing species that develops a sizable canopy. Should it hide a neighboring property? That may call for an evergreen tree with foliage all the way to the ground. Perhaps you'd like a focal point. Look for a tree with striking flowers, foliage, bark, or form. Once you have decided on the tree's purpose, you can narrow your selection.

The most basic distinction between trees is whether they are deciduous or evergreen. Deciduous trees sprout new leaves in spring and carry them throughout the summer. In fall, the leaves may turn brilliant colors before dropping for the winter. Evergreen trees, on the other hand, retain their foliage year-round, making them ideal for screens or as points of interest during winter months. Broad-leafed evergreens, such as Southern magnolias and hollies, have wide leaves similar to many deciduous trees. Needle-leafed evergreens, such as pines and cedars, sport narrow, needlelike leaves.

Once you've decided between deciduous or evergreen, consider the tree's growth rate and ultimate size. A desire for quick shade or instant privacy may tempt you to buy a fast-growing species such as silver maple or cottonwood, but such a vigorous tree can crack sidewalks, invade water lines, or quickly overwhelm the house, calling for replacement at a later date.

Consider, too, a tree's mature shape (above), which may not be obvious when you buy a small sapling at the nursery. A vase-shaped type, such as a Japanese zelkova, makes a good choice for a lawn or street tree, because its ascending branches leave plenty of headroom underneath. Rounded, spreading trees, such as live oaks and Norway maples, need lots of space to extend their branches. Columnar or conical trees, such as eastern red cedar and Arizona cypress, work well in closer quarters.

Many trees offer a spectacular burst of color in fall, but consider their summer and winter foliage tones as well. Deciduous trees with golden, bronze, red, or bluish summer foliage should be treated as accents and used sparingly to avoid a jumble of colors. Likewise, use caution when selecting evergreens with colored foliage, such as many cedars and cypresses.

PLANTING TREES

A. Mature deciduous trees lend an established look and shade the front of the house in summer.

B. Flowering tree in bloom adds color to front entryway.

C. Needle-leafed evergreens screen the driveway year-round.

D. Broad-leafed evergreens offer privacy and shade without excessive leaf litter.

HOUSE

◄ NORTH

CARING FOR TREES

Limbing up. Gradually removing a tree's lower branches reveals the structure of the tree. This practice also increases the amount of sunlight reaching the ground, making it easier to grow grass and flowers around the tree. And it gives more headroom under the tree's canopy. As a general rule, don't limb up more than half of a tree's height, less if possible.

Thinning. Selectively thin the branches of a shade tree to reduce the likelihood of wind damage, open up views, and prevent the tree from forming an overly dense canopy. Remove weak limbs and vertical water sprouts first, and any branches that rub or cross each other. Clear out branches growing toward the center of the tree. Then you can prune selectively along the main limbs, leaving a natural-looking, broad, and bushy top.

Preserving the roots. To keep a tree healthy, start at the bottom. If you build a patio or walkway around the base of a tree, avoid solid materials such as concrete, which prevent air and water from reaching the roots. Select paving that leaves as much open soil as possible around the trunk, use loose materials, or set bricks or paving stones in sand or gravel rather than cement.

If removing soil near a tree to construct a retaining wall or for some other purpose, try to preserve the existing grade around the tree by making any elevation changes beyond the branch spread. For soil-level changes over 2 feet deep, consult an arborist.

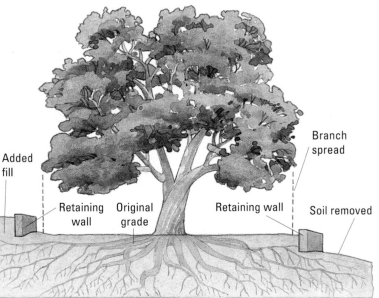

Added fill

Retaining wall

Original grade

Retaining wall

Branch spread

Soil removed

Avoiding problems

It seems obvious, but the easiest way to avoid disappointment with a tree is by selecting one well suited to your climate and soil. Don't try to plant trees that are not reliably cold-hardy in your area or those that need more rainfall than you receive. Sooner or later Mother Nature will get even, and the trees will suffer from cold or drought stress, making them more susceptible to pests and diseases.

Other trees to avoid include those that are prone to pests; those with weak wood that can lose limbs in storms; those that drop messy fruit, seedlings (such as the chinaberry above), or more leaves than you are willing to rake; and those with invasive roots. In addition to the trees listed at right, your local nursery or garden center should be able to advise you on trees that are problematic in your region.

Ten Troublesome Trees

Think twice (or even thrice) about planting the following:

ARIZONA ASH (Fraxinus velutina)
Weak wood; invasive roots

BLACK CHERRY (Prunus serotina)
Messy fruit; pest-prone

BOX ELDER (Acer negundo)
Lots of seedlings; pest-prone

CAMPHOR TREE (Cinnamomum camphora)
Messy seeds; weak wood

CHINABERRY (Melia azedarach)
Messy fruit; lots of seedlings

EASTERN COTTONWOOD (Populus deltoides)
Weak wood; invasive roots

HYBRID POPLAR (Populus)
Invasive roots

MIMOSA (Albizia julibrissin)
Pest-prone; lots of seedlings

SILVER MAPLE (Acer saccharinum)
Weak wood; invasive roots

WHITE MULBERRY (Morus alba)
Messy fruit; lots of seedlings

Why Not Top?

Topping—reducing the height of a mature tree by lopping off its top limbs—is the quickest way to ruin a tree forever. What's more, it doesn't even reduce the height of a tree for very long. Unlike a bushy hedge that soon sprouts new growth after being sheared severely, an older tree does not grow back in a natural-looking way when trunk leaders or top branches are pruned to stubs. Instead, the tree sends out scores of weak shoots from the cutoff points; often these shoots are taller, coarser, and denser than the natural top. Topped trees often develop heart rot, eventually resulting in hollow trunks. This makes them susceptible to storm damage.

Some topped trees might eventually regain their beauty, but the recovery can take decades. A good professional arborist will not top a tree, but will try other techniques to scale it back.

Great Choices for Small Areas

FOR THE UPPER AND MIDDLE SOUTH:

EASTERN REDBUD (Cercis canadensis)

FLOWERING DOGWOOD (Cornus florida)

JAPANESE MAPLE (Acer palmatum)

SERVICEBERRY (Amelanchier)

SOURWOOD (Oxydendrum arboreum)

SWEET BAY (Magnolia virginiana)

FOR THE LOWER SOUTH:

CREPE MYRTLE (Lagerstroemia indica)

FLOWERING DOGWOOD (Cornus florida)

GOLDENRAIN TREE (Koelreuteria paniculata)

JAPANESE MAPLE (Acer palmatum)

SOUTHERN MAGNOLIA
Magnolia grandiflora 'Little Gem'

SWEET BAY (Magnolia virginiana)

FOR THE COASTAL AND TROPICAL SOUTH:

CREPE MYRTLE (Lagerstroemia indica)

DRAKE CHINESE ELM (Ulmus parvifolia 'Drake')

GLOSSY PRIVET (Ligustrum lucidum)

ORCHID TREE (Bauhinia)

PALMS

TEXAS MOUNTAIN LAUREL (Sophora secundiflora)

USING SMALL TREES

When it comes to trees, bigger isn't always better. Many locations, such as courtyards, terraces, patios, and decks, call for small, well-mannered trees that provide much-needed shade and screening but don't drop messy fruits or seeds. The trees listed at left don't harbor insects, and their roots won't pry up paving or damage foundations.

Small, deciduous trees work well, as long as you don't mind sweeping up their autumn leaves. In many places, a crepe myrtle proves the ideal choice, combining quick shade, showy summer flowers, colorful fall foliage, and handsome winter bark. Japanese maple, with its slow growth, elegant form, and beautiful leaves, is another favorite. Other choices are flowering dogwood, Drake Chinese elm, sweet bay, redbud, sourwood, and goldenrain tree.

If you prefer evergreens for year-round color, choose broad-leafed types, such as glossy privet, 'Little Gem' Southern magnolia, yaupon, or Texas mountain laurel. In Florida, many smaller palms, including pindo palm, windmill palm, and Chinese fan palm, serve admirably as patio accents. In general, needle-leafed evergreens aren't recommended for small spaces; their shedding needles require constant sweeping.

Some small trees, such as crepe myrtle and glossy privet, grow quickly, but others, including sourwood and Japanese maple, grow slower than a stalactite. For quick effect, consider starting with a fairly mature specimen.

Perfect view. Sourwood is ideal for planting near the house, deck, or patio, because it suffers from few pests and its roots won't lift paving. For dependable fall color, it's hard to beat.

EVERGREEN TREES

Mainstays of Southern gardens, evergreen trees play a number of roles. Because they hold their foliage year-round, they add constant structure and visual weight to the landscape. They lend color and interest to wintertime, when deciduous trees are barren. During the warmer months they can supply a solid backdrop to show off flowering trees and shrubs. Many make useful windbreaks and tall screens, while others are good shade trees.

Needle-leafed evergreens (often called conifers) include spruce *(Picea),* hemlock *(Tsuga),* true cedar *(Cedrus),* American arborvitae *(Thuja occidentalis),* pine *(Pinus),* Leyland cypress *(Cupressocyparis leylandii),* and eastern red cedar *(Juniperus virginiana).* Common broad-leafed choices include Southern magnolia *(Magnolia grandiflora),* American holly *(Ilex opaca),* glossy privet *(Ligustrum lucidum),* live oak *(Quercus virginiana),* Carolina cherry laurel *(Prunus caroliniana),* and palms (see page 212).

Chief among the drawbacks of evergreen trees is the dense shade they cast, which makes it nearly impossible to grow grass beneath them. And because their low branching structure leaves little headroom, they make poor street, lawn, or courtyard trees. Of course, you can always prune up the lower branches, but this can sacrifice the natural form and beauty of the tree. (Pines are a notable exception; most pines naturally drop their lower limbs as they grow.)

Messiness is another common problem with evergreen trees. While deciduous trees drop leaves and most other litter only in the fall, many evergreens shed leaves, needles, cones, and seeds year-round.

Evergreen trees tend to dominate a garden, so use them judiciously. Planting too many results in a gloomy, overshadowed garden unsuitable for most flowering plants. And be sure you know how tall and wide they'll grow before planting them near the house, street, or sidewalk.

A. Like a gilded spire, golden threadleaf Sawara false cypress *(Chamaecyparis pisifera* 'Filifera Aurea') serves as both a colorful and vertical accent the year round.

B. No finer broad-leafed evergreen tree exists than Southern magnolia. But give it plenty of room, and don't bother trying to grow grass beneath it.

CHINESE FAN PALM (Livistona chinensis) Strongly drooping, dark green leaf tips resemble a fountain. Remains trunkless for years; develops a broad head and reaches 15 ft. tall. Makes a fine patio palm if sheltered from the wind and hot afternoon sun. Hardy to 22°F.

EUROPEAN FAN PALM (Chamaerops humilis) Blue-green or silvery green leaves make this palm outstanding. Forms clumps if not pruned. Hardy to 6°F, yet also endures baking sun and drought. Grows slowly to 20 ft. Leaf stems carry sharp spines.

PINDO PALM (Butia capitata) Hardy, slow-growing palm reaches 10–20 ft. Heavy, patterned trunk; trim stubs on trunk to same length. Has feathery, arching, gray-green leaves and red edible fruit in summer.

PALMS

Like red beans and rice, palms and Florida seem to go together. But except for cabbage palm and a few others, most of the palms we see in Florida aren't native to the Sunshine State. Canary Island date palm, for instance, comes from the waters off northern Africa.

Surprisingly, many palms are cold-hardy. Windmill palm, one of the hardiest, tolerates temperatures as cold as 5 degrees F. Many others can withstand brief periods of freezing temperatures, making them viable candidates for not only Coastal and Tropical South gardens, but also milder areas of the Lower South.

Although palms are not suited to every garden, they can shine in the right setting. They can line an avenue, shade a deck, serve as accents, or form an evergreen backdrop. Some, such as lady palm and European fan palm, stay shrublike for many years, thriving under taller trees, as well as in entryway plantings, mixed borders, and courtyards.

Palms are especially effective near swimming pools, because they don't drop leaves and their roots don't buckle paving. Fronds, whether fanlike or feathery, reflect beautifully in the water. So do the curved trunks of Senegal date palm, which create an atmosphere reminiscent of the tropics.

When carefully placed, palms produce dramatic effects. Night lighting particularly shows off their stateliness and spectacular leaves. You can backlight them, shine spotlights up on them from below, or direct lights to silhouette them against a pale wall (see page 317). Sunlight also casts evocative shadow patterns onto walls.

So many different palms exist for the garden, it's hard to keep up with them all. The modest array presented here represents tried-and-true choices for just about anywhere palms can be grown.

The epitome of grace, Canary Island date palm arches its exotic fronds over the garden. Although tropical, it withstands freezing weather for brief periods.

Cabbage palm   Senegal date palm

PALMS FOR HOME GARDENS

Chinese fan palm

European fan palm

Pindo palm

LADY PALM (Rhapis) Dense palm; multiple stems bear dark green, glossy leaves. Makes good screen but grows slowly. Requires little pruning. R. excelsa grows 5–12 ft., R. humilis to 18 ft. Prefers rich, moist soil and protection from sun and drying winds. Hardy to 22°F.

WINDMILL PALM (Trachycarpus fortunei) Stiff, upright shape; hairy brown trunk. Can reach 30 ft. in warm-winter areas; shorter elsewhere. Looks best in groups of three or more. Fronds get shabby in wind and must be trimmed. Hardy to 5°F.

CABBAGE PALM (Sabal palmetto) Single-trunked and slow growing to 90 ft. Dense, globular head formed by leaves 5–8 ft. across. Tolerates wind, salt spray, and sand; ideal for coastal gardens.

SENEGAL DATE PALM (Phoenix reclinata) Picturesque clumps grow from offshoots, with several curving trunks to 20–30 ft. high; remove offshoots for single-trunked tree; hardy to 28°F.

QUEEN PALM (Syagrus romanzoffianum) Lush, plumelike leaves, 10–15 ft. long. Grows quickly to 30–50 ft. tall. Shelter from winds; needs abundant water and regular fertilizer. May occasionally survive freezing spells down to 25°F.

BAMBOO PALM (Chamaedorea) Several species, most with clumping, bamboolike growth. All grow slowly to 5 ft.–10 ft. Frost tender; needs ample water and a shady spot.

PYGMY DATE PALM (Phoenix roebelenii) Soft, feathery leaves; stem grows slowly to 6 ft. Wind resistant but tender, and suffers below 28°F. Silver date palm (P. sylvestris) is similar in shape, but hardier and grows 20–30 ft. tall.

CANARY ISLAND DATE PALM (Phoenix canariensis) Hardy to 20°F. Big, heavy-trunked plant to 60 ft. tall; gracefully arching fronds can form crown up to 50 ft. wide. Young plants do well in pots.

Queen palm   Lady palm   Windmill palm   Bamboo palm   Pygmy date palm   Canary Island date palm

LAWN TREES

By definition, a good lawn tree is one that casts shade yet allows you to grow grass beneath it. Yet shade is not the only reason to plant a tree in your lawn.

First, the right tree can fill the vertical space above a very large, empty lawn. This reduces the huge expanse of green to a scale that makes an onlooker feel comfortable. Second, it can frame the view of your house to onlookers. Finally, a tree may offer spectacular seasonal color in the form of flowers, foliage, or fruit.

Many trees, while fine ornamentals, make poor lawn trees, unless the lawn is especially large. Dense shade, low branches, surface roots, and messy seeds or fruits either make growing grass beneath them difficult or greatly interfere with mowing. Unsuitable trees for the lawn include live oak (dense shade), Southern magnolia (dense shade, low branches, surface roots), beech (dense shade, surface roots), hemlock (dense shade, low branches), pin oak (low branches), female ginkgo (messy, malodorous fruits), and sweet gum (spiny gum balls). If you insist on growing one of these, consider planting a shade-loving ground cover beneath it. What are some good trees for planting in the lawn? At right are our top ten picks.

Showy in every season, flowering dogwood makes a fine lawn tree in a situation where it is lightly shaded by surrounding tall hardwoods and pines.

Top Ten Lawn Trees

CHINESE ELM
Ulmus parvifolia

CHINESE PISTACHE
Pistacia chinensis

CREPE MYRTLE
Lagerstroemia indica

JAPANESE ZELKOVA
Zelkova serrata

LOBLOLLY PINE (Pinus taeda)

PALMS

RED MAPLE (Acer rubrum)

RED OAK (Quercus rubra)

RIVER BIRCH (Betula nigra)

THORNLESS HONEY LOCUST
Gleditsia triacanthos inermis

STREET TREES

Think about the most beautiful neighborhoods you've ever driven or walked through. What was it that made the experience special? Maybe it was the architecture of the houses, the profusion of flowers, or the sheer perfection of the lawns. But chances are, what really set those neighborhoods apart were the glorious trees lining the streets.

When planting street trees, keep this rule in mind—to maximize impact, minimize variety. A street lined with a single species makes a statement. One planted with a hodgepodge looks weak and accidental. If your neighbors can't agree on a single species for the entire street, consider choosing a single type for each block. When making your selection, remember the following points.

❧ Avoid trees that drop fruit on the street, sidewalk, or parked cars.

❧ Favor trees with ascending branches, such as Japanese zelkova, that leave plenty of headroom underneath. Avoid those with descending branches, such as pin oak, which always get in the way.

❧ Look for trees with outstanding fall color, such as sugar maple, red maple, male ginkgo, Chinese pistache, or Bradford pear.

❧ Consider trees with widespread limbs, which can link with those from the other side of the street to form a canopy above the road. Willow oaks, sugar maples, and Norway maples do this, but the best of all for forming such a dramatic canopy is live oak.

A. For dramatic impact line a street with only one kind of tree, such as these littleleaf lindens in historic Richmond.

B. Majestic live oaks link their branches to form a leafy canopy above this peaceful country drive. Blooming azaleas line the understory.

Enhancing the view

Trees are so valuable to any landscape that they should be incorporated into a view—or used to enhance it—whenever possible. They're wonderful for establishing a sense of perspective for distant vistas, such as mountains or lakes, thereby creating closeness and intimacy within a grand panorama.

Here in the South, a traditional way to frame a view is through the use of an allée—a double row of trees that focuses attention on a distant object, such as a house, gate, or other focal point. Live oaks and eastern red cedars are popular subjects for allées, but employing them requires lots of space. In a typical suburban lot, smaller trees, such as Japanese maples, crepe myrtles, or yaupons, can perform the same function on a modest scale.

Single trees can become beautiful views in their own right, especially when planted so that their form and structure are easily visible, perhaps from several spots around the garden or even within the house. Each species of tree possesses its own distinctive silhouette, usually best appreciated in winter. Then, leafless deciduous trees fully reveal their basic structure, while evergreens don't have to compete for attention with the more showy plants of summer.

A. Pointing the way. This allée of red cedars in St. Michael's, Maryland, directs the eye to the house at the end of the drive.

B. Form and structure can dominate in winter as well as summer, as illustrated by this blue Atlas cedar at Winterthur Museum and Gardens in Delaware.

B

A

B

C

Gardening with shade

It's an unavoidable fact that trees block the sun. And as they grow, the amount of shade they cast increases, sometimes beyond the tolerance of plants growing below. So when selecting trees, keep in mind that not all shade is created equal. Some trees, such as honey locust, palms, loblolly pine, and Chinese pistache, cast a light, dappled shade that is preferred by many understory plants. Others, such as Southern magnolia and beech, cast dense shade that limits your planting choices.

Careful planning matches the amount of shade needed by flowers, shrubs, and ground covers with the tree that will produce it. And although it's true that choices of flowering plants for shade are fewer than those for sun, you can create equally striking effects by combining plants for foliage texture and color.

A. Happy in shade, native blue phlox *(Phlox divaricata)* and white foamflower *(Tiarella cordifolia)* carpet the ground beneath the airy branches of native azaleas.

B. Lush hostas, sensitive ferns *(Onoclea sensibilis),* and Spanish bluebells *(Endymion hispanicus)* form a splendid combination in this shady border.

C. Cold-hardy and colorful, hardy begonias *(Begonia grandis)* prefer light shade and moist, acid soil. They bloom in late summer and often reseed, forming large sweeps of color.

Plantings beneath trees need not be confined to ground covers. Here a profusion of shade-lovers flourishes beneath a crepe myrtle and a Japanese maple.

A Shade Garden

Planting area: 32' × 12'

The Plants

PERENNIALS

A. BEAR'S BREECH
Acanthus mollis **(3)**

B. HARDY BEGONIA
Begonia grandis **(6)**

C. SEDGE
Carex elata 'Bowles Golden' **(3)**

D. COMMON FOXGLOVE
Digitalis purpurea **(6)**

E. AUTUMN FERN
Dryopteris erythrosora **(3)**

F. CORSICAN HELLEBORE
Helleborus argutifolius **(3)**

G. LENTEN ROSE
Helleborus orientalis **(3)**

H. PLANTAIN LILY
Hosta 'August Moon' **(1)**

I. PLANTAIN LILY
Hosta 'Halcyon' **(1)**

J. SPOTTED DEAD NETTLE
Lamium maculatum 'White Nancy' **(3)**

K. BIG BLUE LILY TURF
Liriope muscari 'Big Blue' **(3)**

L. LILY TURF
Liriope muscari 'Monroe's White' **(5)**

TREES AND SHRUBS

M. JAPANESE MAPLE
Acer palmatum 'Osakazuki' **(1)**

N. OAKLEAF HYDRANGEA
Hydrangea quercifolia 'Harmony' **(1)**

O. CREPE MYRTLE
Lagerstroemia indica 'Sioux' **(1)**

SHRUBS

Take away shrubs from your property and you remove not only beauty, but much of what makes the garden comfortable, safe, and livable. Without shrubs, there would be no hedges to keep children and pets safely in bounds and no lilacs or roses to gather for bouquets. House lines would seem stark and angular without the softening effect of familiar shrubs such as holly, crepe myrtle, and boxwood. And shrubs help define the overall shape and limits of the garden, directing traffic, leading the eye to particular features, and dividing various areas of large gardens into more intimate spaces.

Just as furniture defines a room's character, shrubs define a garden's style. Closely clipped hedges lend formality; shrubs with cascading branches make a border look exuberant and free. And blossoming shrubs can form the basis for an overall color palette.

In early spring, Korean azalea bursts into bloom, making it a fine choice for a specimen or accent shrub.

Shrubs have a practical side too. Tall screens and hedges provide privacy, block unpleasant sights and sounds, and bar unwelcome visitors. They also stop winds and help to create microclimates, allowing you to grow tender plants that otherwise might succumb to cold.

Judiciously placed, a single flowering shrub can punctuate the landscape as an accent or a focal point. Other shrubs, when grouped together, add structure to a garden and make a smooth transition from the tree canopy to ground level.

Like trees, shrubs are either evergreen or deciduous. Southerners traditionally favor evergreens, because they give the garden year-round form and substance. They also serve as effective backdrops for plants with showy flowers and foliage. However, deciduous shrubs enjoy a looseness and grace their evergreen counterparts lack. They often compensate for dropping leaves with colorful seasonal displays.

About pruning

Nearly all shrubs need some pruning to maintain their form and vigor. So consider the shrub's growth rate and your own energy level before selecting a plant at the garden center.

Be especially mindful of the shrub's eventual size when placing it near the house. If you have to take loppers to the plant every other week to keep it from devouring a doorway or harpooning an overhang, you've obviously chosen the wrong plant. Fast-growing shrubs that cause frequent problems near the house or other structures include pyracantha (firethorn), Hetz Chinese juniper, thorny elaeagnus, Burford holly, and photinia.

The best time to prune spring-flowering shrubs is immediately after their blossoms fade. Prune summer-flowering shrubs in late winter or early spring. You can prune non-blooming evergreens at almost any time.

Shrubs as Trees

The primary distinction between a tree and a shrub isn't height—it's the number of trunks. Trees usually have just one. Shrubs have many. So by removing most of a shrub's trunks and lower branches, you can train it into a treelike form.

Why do this? Let's say a greatly overgrown Burford holly forms an untidy green mass near the house. You could take a chainsaw and lop it off at the ground. But by removing the lower limbs instead, you reveal the surprisingly sculptural quality of the trunk. The shrub also appears lighter in the landscape and no longer dominates the house.

Removing the branches to show off the plant's form can also turn a single-season shrub, like an evergreen azalea, into one with multiseason interest. And it leaves room beneath the shrub for planting grass, ground cover, or flowers.

Shrubs trained to a single trunk are called standards. Standards range in size from large crepe myrtles and hollies planted in the yard to small plants grown in containers. Good candidates for standards in pots include Chinese hibiscus, rosemary, lantana, juniper, camellia, roses, Indian hawthorn, and princess flower (Tibouchina urvilleana).

Regularly prune limbed-up shrubs and standards, or they will revert to their natural form. This includes removing any suckers that sprout near the base of the trunk.

Removing the lower branches of winged euonymus (above, left) and common boxwoods (above) reveals their sculptural qualities and gives them a lighter look.

A

Foundation plantings

To garden designers, the term "foundation planting" has become a cliché. But to gardeners, it's still an essential part of the landscape. In fact, the first living things a new home-owner usually plants in front of the house are shrubs.

The undeserved reputation of foundation planting began when homebuilders used bushes to hide ugly, exposed concrete foundations. Unfortunately, as house facades improved, foundation plantings didn't. No matter the size or style of house, people plastered the foundation with an impenetrable wall of bushes that darkened windows and obstructed steps. Then, in order to scale down to the lawn or flower beds, there evolved "The Three Bears" style of design—great big Papa plants in back, middle-sized Mama plants in the middle, and wee Baby plants in front.

To be sure, foundation plantings still have their place. They can anchor the house to the site, hide utilities and downspouts, and direct people to the door. But for them to work well at your house, follow these guidelines.

☙ Don't copy the neighbors. Their taste is not your taste, nor is their house an exact copy of your own.

☙ Match the style of the planting to the style of your house. For example, a traditional, symmetrical house calls for a traditional, symmetrical planting.

☙ De-emphasize the negative. Planting tall, narrow ever-greens, such as arborvitae, on the corners of a tall, narrow house only emphasizes its vertical shape. Planting rounded or spreading plants, such as crepe myrtle or boxwood, softens the line and makes the house appear wider.

☙ Simple is better. A planting of three to four plants looks unified. One that has nine or ten looks like a person dressed in a striped shirt, plaid pants, and a spotted tie.

☙ Flower colors should complement, not copy, the house color. For instance, don't plant orange or red azaleas in front of a red brick house (see page 254).

☙ Plant for the future, not just for today. Find out how wide a shrub normally spreads and leave ample space between plants for this growth. Don't cram them together because it looks better today; crowded plants usually become unhealthy plants.

☙ If your house facade is beautiful, show it off. Don't hide it behind a bunker of evergreens. Plant ground covers instead.

A. **Japanese maples, boxwoods,** and a sweep of impatiens decorate this Birmingham home.

B. **Favorites for foundation plantings,** azaleas come in many sizes and colors. Bloom time also varies.

C. **White 'Flower Carpet' roses** wrap around this Maryland home without blocking the view from low windows.

Good under Windows

If you like to see the outdoors from within but you don't like to prune, here are some slow-growing shrubs that won't block the view. Mature heights are given.

AZALEA
Rhododendron, 1–5 ft.

ANDORRA CREEPING JUNIPER
Juniperus horizontalis 'Plumosa', 1½ ft.

INDIAN HAWTHORN
Raphiolepis indica 'Ballerina', 2 ft.

TEXAS SAGE
Leucophyllum frutescens 'Compactum', 3–4 ft.

JAPANESE BARBERRY
Berberis thunbergii 'Crimson Pygmy', 1½ ft.

SHRUB ROSE
Rosa 'Flower Carpet', 1–2 ft.

DWARF CHINESE HOLLY
Ilex cornuta 'Rotunda', 3–4 ft.

EDGING BOXWOOD
Buxus sempervirens 'Suffruticosa', 2–3 ft.

COMMON GARDENIA
Gardenia jasminoides 'Radicans', 1 ft.

DWARF JAPANESE PITTOSPORUM
Pittosporum tobira 'Wheeler's Dwarf', 3–4 ft.

DWARF CAMELLIA
Camellia hiemalis, 2 ft.

DWARF YAUPON
Ilex vomitoria 'Nana', 1–2 ft.

GLOSSY ABELIA
Abelia grandiflora 'Francis Mason', 3–4 ft.

DWARF NANDINA
Nandina domestica 'Harbour Dwarf', 1½–2 ft.

JAPANESE HOLLY
Ilex crenata 'Helleri', 1–2 ft.

HIMALAYAN SWEET BOX
Sarcococca hookerana humilis, 1½ ft.

SPREADING ENGLISH YEW
Taxus baccata 'Repandens', 2–4 ft.

Screening with shrubs

Does your front porch offer a commanding view of your neighbor's RV? Does your pool allow everyone around to check on the progress of your tan? If so, it may be time to install some screening in your garden.

Your first decision regarding screening is whether the screen should be constructed or planted. Screens that have been built, such as fences and walls (see page 180), offer instant privacy. But they can be expensive and require ongoing maintenance and repairs. Planted screens take a few years to fill in completely, but they generally cost less than constructed screens and offer a softer, more natural look.

Planted screens can be formal or informal. "Formal" usually translates into sheared hedges. These may be the epitome of upper-crust style, but if you're considering one for your garden, remember this—you'll practically need a staff to maintain it. A privet hedge in the South, for instance, requires careful shearing four to six times a year.

For most folks, an informal screen is more practical. It requires only occasional light pruning to control its size, while allowing the plant to assume its natural shape. Good candidates for informal screens in the South include Florida leucothoe *(Agarista populifolia),* glossy abelia, holly *(Ilex),* Japanese pittosporum, nandina, oleander *(Nerium oleander),* Texas sage *(Leucophyllum frutescens),* and yellow bells *(Tecoma stans).*

You might notice that all of these suggestions are evergreens. The reason is obvious—you need privacy in winter too. However, that doesn't mean that deciduous shrubs can't be used. Some, such as doublefile viburnum *(Viburnum plicatum tomentosum),* forsythia, and winter honeysuckle *(Lonicera fragrantissima),* have such a thick network of branches, they block the view even without leaves.

Not all screens are for privacy. A few well-placed screens of varying heights can create an air of mystery by directing traffic and revealing the garden in stages. Or you can use screens as "walls" to divide the garden into outdoor rooms. Other screens can focus your view on a vista or garden sculpture or serve as a backdrop for a dynamic focal point.

A. **More for separation** than for privacy, a row of Japanese anise *(Illicium anisetum)* divides two front yards. Behind it grows a row of 'Nellie R. Stevens' hollies.

Parterres

Distinctive components of formal, historic, and herb gardens, parterres traditionally consist of garden spaces defined by rows of neatly clipped, low-growing shrubs. Whether parterres are large or small, they are especially effective when viewed from above. As formal entryways to homes or as charming sections of vegetable or herb gardens, parterres have but one requirement—that they be neatly maintained.

Perhaps the most recognizable form of parterre is the "knot garden," where clipped shrubs create intricate geometric patterns. Shrubs selected to form the knot should be evergreen and tolerant of pruning. Probably the two most common choices are germander (Teucrium chamaedrys) and edging or English boxwood (Buxus sempervirens 'Suffruticosa'). To introduce color in the knot garden, designers often add red-leafed 'Crimson Pygmy' Japanese barberry (Berberis thunbergii 'Crimson Pygmy'), gray-leafed English lavender (Lavandula angustifolia), and silvery gray lavender cotton (Santolina chamaecyparissus). Hard pruning during hot summer months can cause dieback, so trim these shrubs lightly throughout the year, but often.

Once shrubs have established the "bones" of the parterre, feel free to fill in with seasonal color by planting annuals or bulbs. But you can also try low-growing vegetables with attractive foliage, such as bright green lettuces or purple-leafed cabbages, as well as herbs, perennials, and ground covers.

Don't forget to add a focus. The center of a parterre can be the perfect spot for an urn, a fountain, a sundial, a gazing ball, or classic statuary.

B. Among the most popular plants for screens, hollies have handsome evergreen foliage and tolerate pruning.

C. Screens needn't be evergreen. Here, a row of limbed-up crepe myrtles helps to hide a neighbor's house.

SHRUBS IN BORDERS

Borders filled with many different plants allow you to show off a shrub's best features without forcing the shrub to be the dominant element. All shrubs, especially evergreens, lend permanence to flowering borders that change with the seasons. Within a border, shrubs can be accents or serve as backgrounds for showier plants. Shrubs that reflect the color or texture of nearby trees link the planting scheme to the surrounding garden. And many require less maintenance than perennials or annuals.

The border at right has several different flowering shrubs, including 'Snowflake' oakleaf hydrangea, butterfly bush, and two roses. The accompanying plants add blooms from late winter to fall.

A. Like a shower of white, this fragrant mock orange cascades over a mixture of poppies, daisies, and phlox.

B. Welcome to my garden. Shrub roses, ornamental grasses, and perennials greet visitors at the head of this gravel path, leading them onward to a garden shelter.

C. Backlighting the border, the yellow needles of golden Hinoki false cypress illuminate a daylily's apricot blossoms.

A MIXED BORDER

Planting area: 24' × 12'

The Plants

A. ORANGE-EYE BUTTERFLY BUSH
Buddleia davidii 'Black Knight' **(1)**

B. BLUE MIST
Caryopteris clandonensis
'Longwood Blue' **(1)**

C. DWARF PLUMBAGO
Ceratostigma plumbaginoides **(3)**

D. CHEDDAR PINK
Dianthus gratianopolitanus
'Bath's Pink' **(3)**

E. WALLFLOWER
Erysimum 'Bowles Mauve' **(1)**

F. OAKLEAF HYDRANGEA
Hydrangea quercifolia
'Snowflake' **(1)**

G. GOLD FLAME HONEYSUCKLE
Lonicera heckrottii **(1)**

H. MAZUS
Mazus reptans **(24)**

I. ROSE
Rosa 'French Lace' **(1)**

J. ROSE
Rosa 'New Dawn' **(1)**

K. MEXICAN PETUNIA
Ruellia brittoniana 'Katie' **(6)**

L. MEALY-CUP SAGE
Salvia farinacea 'Victoria' **(3)**

M. COMMON SAGE
Salvia officinalis **(3)**

N. LAVENDER COTTON
Santolina chamaecyparissus
'Nana' **(3)**

O. FANFLOWER
Scaevola aemula 'Blue Wonder' **(2)**

P. BUMALDA SPIRAEA
Spiraea bumalda 'Limemound' **(1)**

Q. GERMANDER
Teucrium chamaedrys
'Prostratum' **(5)**

R. NARROW-LEAF ZINNIA
Zinnia angustifolia (white) **(5)**

GREAT GARDEN ROSES

Roses, long a gardener's favorite and our country's National Flower, still suffer from the reputation of being hard to grow. In reality, roses are tough, long-lived, flowering shrubs. No plant is more flexible, more versatile, and more fun than the rose in all its myriad forms.

Southern gardeners now have access to a broader selection of easy-care roses than ever. Now widely available through nurseries and mail order are modern selections specifically developed for heavy, repeated bloom and easy care, as well as heirloom favorites that have always been sound landscape performers.

Rose enthusiasts can fill your head with boundless information regarding these beloved plants. But for beginning and weekend gardeners, there's no need to get picky about what class a rose belongs to or when it was introduced. Whether a rose is new or old, its most important feature is how it performs in your garden. Choose the right rose, and you can fill any niche or empty spot in the garden with just about any color and size you desire.

Planting roses with other flowers heightens their beauty and can even keep them healthier. Here, the rich apricot tones of 'Abraham Darby' are enhanced by purple clematis and pink peonies.

A. **'Ballerina'**, a hybrid musk rose, bursts with plenty of single, white-and-pink blooms.

B. **'Sun Flare'** is a fragrant, yellow floribunda.

C. **'Sombreuil'** offers creamy white flowers that are long lived and nearly everblooming.

D. **Multicolored miniature 'Rainbow's End'** blends with other perennials, adding a bright note to a low border. Roses of all sizes are effective in the garden.

E. **Cascading over a rustic fence,** the rich pink flowers and lush foliage of 'Zéphirine Drouhin' add romance to a setting. Climbing roses have the potential to expand the limits of a garden view.

A

Roses in the garden

Roses offer much more than simple beauty. For example, climbing roses on trellises can form the walls of outdoor "rooms" or create a passageway underneath a series of arched arbors. Thorny shrub roses can function as protective hedges. Roses clambering atop an arbor can supply needed summer shade. And roses that form colorful hips can attract birds and other wildlife.

If roses and other flowering plants are to be a highlight of your garden, then arrange the structures, seating areas, and pathways to focus attention on these plants. For instance, an arbor draped with a climbing rose can form a focal point at the end of an allée or a walkway. A border filled with roses and perennials could be placed where it can be seen from the deck or patio where you usually sit. Or roses can be made to scramble around windows or doorways, offering fragrance indoors and out.

Make sure the rose planting works visually both from a distance and from up close. Strong colors such as crimson and yellow are more striking when seen from farther away;

subtler colors work better in borders or where they will be viewed at close quarters.

Don't forget that roses can be used in place of many different plant types. Miniatures can be used to edge beds and pathways, climbers can take the place of vines, standards can work as accents or focal points in place of flowering shrubs or ornamental grasses, and many shrub roses can be mixed in with other plants to form spectacular borders or foundation plantings. Use drifts of roses in place of annuals and long-flowering perennials, or mix them with a single plant, such as lavender or clematis, for dramatic contrasts. Roses can even bring color into the vegetable or herb garden.

Roses are vigorous plants, and they need sufficient space to grow and develop. When choosing roses, pay attention to the size given for the ultimate height of the plant. And if you decide to move a rose because it has grown too big or unwieldy, do so during the dormant season. Because most roses require at least a yearly grooming, make sure that you can reach them as needed.

A. Why settle for vines when you can dine beneath the heady fragrance of climbing roses in full bloom? Just a few plants of vigorous 'New Dawn' cover this pergola with waves of perfumed flowers during our long growing season.

B. Roses of different habits can be mixed to create a multitextured planting. The delicate-looking single flowers of 'Ballerina' contrast with the full-blown blooms of 'Old Blush', while *Rosa multiflora carnea* arches overhead with clusters of spring beauty.

C. The vivid red flowers of 'Dortmund' make an eye-catching frame for a rustic birdhouse. The prickly canes also help protect the resident birds, and the rose hips that follow flowers offer winter forage.

D. Easy to grow in containers, individual roses make great accent plants for decorating different aspects of a garden. 'Bonica' in full bloom brightens a garden corner.

MEDIUM HEDGES, BORDERS, SPECIMENS. These grow 4 to 5 feet tall and wide: 'Iceberg' (white), 'Europeana' (red), 'La Marne' (pink and white), 'Perle d'Or' (apricot), 'Valentine' (red), 'Carefree Wonder' (pink), 'Ballerina' (pink and white), 'Belinda's Dream' (pink), 'Archduke Charles' (red and pink), and 'Bonica' (pale pink).

TALL HEDGES, BORDERS, SPECIMENS. Big bushes that grow 6 feet tall and wide or more include 'Sally Holmes' (pale peach), 'Sparrieshoop' (light salmon pink), 'Mutabilis' (multicolored), 'Hansa' (mauve), 'Westerland' (orange), 'Graham Thomas' (mustard yellow), 'Heritage' (pale pink), 'Queen Elizabeth' (salmon pink), 'Mrs. B.R. Cant' (soft crimson) and 'Linda Campbell' (red).

GROUND COVERS. Some roses sprawl on the ground or form low, graceful mounds. They cover banks, cascade over walls, or fill large containers: 'Ralph's Creeper' (red and white), 'Magic Carpet' (mauve), 'Alba Meidiland' (white), 'Pearl Drift' (pale pink), 'The Fairy' (pink), 'Memorial Rose' (white), 'Red Cascade' (red), 'Flower Carpet' (pink, white, and red).

Great choices

What most people want out of a rose is repeated blooming. Many, but not all, of the roses listed here meet this requirement. But you should also consider roses that resist disease and need little spraying (see the *Southern Living Garden Problem Solver*), as well as how a particular rose can be best used in a garden. The following lists suggest specific roses for a variety of common garden situations.

SMALL HEDGES, BORDERS, CONTAINERS. Little roses that bloom constantly will never go out of fashion; they're just too effective in too many settings. They can be used in drifts like perennials, as color accents in containers, as low hedges or borders along a bed, path, or driveway. Superb choices include miniatures, polyanthas, and floribundas such as 'Magic Carrousel' or 'Sweet Vivien' (pink and white), 'Green Ice' (green and white), 'Rise 'n' Shine' or 'Fairhope' (yellow), 'Baby Faurax' or 'Sweet Chariot' (mauve), 'White Pet' or 'Katharina Zeimet' (white), 'Margo Koster' or 'Millie Walters' (coral), 'Pinkie' or 'China Doll' (pink), 'Grüss an Aachen' or 'Jean Kenneally' (pale apricot), 'Impatient' or 'Pride 'n' Joy' (orange), 'Martha Gonzales' or 'Beauty Secret' (red), 'Show Biz' (scarlet). Expect these roses to form bushy plants 1½ to 3 feet high.

A. **Unusual gold flowers** combined with a heady fragrance make 'Graham Thomas' a garden favorite. This rose performs well either as a tall shrub or pruned back to flower heavily in a border.

B. **'Oklahoma'** is a dark red rose with a sweet, peppery fragrance.

C. **'Margo Koster'**, a Polyantha rose, has cupped, coral-orange blooms.

D. **'Mutabilis'**, a Southern heritage rose, offers yellow blooms that change to pink and crimson.

E. **Hybrid tea 'Fragrant Cloud'** has highly fragrant, orange blooms.

SUPERFRAGRANT. Distinctively scented roses are a double delight. Place them where you can enjoy the beauty and perfume close-up. Good choices include 'Hermosa' (blue-pink), 'Mrs. Oakley Fisher' (apricot), 'Souvenir de la Malmaison' (pale pink), 'Sun Flare' (yellow), 'Fair Bianca' (white), 'Ambridge Rose' (pale peach), 'Bayse's Blueberry' (dark pink), 'Kronprincessin Viktoria' (white), 'Clotilde Soupert' (creamy pink), 'Belle Story' (creamy peach), 'La France' (silvery pink), 'Rose de Rescht' (dark pink), 'Angel Face' (lavender), 'Fragrant Cloud' (orange), 'Madame Isaac Pereire' (dark pink), 'Oklahoma' (dark red), 'Double Delight' (red and white).

SHORT CLIMBERS (8 to 10 feet) FOR PILLARS. 'Don Juan' (dark red), 'Abraham Darby' (apricot-pink), 'Golden Showers' (yellow), 'Prosperity' (white), 'Aloha' (pink), 'Maggie' (soft crimson), 'Madame Isaac Pereire' (dark pink).

MEDIUM-SIZE, FLEXIBLE CLIMBERS (10 to 12 feet) FOR FENCES, TRELLISES. 'Red Fountain' (red), 'Sombreuil' (white), 'Compassion' (peach), 'Buff Beauty' (apricot), 'Climbing Angel Face' (lavender), 'Parade' (pink), 'Yellow Blaze' (yellow).

LARGE, VIGOROUS CLIMBERS (12 to 20 feet) FOR ARBORS, WALLS. 'Climbing Queen Elizabeth' (salmon pink), 'Climbing Iceberg' (white), 'Madame Alfred Carriére' (cream), 'Climbing Crimson Glory' (red), 'Dortmund' (red), 'New Dawn' (pale pink), 'Mermaid' (yellow).

THORNLESS ROSES. Lady Banks (white or yellow climber), 'Aimée Vibert' (white climber), 'Crepuscule' (apricot climber), 'Zépherine Drouhin' (deep pink climber), 'Climbing Pinkie' (pink climber), 'Heritage' (light pink bush), 'Paul Neyron' (cerise pink bush), 'Reine des Violettes' (purple bush), 'Mrs. Dudley Cross' (yellow and pink bush), 'Marie Pavié' (white bush), 'Smooth Prince' (red bush), 'Veilchenblau' (purple rambler).

ROSES THAT BLOOM IN LIGHT SHADE. 'Lavender Lassie' (lavender-pink climber), 'Climbing Cécile Brunner' (pale pink), 'Old Blush' (pink bush or climber), 'Marie Pavié' (white bush), 'Penelope' (pale apricot bush), 'Eutin (red bush).

F. The soft lines of rose hedges in bloom add color and interest to a pathway at the Birmingham Botanic Gardens. Both 'Bonica' (left) and 'Carefree Wonder' (right) are excellent choices for this type of traditional landscape design.

LAWNS

In most Southern neighborhoods it's hard to find a home without a lawn. It serves as the foundation for the entire garden, providing a comfortable venue for outdoor parties, touch football games, casual conversations, and just enjoying the surrounding trees, shrubs, and flowers.

A lawn should both look good and serve a practical function. Achieving these goals, however, isn't as easy as it sounds. For example, if your yard contains low-branching or shallow-rooted shade trees, growing grass beneath them may be impossible. Not only does grass grow best in full sun, but large trees compete with grass roots for moisture and nutrients. If you want to keep your trees, planting a shade-loving ground cover beneath them is a better option.

Slopes present another problem. Grass does a fine job of stabilizing slopes to prevent erosion. But steep slopes are too dangerous to mow. How steep is too steep? Many landscape architects will tell you not to mow a slope with a greater than 30 percent grade—that is, the grade rises 3 feet for every 10 feet of slope. By planting the slope with a ground cover or terracing it with retaining walls, you'll save time, effort, and maybe a couple of toes.

After you've evaluated your site, it's time to study how you and your family will use the lawn. If you have children, you'll likely want a large lawn on which they can play. But if it's just the two of you, you may be happier with a small lawn or no lawn at all. Remember to cover areas subject to heavy foot traffic with permanent walkways or terraces, so you won't be faced with a series of worn trails.

Also consider how much work you're willing to put into your lawn. A lush lawn is rather like a baby—it demands constant care. Its weekly and monthly demands include watering, fertilizing, raking, mowing, and pest and disease control. If you don't have the time or energy for this, consider a smaller lawn (see page 236).

A well-manicured lawn (above, right) reinforces this garden's formal design, while tough and drought-tolerant buffalo grass (right) creates the perfect lawn in Texas.

Designing your lawn

A well-designed lawn enhances the garden in several ways. Its fine texture brings out the bold nature of coarsely leafed shrubs and perennials around it. Its bright green color can complement the dark green leaves of English ivy, mondo grass, and Asian star jasmine, as well as the light green fronds of Southern shield fern or the silvery blue needles of Colorado blue spruce. Finally, its formal, closely cropped look can emphasize the natural character of informal plantings.

Probably the most common design seen in suburbia today is letting each lawn on the street simply flow into the next. Essentially, the lawn becomes an amorphous green blob without boundaries. You can avoid this pitfall by using borders of shrubs, trees, and ground covers to surround the lawn. This not only gives the lawn shape, it also provides a feeling of containment, making the lawn a carpet for an outdoor room.

The shape a lawn finally assumes depends on topography, existing plants, architectural styles, and personal preference. For example, in Charleston, New Orleans, and Savannah, the landscape is flat, most gardens are small, and the houses are largely formal. Small, geometric panels of grass are a popular option there. On the other hand, the hills and larger lots around Birmingham and Atlanta present entirely different opportunities. There, lawns often assume sweeping, curvilinear shapes.

Whatever shape you choose for a lawn, the line formed by its edge will have the greatest visual impact. If this line doesn't please the eye, the lawn won't please you. Establishing a graceful curvilinear line can be especially difficult. Often, the result is too many wiggles worming their way across the yard. Instead, the edge should flow smoothly, using broad, sweeping curves.

An easy way to establish a curving line is to lay a garden hose upon the ground and use it as an imaginary border. Adjust it back and forth, nudging it here and there, until it forms the line you want. Then spray some marking paint on the ground beside it. If you make a mistake, don't worry—the paint isn't permanent and you can always start over.

Southern Grasses

Lawn grasses for the South belong to two groups—warm-season grasses (Bahia, Bermuda, buffalo grass, carpet grass, centipede grass, St. Augustine, and zoysia) and cool-season grasses (Kentucky bluegrass, perennial ryegrass, and tall fescue).

Warm-season grasses grow vigorously when daytime temperatures soar above 90 degrees and night temperatures remain above 70 degrees. Freezing weather turns these grasses brown and may even kill some of them if it's cold enough. Cool-season grasses, on the other hand, thrive when day temperatures are in the 70s and 80s and nighttime temperatures are 10 to 20 degrees cooler. They stay green all winter, but suffer greatly in stretches of hot, dry weather.

The map above is a general guide for determining which grass is better for your region. The unbroken line separates the South into warm-season and cool-season zones. The shaded area on either side marks the transition zone where warm-season grasses may be grown in sunny, protected locations and cool-season grasses may be grown in shady spots, at higher elevations, or with frequent watering. Transitional grasses include Bermuda, buffalo grass, Kentucky bluegrass, perennial ryegrass, tall fescue, and zoysia.

Of course, a map this size can't begin to determine the exact, best grass for your particular yard. Local features such as bodies of water, prevailing winds, topography, and existing vegetation often create microclimates where conditions vary greatly from those of nearby surroundings. So ask your neighbors, Cooperative Extension agent, or nurseryman about which grasses perform well in your area. For more information about different types of grasses, consult the Southern Living Garden Book *and the* Southern Living Garden Problem Solver.

Nice lawn, less work

Follow these simple rules to reduce lawn maintenance.

~ Minimize sharp corners in your lawn. Pushing your lawn mower in and out of tight spaces and having to change directions wastes time and energy.

~ Install a mowing strip between the lawn and planting

beds. A ribbon of brick, concrete, or stone, just wide enough to accommodate the wheels of a mower, will allow you to neatly trim the edge of the lawn. Grass that spreads onto the mowing strip is easy to remove by using a string trimmer or spraying with glyphosate (Roundup) according to label directions.

~ Keep obstructions such as lamp posts, mailboxes, and birdbaths out of the lawn. They add to mowing and trimming time. Locate them in planting beds or mulched areas.

~ Use a bed of ground cover to link groups of small trees in the lawn, so you won't have to maneuver the mower between them.

~ To minimize insect, disease, and other problems, choose a grass that's well-suited to your climate and the demands you'll place on your lawn. For detailed information on the different grasses available, refer to the *Southern Living Garden Book* or the *Southern Living Garden Problem Solver.*

~ Mow your grass a little higher than normal during dry summer weather. You won't have to water it as often to keep it green.

~ If you hate dragging hoses and sprinklers across the lawn, consider installing an irrigation system (see page 358). If possible, install the system before you put in the lawn. Because sprinkler heads and valves tend to break over time, be sure you make or receive a complete plan of your system, so you can quickly locate the source of any problem.

A

A. Just minutes to mow. Bordered in brick, this small zoysia lawn is quick and easy to trim.

B. The lawn in the center of this sunken garden is easy to mow and serves as a transition between different levels of the hillside garden.

C. Like a river of green, tall fescue flows between house and woods. Mulched beds on either side form crisp, clean lines.

The Lawn in Winter

Lawns can be just as striking in winter as they are in summer. Warm-season grasses, such as Bahia, buffalo grass, Bermuda, carpet grass, centipede grass, St. Augustine, and zoysia, turn handsome shades of beige and tan in winter, becoming an outdoor carpet (such as the one above). You can enhance this effect by bordering them with an evergreen ground cover like English ivy or Asian star jasmine. Cool-weather grasses, such as Kentucky bluegrass, tall fescue, and perennial ryegrass, stay green in winter. When surrounded by the bare silhouettes of deciduous trees and shrubs, lawns of cool-season grasses become the dominant element of the winter garden.

LAWN ALTERNATIVES

Grass may be the ultimate ground cover, but it may not be the one for you. Maybe you hate mowing, watering, and fertilizing. Maybe grass won't grow in your yard. Maybe you have no need for grass. Or maybe you'd just rather plant something else.

Whether you're covering large areas, stabilizing a bank, or uniting various planting beds, ground covers offer numerous possibilities for combining textures and colors. Some have variegated leaves. Others feature showy flowers. And just about all are tough, long-lived, and easier to grow than grass, therefore requiring less maintenance.

Your first consideration in choosing a ground cover is whether it suits the climate in your area. For example, liriope and junipers grow just about everywhere. But Japanese ardisia loathes long, cold winters, while Japanese pachysandra abhors the hot summer months. See the zone ratings on the opposite page.

Also consider the purpose of the ground cover. To blanket large areas, English ivy, Algerian ivy, and Asian star jasmine work well, because they fill in quickly and grow so thickly that they choke out weeds. To hold a bank requires either a prostrate shrub with wide-spreading branches, such as shore juniper *(Juniperus conferta)*, or a ground cover that roots as its goes, such as wintercreeper euonymus. Low-growing herbs, such as various thymes, work well between stepping-stones, because they tolerate light foot traffic and emit a pleasant fragrance when stepped on.

Many folks with shady lawns fight a never-ending battle against moss. Lack of sun and compacted, poorly drained soil take a toll on the grass, leaving the door open for mosses, which like these conditions. If this sounds like your lawn, you might consider going with the flow and growing a moss lawn. Mosses come in many different shades of green and can be absolutely beautiful blanketing a shady corner. And you'll never have to mow or fertilize a moss lawn.

Mulch provides a final alternative to grass. A bed mulched with either bark or pine straw can visually unite a planting of trees, shrubs, or perennials, while its neutral color helps highlight flowers and foliage. As long as you replenish it now and then, you won't be bothered with pulling weeds.

Don't fight Mother Nature. If a moist, shady area grows mostly moss, make a "lawn" of it. You'll never need to mow or fertilize it.

Nearly foolproof, mondo grass is another superb substitute for grass in shady areas. Dwarf forms grow only 3 inches tall.

A GROUND COVER SAMPLER

NAME	LIGHT	ZONES	COMMENTS
Algerian ivy *Hedera canariensis*	Shade	CS,TS	Spreads quickly, will climb; grows 8–10 in. tall.
Asian star jasmine *Trachelospermum asiaticum*	Sun/shade	LS,CS,TS	Tough; spreads quickly, will climb; grows 10–14 in. tall.
Big blue liriope *Liriope muscari*	Part sun/shade	All	Showy summer flowers; variegated forms; grows 12–15 in. tall.
Carpet bugleweed *Ajuga reptans*	Sun/shade	US,MS,LS	Blue spring flowers; green or bronze foliage; grows 2–3 in. tall.
Common periwinkle *Vinca minor*	Shade	All	Blue spring flowers; plant spreads quickly; grows 3–6 in. tall.
Cotoneaster *Cotoneaster*	Sun	US,MS,LS	Deciduous or evergreen; showy red berries; grows 1–3 ft. tall.
English ivy *Hedera helix*	Shade	US,MS,LS,CS	Spreads quickly, will climb; grows 6–10 in. tall.
Japanese ardisia *Ardisia japonica*	Part sun/shade	LS,CS	Glossy evergreen foliage, red berries; grows 6–12 in. tall.
Japanese pachysandra *Pachysandra terminalis*	Shade	US,MS,LS	Needs moist, acid, fertile soil; spreads slowly; grows 8–12 in. tall.
Juniper *Juniperus*	Sun	US,MS,LS,CS	Tolerates drought, poor soil; grows 3–36 in. tall, depending on type.
Mazus *Mazus reptans*	Sun/part shade	US,MS,LS,CS	Showy spring flowers; likes growing between rocks; reaches 1–2 in. tall.
Mondo grass *Ophiopogon japonicus*	Part sun/shade	MS,LS,CS,TS	Carefree appearance like dark green grass; grows 3–8 in. tall, depending on selection.
Sprenger asparagus *Asparagus densiflorus* 'Sprengeri'	Part sun/shade	CS,TS	Light green fronds, fine texture, red berries; grows 1–3 ft. tall.
Thyme *Thymus*	Sun/part shade	US,MS,LS,CS	Fragrant foliage; good for growing between stepping-stones; reaches 2–12 in. tall, depending on type.
Wedelia *Wedelia trilobata*	Sun/part shade	CS,TS	Showy yellow flowers; can be invasive; grows 12–18 in. tall.
Wintercreeper euonymus *Euonymus fortunei*	Sun/shade	US,MS,LS,CS	Tough; spreads quickly, will climb; grows 4–8 in. tall.

Japanese pachysandra

Thyme   *Wedelia*   *Liriope*

DISPLAYING VINES

Lightweight wooden or metal trellises can hold only well-behaved climbers such as clematis. Stronger trellises have posts that can be anchored in the ground or in a large container.

Freestanding arbors support permanent vines with hard, woody stems, such as muscadines or wisteria. The stems twirl up the posts, and the spreading foliage provides shade.

A sturdy fence or wall bears the weight of vigorous vines such as Lady Banks's rose, bougainvillea, or trumpet vine. Prune and tie to keep the vine in check.

VINES

Whether draping an arbor, twining through a trellis, or clambering over a wall, vines bring color and grace to Southern gardens. The rampant growth of many vines makes them ideal candidates for temporary screens as well as more permanent features. They can entirely blanket a large structure, such as a fence, or weave a delicate tracery on a courtyard wall. Many make excellent container plants, whether trailing from hanging baskets or spilling from the rim of a large pot. And many vines feature colorful flowers, foliage, and fruits.

While vines produce a delightful softening effect, they also have their down side. Their very nature makes most of them aggressive spreaders, necessitating steady maintenance to keep them in bounds. Those that escape to nearby trees and natural areas often become invasive. Muscular, twining vines, such as wisteria, can crush a trellis or throttle a young tree. Vines with aerial rootlets, such as English ivy, can damage mortar in brick walls. No vine should be allowed to climb wooden siding, as trapped moisture and debris will cause the wood to rot.

Unlike its unruly Japanese cousins, native trumpet honeysuckle (Lonicera sempervirens) *decorates without taking over. Its tubular, bright red flowers attract hummingbirds in spring.*

Vines Can Do Many Things

Embellish a wall. Bare walls can often appear featureless and stark. Training a flowering vine to grow against the wall gives the structure texture, depth, and added color. Smaller and less aggressive than its oriental counterparts, this American wisteria *(Wisteria frutescens)* adorns a wall without damaging the lattice that supports the plant.

Brighten an entry. Train woody vines such as crossvine, trumpet vine, climbing roses, or common allamanda (above) to frame entryways, gables, railings, and balconies. Their flowers dress up plain house walls or soften angular decks or railings. Wires fastened to eye screws will hold main branches to the wall, or the vine may be trained up porch or deck posts.

Screens and boundaries. Quick climbers such as morning glory or more permanent perennials such as ivy, trumpet vine, clematis (above), or Virginia creeper can cover plain fences and walls with color. Vines covering a boundary fence increase the feeling of enclosure on the garden side, while the thick cover of greenery also serves as a privacy screen.

Shade and fragrance. A sturdy arbor becomes a haven when used as a support for vines that cast cooling summer shade. Fragrant vines suitable for arbors include Carolina jessamine, Armand clematis, Confederate jasmine, as well as climbing roses. Tie the growing vines or canes to the structure with tree tape or strips of soft cloth until the plant has established good contact with the frame. To shade porches during hot summers, train annual vines such as moonflower up lengths of twine or garden netting.

BUILD BETTER BORDERS

A successful flower border results from good marriages between plants. Which plants you choose depends on your personal taste, the amount of room you have, and how much upkeep you're willing to take on. But all borders benefit from adherence to a few simple principles.

Purple coneflower

Forget the maxim admonishing you to "always put tall plants in the back, medium-sized plants in the middle, and low-growing plants in front." This can end up producing a border that looks like stair steps rather than a flowing composition. While you clearly don't want to hide tiny plants behind enormous ones, don't be afraid of moving a few medium-sized plants to the front and a few tall ones to the middle; the result can be a border with depth, interest, and surprise.

Place plants together that enjoy similar conditions, whether this involves sun versus shade, moist soil versus dry soil, or rich soil versus poor soil.

For example, don't plant moisture-loving astilbes and cardinal flower *(Lobelia cardinalis)* next to drought-tolerant lamb's ears and yuccas. Either the former will dry up or the latter will rot.

Develop an appreciation for foliage textures. Juxtaposing perennials with finely textured leaves (ornamental grasses, Siberian iris, pinks, thyme) against those with large, coarsely textured leaves (hostas, hellebores, cannas, hollyhocks) maintains the border's appeal, even when plants aren't blooming. Perennials with very large leaves can become dynamic focal points.

Use flower colors that complement each other, rather than clash or compete. For more advice on using color effectively, see page 254.

Most flower borders peak in spring or summer, but don't neglect the other seasons. Asters, goldenrods, mums, ornamental grasses, salvias, ironweed *(Vernonia noveboracensis)*, Joe-Pye weed *(Eupatorium purpureum)*, confederate rose *(Hibiscus mutabilis)*, and other fall bloomers put on spectacular autumn shows. For winter interest, try perennials with winter blooms, such as lenten rose *(Helleborus orientalis)* or 'Bowles Mauve' wallflower *(Erysimum* 'Bowles Mauve'), or those with evergreen foliage.

Don't be afraid to add shrubs, annuals, and tropical plants to your border to extend its allure. Plants such as floribunda roses, butterfly bush *(Buddleia)*, yellow shrimp plant *(Pachystachys lutea)*, and narrow-leaf zinnia *(Zinnia linearis)* are excellent choices, because they bloom for as long as the weather stays warm.

Finally, remember that you want your border to look like a composition, not a collection. So repeat certain plants or plant combinations. Repetition will tie the border together and establish a visual rhythm.

A. Summerlong show.
Perennials and shrubs
bloom together in this
sensational mixed border
in Virginia. Featured plants
include perennial phlox,
speedwell *(Veronica)*,
coreopsis, ox-eye *(Heliopsis
helianthoides)*, salvias,
sedum, and oakleaf
hydrangea.

B. Boon companions.
Pink crepe myrtle provides a
glorious backdrop to hardy
hibiscus, purple loosestrife,
black-eyed Susans, purple
coneflowers, coreopsis, and
other perennials.

PERENNIAL SUCCESS

Convincing folks to try perennials for the first time is usually pretty easy. All you have to do is say, "Just think, perennials come back year after year, so you only have to buy them once," and they're hooked.

If only it were that easy. But as anyone who has grown perennials for years can tell you, it's a bit more complicated.

To begin with, a "perennial" is seldom perennial everywhere. For example, delphiniums and lupines are perennial in the Upper South, but cool-weather annuals everywhere else. Conversely, Mexican heather and four o'clocks are annuals in the Upper and Middle South, but perennials in the Lower, Coastal, and Tropical South. To determine whether a plant is long-lived in your area, consult the *Southern Living Garden Book.*

Secondly, unlike annuals, which grow to a predetermined size and then die, perennials endure for years and get bigger. Thus, a plant you purchased in a 4-inch pot may eventually grow to be 4 feet tall and wide. So you may soon find that those 10 perennials you planted in a 20-foot-long border have filled up the whole thing, leaving you no room to add anything else.

Another problem associated with perennials is that relatively few bloom continuously. Devoting an entire border to herbaceous (nonwoody) perennials may mean long stretches of mostly foliage. For this reason, it's a good idea to mix annuals with perennials, so you'll always have plenty of color during the growing season. See "Flowers Forever" on pages 248–249 for more ideas on extending the bloom season.

Purple coneflowers (Echinacea purpurea), *black-eyed Susans* (Rudbeckia hirta), *purple loosestrife, and mealy-cup sage* (Salvia farinacea) *form a dazzling combination in this Dallas border.*

Showers of Flowers

The following perennials bloom for months on end:

AUTUMN SAGE
Salvia greggii

BALLOON FLOWER
Platycodon grandiflorus

CANNA

COREOPSIS

FIRECRACKER PLANT
Russelia equisetiformis

FOUR O'CLOCK
Mirabilis jalapa

FRENCH HOLLYHOCK
Malva sylvestris

GAURA
Gaura lindheimeri

INDIAN BLANKET
Gaillardia pulchella

LANTANA

MEALY-CUP SAGE
Salvia farinacea

MEXICAN HEATHER
Cuphea hyssopifolia

MEXICAN PETUNIA
Ruellia brittoniana

ORNAMENTAL GRASSES

PENTAS
Pentas lanceolata

PERENNIAL PHLOX
Phlox paniculata

PURPLE CONEFLOWER
Echinacea purpurea

SOCIETY GARLIC
Tulbaghia violacea

More than Flowers

Don't focus on flowers alone when planning your perennial garden. Many perennials sport handsome evergreen foliage.

AUTUMN FERN
Dryopteris erythrosora

BUSH DAISY
Euryops

CHRISTMAS FERN
Polystichum acrostichoides

EVERGREEN CANDYTUFT
Iberis sempervirens

HOLLY FERN
Cyrtomium falcatum

IRIS

JERUSALEM SAGE
Phlomis fruticosa

LAMB'S EARS
Stachys byzantina

LAVENDER
Lavandula

LENTEN ROSE
Helleborus orientalis

LILY OF CHINA
Rohdea japonica

LILY-OF-THE-NILE
Agapanthus africanus

PINK
Dianthus

ROSEMARY
Rosmarinus officinalis

SANTOLINA

THRIFT
Phlox subulata

WALLFLOWER
Erysimum 'Bowles Mauve'

YUCCA

A. **Perennial favorites,** four o'clocks come in many different colors, and perfume the evening with their sweet fragrance.

B. **Even after the flowers fade,** lenten roses display attractive, evergreen leaves that lend color to every season.

PLANTS FROM

Southerners, perhaps more than folks from any other region, share a clear sense of their history and land. Although migration from the North and West has swelled our ranks, Southerners' roots remain firmly planted in the Carolina sandhills, the Mississippi Delta, the Kentucky bluegrass, the Hill Country of Texas, the Virginia tidewater, and the Louisiana bayous.

When Southerners settle down, they tend to stay. It's not uncommon to find people who can trace their family back in one county for six to eight generations. And when they find plants that bloom and survive despite the worst vagaries of weather, they pass them along to neighbors and kin. This tradition of sharing enriches our gardens, since many plants unique to the South survive only by being propagated and shared. It also enriches our memories, because when we look at an heirloom plant thriving in our gardens, we immediately recall when we received it and who gave it to us. This can establish links that may span a century or more.

Bulbs are made-to-order pass-along plants. Many go dormant shortly after they bloom, so they aren't as affected by droughts, heat spells, or sudden freezes as other plants. They spend a

A.–B. Southern treasures. Daffodils and jonquils are favorites because they're easy to share and are perfectly attuned to our climate. Those at right include 'Butter and Eggs', 'Pheasant's Eye', 'Trevithian', hoop petticoat, and double jonquil.
C.–E. Common camellia, 'Festiva Maxima' peony, and lace cap hydrangea.

THE PAST

good deal of their lives below ground, protected by the soil. Thus, it isn't surprising to find a clump of daffodils or crinum lilies blooming beside the crumbled foundation of a home that burned decades ago. In fact, some selections of bulbs perfectly suited to the Southern climate made it into the market only after being rescued from abandoned homesites.

Vines and ground covers lend themselves to sharing, because they'll share themselves with all of your neighbors anyway if you don't beat them to it. Ajuga, Carolina jessamine, moon vine, and cypress vine are just a few of these gifts that keep on giving. So keep an eye on these plants, lest you quickly find yourself with too much of a good thing.

Many old-fashioned favorites, such as ginger lilies, sweetshrub, banana shrub, gardenia, and four o'clocks, boast fragrant flowers. Planting them near porches, under screened windows, and around seating areas lets them bathe you in sweet perfume. Other fragrant pass-alongs, such as winter honeysuckle and mock orange, aren't much to look at after they've bloomed. They're best confined to the back of the border or concealed behind a wall, where their scent can still call to you for the few weeks it's present.

Where can you get such plants of the past? The first people to ask are your family and gardening friends. Most true gardeners are only too happy to share their treasures, almost all of which come with a good story and a piece of gardening advice. Next, search "mom and pop" garden centers, the ones that have been in business for decades and know their customers by name. Such small, family-run businesses are more likely to carry old-fashioned, one-of-a-kind plants. Make sure you check out mail-order catalogs, such as those listed in the back of the *Southern Living Garden Book*. Finally, give the mass-merchandisers a look. Some formerly "off the wall" plants are now returning to mainstream gardening.

FLOWERS FOREVER

Too many flower gardens act like supernovas. They shine brightly for a few weeks, then quickly burn out. To ensure long-lasting color, plant an assortment of flowering plants that bloom in spring and summer. This mixed border, designed in the English country style, makes it easy. Two white-flowering shrubs, spiraea and mock orange, and the everblooming Polyantha rose 'China Doll' anchor the composition. A combination of sun-loving spring- and summer-flowering perennials fills out the border with blue, purple, pink, and apricot, with accents of red, yellow, and white.

A. Start spring with a bang. Sweeps of blue phlox and purple pansies make a splendid combination in March and April.

B. Blooming nonstop in warm weather, pentas is also a premier attraction for butterflies.

C. The long-spurred blooms of yellow columbine arc like shooting stars above scalloped foliage in late spring and early summer.

The Plants

A. COMMON YARROW
Achillea millefolium **(2)**

B. HOLLYHOCK
Alcea rosea
'Country Garden Mix' **(5)**

C. COLUMBINE
Aquilegia McKana Giants **(3)**

D. BUTTERFLY BUSH
Buddleia 'Lochinch' **(2)**

E. CHIVES (6)

F. GAURA
Gaura lindheimeri
'Siskiyou Pink' **(2)**

G. CRANESBILL
Geranium 'Johnson's Blue' **(3)**

H. EVERGREEN CANDYTUFT
Iberis sempervirens **(3)**

I. TALL BEARDED IRIS
Iris 'Beverly Sills' **(3)**

J. SIBERIAN IRIS
Iris 'Super Ego' **(5)**

K. RED-HOT POKER
Kniphofia uvaria 'Maid of Orleans' **(3)**

L. CATMINT
Nepeta faassenii **(3)**

M. PEONY
Paeonia 'Festiva Maxima' **(1)**

N. PENTAS
Pentas lanceolata (pink) (3)

O. VIRGINAL MOCK ORANGE
Philadelphus virginalis 'Natchez' **(1)**

P. CAROLINA PHLOX AND PERENNIAL PHLOX
Phlox maculata 'Miss Lingard' **(2)**
and P. paniculata 'Mt. Fuji' **(1)**

A SPRING-SUMMER SHOW

Q. BALLOON FLOWER
Platycodon grandiflorus **(4)**

R. ROSE
Rosa 'China Doll' **(3)**

S. PINCUSHION FLOWER
Scabiosa columbaria
'Butterfly Blue' **(3)**

T. BABY'S BREATH SPIRAEA
Spiraea thunbergii **(1)**

U. LAMB'S EARS
Stachys byzantina **(2)**

V. STOKESIA
Stokesia laevis 'Blue Danube' **(4)**

W. SPEEDWELL
Veronica 'Sunny Border Blue' **(3)**

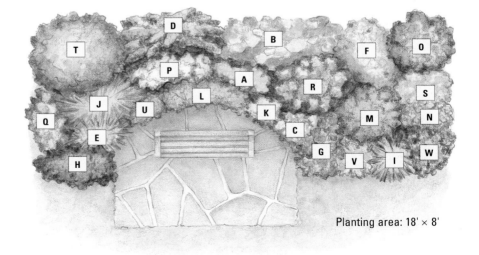

Planting area: 18' × 8'

BORN FREE

Just as dogs need to roam, a garden needs its freedom. Regiments of bedding plants held in strict formation by clipped boxwoods and barberries may work for historic, colonial gardens. But the soul of the Southern cottage garden rests in rebellion. Here, lanky, untamed flowers jostle for sunlight and invade each other's space. The object is a sort of organized chaos, where color abounds and plant combinations look both accidental and planned.

Southern cottage gardens take their cue both from English gardens and those of our rural neighbors. Lawn is considered a waste of good soil. Flowers claim every available inch. Plants are allowed to reseed between stepping-stones. Hardy native perennials and biennials, such as Queen Anne's lace, gaura, and bee balm, frequently appear, often received as seeds or divisions from other gardeners.

A true cottage garden needs some sort of enclosure, such as a fence, hedge, or wall, to give it form. An architectural piece, such as a fountain or sundial, can serve as a focal point. But details needn't be expensive. A birdhouse, gazing globe, or painted chair can achieve the same result.

A. Punctuating the air with spears of blossoms, rangy foxgloves defy the neatly clipped hedges behind them. For a good show each year, set out new foxgloves in the early summer or fall.

B. Warm and cool colors collide in this vibrant collage of perennials and shrubs. Stepping-stones occupy the only ground not claimed by plants.

C. Law and disorder. There are no rules for planting a cottage garden. Put in as many plants in as much variety as you like. The more different blooms and colors, the better.

A Cottage Garden

The Plants

A. SNEEZEWORT YARROW
Achillea ptarmica 'The Pearl' **(5)**

B. ARTEMISIA 'POWIS CASTLE' (2)

C. QUEEN ANNE'S LACE
Daucus carota **(5)**

D. SWEET WILLIAM
Dianthus barbatus **(10)**

E. GAURA
Gaura lindheimeri **(1)**

F. DAME'S ROCKET
Hesperis matronalis **(6)**

G. BEE BALM
Monarda didyma
'Marshall's Delight' **(3)**

H. LOVE-IN-A-MIST
Nigella damascena
Persian Jewels **(12)**

I. THRIFT
Phlox subulata **(5)**

J. BALLOON FLOWER
Platycodon grandiflorus
mariesii **(6)**

K. ROSE
Rosa 'Climbing Cécile Brunner' **(2)**

L. ROSE
Rosa 'Grüss an Aachen' **(2)**

M. VERBENA
Verbena bonariensis **(6)**

N. PANSY
Viola wittrockiana
Imperial Antique Shades **(18)**

Planting area: 15' × 10'

WATER SAVERS

Water may be at a premium in parts of Oklahoma and Texas, but most of the South has all that it needs. The problem for gardeners is that the majority of rain falls during winter and spring, leaving the hot summer months bone-dry for weeks at a time. And extended droughts often force communities to restrict outdoor watering just at the time your garden needs it most.

Fortunately, many plants thrive with little water, once their root systems are established. Star performers include native perennials, such as butterfly weed *(Asclepias tuberosa)*, autumn sage *(Salvia greggii)*, and blanket flower *(Gaillardia grandiflora)*. These plants actually prefer dry weather and quickly decline if the soil stays too wet.

Many dry-soil plants come from the Mediterranean region, Australia, southern Africa, and Mexico, where dry summers are the norm. Bearded iris, cape plumbago, rosemary, bougainvillea, juniper, oleander, bear grass *(Nolina erumpens)*, and lily-of-the-Nile *(Agapanthus)* are all exotic, drought-tolerant plants.

When choosing plants for a dry garden, look for those with gray or silvery foliage. Tiny hairs on the leaves and stems responsible for the color reduce transpiration and the need for added water. Also consider succulent plants, such as yuccas, sedums, and agaves.

Heavy, wet soil will rot the roots of many drought-tolerant plants. To improve drainage, till the bed to a depth of at least 12 inches before planting and add plenty of builder's sand, sharp gravel, ground bark, and expanded shale. Grade the bed so that excess rainfall runs off.

A. Weeks of drought won't faze yellow fernleaf yarrow or red-and-yellow blanket flower, but too much water can kill them.

B. Dry, gritty soil is what many herbs prefer. The lack of water concentrates their oils and improves their flavors. This garden features rosemary, lemon thyme, and silvery-leafed butterfly bush.

C. Failsafe combination. Plant black-eyed Susans, showy sedum, and ornamental grasses in a sunny spot in well-drained soil and you can't miss. Frequent watering isn't necessary.

A WATERWISE BORDER

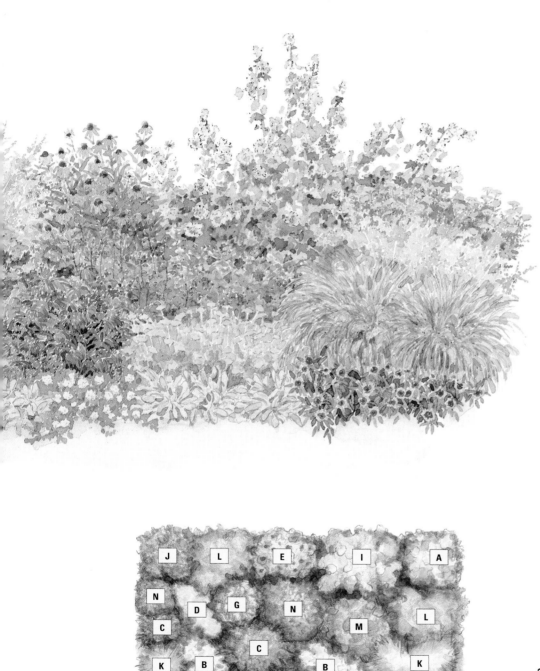

Planting area: 6' × 11'

The Plants

A. FERNLEAF YARROW
Achillea filipendulina
'Coronation Gold' **(1)**

B. YARROW
Achillea 'Moonshine' **(4)**

C. BUTTERFLY WEED
Asclepias tuberosa **(4)**

D. LANCE COREOPSIS
Coreopsis lanceolata **(2)**

E. PURPLE CONEFLOWER
Echinacea purpurea
'Bright Star' **(1)**

F. BLANKET FLOWER
Gaillardia grandiflora
'Baby Cole' **(6)**

G. CRANESBILL
Geranium endressii
'Wargrave Pink' **(1)**

H. COMMON LANTANA
Lantana camara
'Dwarf White' **(1)**

I. TREE MALLOW
Lavatera thuringiaca
'Barnsley' **(1)**

J. SPIKE BLAZING STAR
Liatris spicata 'Kobold' **(3)**

K. CHINESE PENNISETUM
Pennisetum alopecuroides
'Hameln' **(3)**

L. RUSSIAN SAGE
Perovskia 'Blue Spire' **(6)**

M. MEXICAN PETUNIA
Ruellia brittoniana **(1)**

N. AUTUMN SAGE
Salvia greggii
'Raspberry Royal' **(3)**

O. LAMB'S EARS
Stachys byzantina
'Silver Carpet' **(5)**

COLOR IN THE GARDEN

If you're one of those rare folks who has never had a headache, embroil yourself in color theory and you'll soon experience one. For despite an overwhelming number of intimidating rules about color combination, a simple fact remains—beauty rests in the eye of the beholder.

When working with color in the garden, however, it's worthwhile to understand some basic concepts and familiarize yourself with certain terms. *Primary colors*—red, blue, and yellow—share nothing in common; they are the colors from which all others are derived. Mixing two primary colors creates the *secondary colors,* green, purple, and orange. Mixing a primary and secondary color creates a *tertiary color,* such as yellow-green or orange-red.

Contrasting colors (often called "complementary" colors, to everyone's confusion) lie directly opposite each other on the color wheel. Examples include red and green, blue and orange, and yellow and purple. Contrasting colors intensify each other and make a bold statement. Adding a close neighbor of one of the contrasting colors—say, purple and yellow with yellow's neighbor, yellow-orange, makes a harmonious composition.

Warm colors include red, orange, yellow, and the tertiary colors in-between. They're visible from afar, dominate the scene up-close, and bring excitement and energy to the garden. They're great for accents and focal points. Against a quiet background, they combine well with each other, and individually each pairs well with blue.

Cool colors consist of blue, purple, green, and their tertiary colors. Many garden designers also place white among them (although purists define white as the absence of color). Cool colors lend the garden a sense of calm and repose. They also prove effective buffers between clashing colors like orange and magenta. One problem with cool-color borders is that, except for white, cool colors tend to disappear with distance or in dim light, making the border look washed-out. Adding just a few warm colors to the mix solves this without compromising tranquility.

Contrasting colors
Pairing the blossoms of yellow coreopsis with those of blue-purple mealy-cup sage makes both look more vivid.

Cool colors
Backed with green foliage, the frosty lavender and purple blooms of this clematis generate calm and serenity.

Warm colors
Visible from a distance, the lively reds, pinks, oranges, and yellows of zinnias and globe amaranth battle for attention.

White
This is the color of purity, grace, and joy. It combines well with every other color and buffers clashing colors. It's hard to have too much white in any garden.

Shown: Tulips, deutzia, and azaleas

Gray
Like white, gray and silver are garden peacemakers, mellowing the heat of competing magentas, pinks, reds, and oranges. Gray helps these and other colors blend together better.

Shown: Lamb's ears

Green
Foliage comes in many shades—yellow-green, bright green, blue-green, chartreuse. Green usually serves as a backdrop for flowers, but green combinations are also striking.

Shown: Bearded iris and 'Goldflame' spiraea

Blue
This is the rarest color in horticulture (and the most difficult to photograph), but it is welcome in any garden. Blend it with all colors, especially apricot, pink, orange, and yellow.

Shown: Bachelor's buttons

Red
Red is the color of fire and passion. When backed by green, it positively glows. Red dominates other colors, so use it judiciously to attract attention to specific focal points.

Shown: Common camellia

Yellow
Yellow catches the human eye faster than any other color. The hue of the midday sun, it brightens the border and creates feelings of well-being and cheer. But be careful when combining it with pink.

Shown: Black-eyed Susan

Orange
A combination of red and yellow, orange goes well with either of its parent colors. It's a perfect foil for blue and purple. Like red and yellow, it sizzles with energy and a little goes a long way.

Shown: Butterfly weed

Pink
An enchanting blend of red and white, pink is the color of spring, suggesting youth and renewal. Pair it with blue, purple, white, and gray, but think twice before trying it with red, orange, or yellow.

Shown: 'Stargazer' lily

When planning your garden, try these tricks:

∾ Use warm colors in the distance to draw your eye to an object or destination.

∾ Use cool colors up close to bring calm to a secluded sitting area.

∾ Repeat favorite colors to move your eye along a border.

∾ Make lavish use of "garden peacemakers"—plants with flowers or foliage of white, silver, gray, green, chartreuse, bronze, blue, or purple—to separate colors that often fight, such as pink and yellow.

And remember, every gardener has to move things around; no one gets it right the first time. In the words of Atlanta landscape architect Dan Franklin, "For the first few years, your garden will be on roller skates."

Getting started with color

Before deciding on a palette, take a look around. Do you live in the mountains or on the coast? The city or the suburbs? Kentucky or Louisiana? Where you live does affect the colors you see. Beach homes painted canary, aquamarine, and lavender imply a relaxed attitude toward color. Red brick homes in the Blue Ridge Mountains imply just the opposite. Gardeners in the Southwest tend to favor warm, bright colors. Choose colors that complement your surroundings and home and express your personality.

But if you're a beginner, temper your enthusiasm just a bit. Don't plant one flower of every color you can find at the garden center. Instead, plant masses of single colors or drifts of colors that ease into each other. Make a favorite color or combination of colors your basic theme and work within a narrow framework of harmonious colors.

A. Excitement and energy are brought to this border by bright red petunias and yellow flowering sedum.

B. Like a spotlight, the white-and-green leaves of variegated ribbon grass illuminate a combination of burgundy coleus and purple 'Blackie' sweet potato vine.

C. Sulfur yellow 'Moonshine' yarrow shines even brighter against the contrasting purples of Siberian iris and purple heart.

D. Orange tulips seem to catch fire when paired with deep blue pansies.

Colorful queries

How can I get color in the garden from something other than flowers?

The most obvious option is to look for plants with colorful or variegated foliage, such as coleus, caladiums, crotons, and hostas. One big advantage of colorful foliage is that it lasts longer than flowers. But color in the garden isn't restricted to plants. Painted chairs and benches can make superb accents or echo the colors of flowers or foliage. Colored ornaments, such as gazing globes, can do the same. Brightly colored berries can wake up a garden too, particularly in late fall and winter.

Is green a color?

The obvious answer is "yes," but many gardeners fail to see it that way. In fact, they don't see green at all— it's just what makes up the background. But if you don't think green can be a dynamic color, take a look at a green fescue lawn in winter, when all the surrounding trees and shrubs are bare.

Many wonderful forms of green exist—chartreuse, lime, emerald, blue-green, and more. While they combine effectively with other colors (chartreuse and burgundy are splendid together), different shades of green make great combinations too. Try pairing the light green fronds of Southern shield fern with the dark green leaves of cherry laurel or boxwood. Or edge a medium green lawn with a dark green sweep of English ivy or Asian star jasmine.

Can I have color in shade?

Sure. Many colorful plants, such as impatiens, coleus, hostas, caladiums, sedge *(Carex)*, carpet bugleweed *(Ajuga)*, hydrangeas, and Japanese painted fern, enjoy the shade. Plants with variegated foliage often prefer some shade. And don't forget what we just said about all the types of green. Try pairing shade-loving plants with yellow-green or blue-green foliage with those sporting bright green foliage.

How can I maximize color impact on a budget?

If you're gardening on a budget and 24 flats of impatiens aren't an option this year, concentrate color in high visibility areas. Examples include window boxes, planters on the porch or deck, or small beds by an entry. For greatest impact, use a single color. And remember, warm colors carry farther visually than cool colors.

Is there a color combination that always works?

It's hard to go wrong with pink, blue, and white. Blue and white also go well with just about all other colors.

Which color combinations are a disaster?

Well, some gardeners think pink and yellow look awful together, as well as pink and orange. But there are ways to work things out. For example, pink and orange can peacefully coexist if you separate them with a transitional color that combines both pink and orange, such as salmon or peach. However, don't worry about breaking these and other "rules." In the end, the only judge that matters is you. So feel free to experiment.

A. Beacons of bright yellow, the golden spires of yellow loosestrife *(Lysimachia punctata)* illuminate a shaded garden.

B. Ivy of deepest green provides the perfect stage for the pinks and purples of caladiums, impatiens, bromeliads, and 'Black Cardinal' philodendron.

C. Purple old-fashioned perennial phlox is a pretty foil for the yellow blossoms of fernleaf yarrow.

ANNUALS

Unlike perennials, annuals may not come back year after year, but they have a number of distinct advantages. First, they bring instant, showy color to a garden. Second, on average they bloom for a much longer time than perennials. Indeed, many bloom nonstop for months on end. Third, there's a fantastic array of annuals from which to choose in practically every color. Finally, the fact that annuals die at the end of a growing season means you get the opportunity to try something new.

Depending on the type of weather they prefer, annuals are classified as either warm-season or cool-season. Warm-season annuals are planted in spring and include such favorites as impatiens, zinnias, marigolds, wax begonias, ageratum, and salvia. Cool-season annuals are planted in fall and among their ranks are pansies, violas, pot marigold *(Calendula officinalis),* Shirley poppy, larkspur, sweet William, and flowering cabbage and kale. Petunias can be either warm- or cool-season bloomers, according to where they're grown — summer flowers in most places, but winter flowers in Florida.

Some cool-weather annuals are really perennials that die when our hot weather begins. Delphiniums, snapdragons, and lupines are good examples. And tropical perennials, such as pentas, Mexican heather, and coleus, become annuals as soon as freezing weather strikes.

There is hardly any limit to the ways you can use annuals. They're ideal for massing in large, prominent beds for blazing impact or planting in graceful, curving sweeps that tie the garden together. You can spot them throughout the garden in pots, hanging baskets, and window boxes. They're also superb for filling the gaps in mixed borders or providing temporary or seasonal color to perennial and rose gardens.

For maximum impact, don't be stingy when setting out annuals. Plant in masses of six or more. Annuals come in inexpensive market packs, making this easy to do. It's also a good idea to plant in blocks of single colors, rather than creating a mish-mash. Exceptions always exist, of course. Mixed colors of Shirley poppies, bachelor's buttons, pastel cosmos, and large-flowered zinnias look just great.

Certain flower colors just seem to work better together. For more information on combining colors, see pages 254–257. But you can also heighten interest by blending flowers of different shapes. For example, try juxtaposing the flat, rounded, daisylike blooms of common zinnias with the vertical spikes of mealy-cup sage *(Salvia farinacea).*

The color never stops in this raucous cottage garden, thanks to such long-blooming annuals as sunflowers, zinnias, blue salvia, globe amaranth, and verbena, among others.

Sure Things

Here are carefree, dependable, can't-miss annuals for the South.

CALADIUM*

COLEUS*

COMMON ZINNIA (Zinnia elegans)

GLOBE AMARANTH
Gomphrena globosa

IMPATIENS*

LANTANA

NARROW-LEAF ZINNIA
Zinnia angustifolia

PANSY

SALVIA

WAX BEGONIA

*Prefers partial to full shade

Sweet Success

These annuals combine color and fragrance.

ENGLISH WALLFLOWER
Erysimum cheiri

FLOWERING TOBACCO (Nicotiana)

FOUR O'CLOCK*

NASTURTIUM

PETUNIA

STOCK

SWEET ALYSSUM

SWEET PEA

*Perennial in Lower, Coastal, and Tropical South

Snapdragons

Zinnias

Larkspurs

Easy Starters

Starting these annuals from seed is a snap.

BACHELOR'S BUTTON
Centaurea cyanus*

COSMOS*

ENGLISH WALLFLOWER
Erysimum cheiri

LARKSPUR*

MARIGOLD

MEXICAN SUNFLOWER
Tithonia rotundifolia*

MORNING GLORY

SHIRLEY POPPY
Papaver rhoeas*

SPIDER FLOWER
Cleome hasslerana*

SUNFLOWER

ZINNIA*

*Can be sown in the ground. Larkspur and Shirley poppies should be sown in fall, the others in spring.

Easy color

If you like a long season of show without long hours of care, here is a garden plan for you. It features no-fuss annuals whose only requirements are well-drained soil and lots of sun. Although the dominant color is white, repeating the color of the fence, blues and yellows add interest and excitement. Repeating plants creates balance and rhythm. Tall, white spider flowers anchor each end of the display, while a mass of 'Burgundy Giant' pennisetum in the center acts as a focal point. Periodic "deadheading" (removing spent flowers) keeps the spider flowers and mealy-cup sage blooming; the lantana, narrow-leaf zinnias, and pennisetum will bloom nonstop until frost.

A. Cut and come again. Old-fashioned zinnias provide a bounty of cut flowers throughout summer. The more you snip, the more blossoms they produce.

B. Sage advice. Mealy-cup sage *(Salvia farinacea)* and scarlet sage *(Salvia splendens)* will supply your garden with colorful blooms from spring until frost.

C. Sun-loving spikes of tall spider flower *(Cleome hasslerana)* and old-fashioned flowering tobacco *(Nicotiana sylvestris)* make dramatic accents. Sow seeds of these fast-growing annuals near a wall, in large containers, or at the back of a border. Both plants reseed readily.

AN ANNUAL DISPLAY

The Plants

A. SPIDER FLOWER
Cleome hasslerana 'White Queen' **(6)**

B. COMMON LANTANA
Lantana camara 'Dwarf Yellow' **(2)**

C. FOUNTAIN GRASS
Pennisetum 'Burgundy Giant' **(2)**

D. MEALY-CUP SAGE
Salvia farinacea 'Victoria' **(10)**

E. NARROW-LEAF ZINNIA
Zinnia angustifolia 'Crystal White' **(12)**

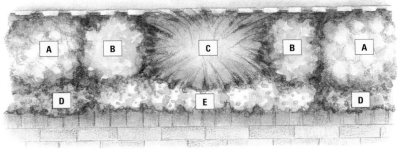

Planting area: 12' × 3'

BULBS

Some of our best-loved garden flowers, such as daffodils and tulips, arise from bulbs—or from similar corms, tubers, rhizomes, or tuberous roots. Although most familiar in dazzling spring displays, many bulbs bloom in late winter, summer, or fall.

You can use bulbs in either informal or formal designs. Bulbs that multiply freely, such as jonquils, grape hyacinths, Spanish bluebells, and spider lilies, can be "naturalized" in woodland gardens, lawns, and grassy meadows. They'll gradually form loose drifts. New bulbs will pop up to surprise you each year. However, bulbs with long, sturdy stems and big flowers, including tulips, Dutch hyacinths, and true lilies, look better in more ordered circumstances, such as patterns, mass displays, and mixed borders.

Bulb blossoms may be spectacular, but they're also fleeting; many bloom for only a week each year. There are several tricks you can use to extend the bulb season. First, plant early, midseason, and late-flowering selections of the same type of bulb (for example, 'Saint Keverne', 'Professor Einstein', and 'Roseworthy' daffodils). Or you can plant some summer-flowering bulbs, such as glads and calla lilies, at two-week intervals in spring. Finally, you can combine spring-, summer-, and fall-flowering bulbs within a mixed border.

Using bulbs in design is a bit like using annuals. For big impact, you need to plant them by the dozens. To make sure they all bloom at the same height, be sure to plant all the bulbs at the same depth. Don't mix up lots of colors or your bed will end up looking like a clown's pants. Instead, plant drifts of single colors.

One common problem with spring-flowering bulbs is that their foliage becomes unsightly after the flowers fade. This isn't a concern with tulips, which are treated as annuals in most of the South. After they finish blooming, you simply yank them up. But the foliage of perennial bulbs, including crocus, daffodil, and Spanish blue-bells, must be left in place until it yellows. Fortunately, a little advance planning

Like magic, naked ladies (Lycoris squamigera) *suddenly appear in late summer, holding pink trumpets atop leafless stems.*

effectively disguises this. After you plant these bulbs in the fall, plant pansies, violas, forget-me-nots, pot marigolds, and other cool-weather annuals on top of them. These long-blooming flowers will camouflage the withering bulb foliage. Or plant bulbs amid an ever-green ground cover, such as English ivy, mondo grass, or common periwinkle.

A. Surprisingly cold-hardy and needing no winter chill, paperwhite narcissus supply fragrant winter blooms outdoors in the Lower, Coastal, and Tropical South.

B. Dramatic cannas combine gaudy foliage and flowers and tolerate wet or well-drained soil.

C. Heralds of spring, crocuses often open in late winter, forecasting warmer weather soon to come.

D. Tiger lilies love Southern climates and thrive for decades with little care.

Come Back for More

While some bulbs poop out after a season or two, others return dependably year after year. So if you're tired of replanting, here are some bulbs you can count on.

CANNA+

CRINUM+

CROCUS

DAFFODIL

GRAPE HYACINTH (Muscari)

LOUISIANA IRIS

SIBERIAN IRIS

SNOWFLAKE (Leucojum)

SPIDER LILY (Lycoris radiata)*

SPANISH BLUEBELL
Endymion hispanicus

TIGER LILY (Lilium lancifolium)

+ Not winter-hardy in the Upper and the Middle South

** Not winter-hardy in the colder areas of the Upper South*

Stylish and easy

This plan focuses on bulbs and bulb-like plants that fare especially well in Southern climates, including bearded iris, Louisiana iris, summer snowflake, and Spanish bluebell. 'Apricot Beauty' tulips are reliable bloomers, but still should be treated as annuals and replanted each fall. Above the bed, 'Henryi' hybrid clematis sports huge, white blossoms, but won't tear down the fragile lattice that supports it. The garden is shown at the height of spring. When warmer weather arrives, summer annuals will replace the cool-season flowers, such as pansies and forget-me-nots, and grow among yellowing bulb foliage to disguise it.

A. Long-lived and dependable, daffodils are the best all-round spring bulbs for the South. Underplanting them with pansies helps hide their foliage after the flowers fade.

B. Bearded irises supply nearly every color in the rainbow. In well-drained fertile soil, they multiply rapidly, forming dense borders.

C. You can't beat tulips for spectacular color. For the best show, dig them up after they finish blooming and plant new bulbs the following fall.

Pinks, blues, and whites adorn this lovely garden corner. Roses and clematis provide a sparkling backdrop for irises, tulips, and bluebells. Pansies, petunias, poppies, primroses, and forget-me-nots carpet the ground around the bulbs.

SPRINGTIME SPECTACULAR

The Plants

A. CLEMATIS 'HENRYI' (4)

B. SPANISH BLUEBELL
Endymion hispanicus
'Excelsior' **(30)**

C. TALL BEARDED IRIS
Iris 'Celebration Song' **(8)**

D. LOUISIANA IRIS
Iris 'Marie Caillet' **(12)**

E. SIBERIAN IRIS
Iris 'Orville Fay' **(6)**

F. SUMMER SNOWFLAKE
Leucojum aestivum **(24)**

G. FORGET-ME-NOT
Myosotis sylvatica 'Music' **(10)**

H. SHIRLEY POPPY
Papaver rhoeas
'Mother of Pearl' **(22)**

I. PETUNIA
Petunia hybrida (white) **(10)**

J. POLYANTHUS PRIMROSE
Primula polyantha (blue) **(15)**

K. ROSE
Rosa 'Iceberg' **(1)**

L. TULIP
Tulipa 'Apricot Beauty' **(18)**

M. PANSY
Viola wittrockiana
'Crystal Bowl White' **(24)**

N. PANSY
Viola wittrockiana
Imperial Antique Shades **(10)**

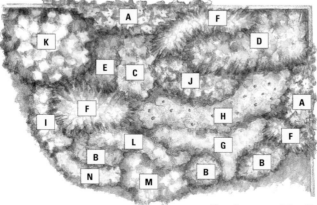

Planting area: 14' × 9'

FRUITS AND VEGETABLES

It's easy to create a productive vegetable garden. The trick is making one that doesn't look perfectly awful. There are many ways to accomplish this. First, add a structure, such as paving, a trellis, or a bench, that gives the area a defined form. Second, add color, either with flowers or with colorful foliage and fruits. Finally, don't plant everything in straight rows. Plant in blocks of varying size, combining vegetables with fruits and herbs. The more intensive the plantings, the more you can harvest even from a small kitchen garden.

Choose fruit selections that are well-adapted to the climate and soils in your area. For example, if your soil is neutral or on the alkaline side, don't plant acid-loving blueberries—instead plant thornless blackberries, such as 'Arapaho' or 'Navaho'. Also, plant at least two different selections of certain fruits, such as blueberries and apples, for cross-pollination.

Flowers can bring more than color to the vegetable garden. Many flowers are edible, including marigolds, daylilies, nasturtiums, pansies, violas, pot marigolds *(Calendula)*, bee balm, roses, chives, and squash blossoms.

A. **'Red Russian' kale** is winter-hardy and actually tastes better after being touched by frost. The surrounding daffodils add a second cheery color to the garden.

B. **Yellow-orange signet marigolds** bring out the color of pumpkins engulfed by the foliage of peppers and beans.

C. **Colorful and aromatic,** green- and purple-leafed basils are among the easiest of herbs to grow.

A KITCHEN GARDEN

The Plants

A. **APPLE (DWARF)** (2)

B. **BLUEBERRY** (2)

C. **CHIVES** (6)

D. **DAYLILY**
Hemerocallis
'Happy Returns' **(5)**

E. **BAY**
Laurus nobilis **(1)**

F. **BEE BALM**
Monarda didyma
'Gardenview Scarlet' **(2)**

G. **SWEET BASIL**
Ocimum basilicum
'Dark Opal' **(4)**

H. **OREGANO**
Origanum vulgare **(3)**

I. **PEPPER 'VALENCIA'** (5)

J. **SQUASH 'PARK'S
CREAMY HYBRID'** (3)

K. **SIGNET MARIGOLD**
Tagetes tenuifolia
'Lemon Gem' **(4)**

L. **TOMATO 'CELEBRITY'** (3)

Ripe for the picking: This richly
textured garden shows a cornucopia of
vegetables, herbs, and fruits. A "living
fence" created by two espaliered apple
trees within easy reach of the pathway
serves as a focal point. The garden is
shown here in midsummer.

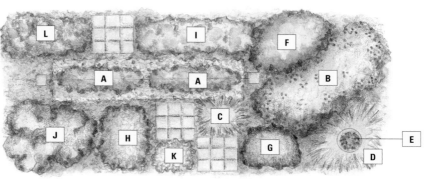

Planting area: 30' × 12'

HERBS

Gardeners have valued the culinary and medicinal properties of herbs for thousands of years. Today, we also value them as ornamentals—planted in containers, mixed with annuals and perennials in a scented garden, or used as a ground cover. Given plenty of sun and good drainage, most herbs are easy to grow. Many develop more intense flavor and fragrance when grown in dry, even rocky soil.

The compact herb garden below delivers both good looks and snippets of foliage for seasoning soups, salads, and grilled meats. It pairs herbs and flowers in a classic yellow and blue combination. A terra-cotta pot adds a Mediterranean touch, while the China rose 'Hermosa' adds a colorful focal point from spring through fall. Plant this mixture in full sun and water sparingly.

A Fragrant Nook

The Plants

A. CHIVES (3)

B. CATMINT
Nepeta faassenii **(3)**

C. SWEET MARJORAM
Origanum majorana **(1)**

D. OREGANO
Origanum vulgare **(1)**

E. ROSE
Rosa 'Hermosa' **(1)**

F. ROSEMARY
Rosmarinus officinalis
'Collingwood Ingram' **(1)**

G. COMMON SAGE
Salvia officinalis 'Icterina' **(3)**

H. LAVENDER COTTON
Santolina chamaecyparissus
'Nana' **(3)**

I. MEXICAN MINT MARIGOLD
Tagetes lucida **(3)**

J. LEMON THYME
Thymus citriodorus 'Aureus' **(1)**

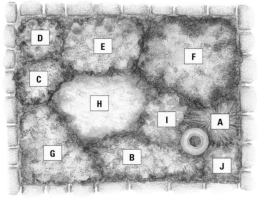

Planting area: 8' × 6'

A FORMAL CIRCLE

The Plants

HERBS

A. SWEET BASIL
Ocimum basilicum 'Minette' **(20)**

B. COMMON SAGE
Salvia officinalis 'Icterina' **(8)**

C. COMMON SAGE
Salvia officinalis
'Purpurascens' **(16)**

D. COMMON SAGE
Salvia officinalis 'Tricolor' **(16)**

E. LEMON THYME
Thymus citriodorus **(16)**

F. COMMON THYME
Thymus vulgaris **(16)**

G. COMMON THYME
Thymus vulgaris 'Argenteus' **(16)**

SHRUB

H. GERMANDER
Teucrium chamaedrys **(30)**

Formal herb plantings vary in design, from intricate "knot" gardens filled with geometrical planting beds and gravel paths (see page 225) to "sundial" gardens composed of flowering herbs that open at different times of the day. Formal gardens require precise planting. Start hedges with small plants spaced closely and place herb plants according to a carefully orchestrated pattern. Maintaining such an orderly garden requires more work than for informal beds, but an assembly of neatly edged plants creates a uniquely peaceful setting.

A formal herb garden need not be large. In the garden shown here, the different textures and colors of the foliage—yellows, greens, purples, and gray—create a "stained-glass window" effect. The warm tones of flagstone and brick, traditional paving materials for this type of garden, blend well with the herbs. Benches and a sundial on a pedestal add height and give the garden a focal point.

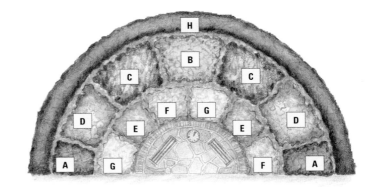

Planting area: 26' × 13'

ORNAMENTAL GRASSES

The fact that many Southern gardeners still think ornamental grasses look weedy proves how enamored we've become of our lawns. True, ornamental grasses won't produce an even, green carpet. But they have much more to offer than simple conformity.

Their slender leaves lend the garden a fine, soft texture. Many have long-lasting, showy plumes that add striking vertical form, blend well with daisy-shaped flowers, and sway gracefully in the breeze. Some ornamental grasses develop outstanding fall color. Finally, these plants are generally easy to grow and require little care.

Ornamental grasses work well in informal, naturalized areas. They're also choice plants for the beach or

Chinese pennisetum and maiden grass add color and grace to this mixed autumn border in a Maryland garden.

water's edge. In small gardens, use them as specimens or as accents. (Variegated forms are excellent for this.) In large gardens, fill wide borders with them. Taller grasses, such as pampas grass, maiden grass, and ravenna grass, can make effective informal screens.

Of course, grasses aren't perfect. While many are well-behaved, others can be invasive. For example, maiden grass and river oats self-sow prolifically. Giant reed and ribbon grass *(Phalaris arundinacea)* spread quickly through the garden by underground rhizomes. So research these hardy perennials before you plant them in your garden. The chart at right should help you make the best choices for your area.

AN ORNAMENTAL GRASS SAMPLER

NAME	LIGHT	SIZE	DESCRIPTION/LANDSCAPE USES
Blue fescue *Festuca ovina* 'Glauca'	Full or partial sun	4–11 in.	Forms blue-gray tufts. Useful for edging, massing, accents. Best in US and MS.
Chinese pennisetum *Pennisetum alopecuroides*	Full or partial sun	2–4 ft.	Plumes can be tan, white, or dark purple, depending on selection; yellow or orange fall foliage. Use with perennials or in solid borders. Very dependable.
Feather reed grass *Calamagrostis acutifolia* 'Stricta'	Sun	3–4 ft.	Bright green foliage; tall, erect flower spikes are very showy, but blooms better in US and MS. Makes splendid vertical accent; effective in masses.
Fountain grass *Pennisetum* 'Burgundy Giant'	Sun	4–5 ft.	Handsome burgundy foliage with showy red-purple plumes. Makes striking color accent. Annual in US, MS, and LS.
Giant reed *Arundo donax*	Sun	10–20 ft.	Enormous grass planted for bold effects. Can be used as a windbreak or informal screen. Types with variegated foliage are quite common. Spreads aggressively by rhizomes.
Gulf muhly *Muhlenbergia filipes*	Full or partial sun	4–5 ft.	Clumping native grass, spectacular in fall as wispy plumes held above foliage turn reddish pink. Tolerates poor, dry soil.
Japanese sedge *Carex morrowii expallida*	Full or partial shade	1 ft.	Small, mounding plant good for edging, rock gardens, mixed borders, containers. Likes moist soil; effective near water. Variegated forms have gold- or white-striped leaves.
Lindheimer's muhly *Muhlenbergia lindheimeri*	Full or partial sun	3–5 ft.	Showy, silvery-gray plumes stand atop narrow, blue-green leaves in fall. Nice textural accent; good for naturalized areas; tolerates both wet and dry soil.
Little bluestem *Andropogon scoparius*	Full or partial sun	2–3 ft.	Clumping grass with blue-green leaves that turn coppery red in fall. Good for naturalizing, but will self-sow. Tolerates wet or dry soil.
Maiden grass *Miscanthus sinensis* 'Gracillimus'	Full or partial sun	5–6 ft.	Slender weeping foliage with narrow, white midrib; reddish plumes; leaves orange in fall. Forms large clump. Use in mixed borders, near water, or as informal screen. Dependable.
Oriental fountain grass *Pennisetum orientale*	Full or partial sun	1–1½ ft.	Clumping grass topped with pinkish plumes. Front of the border plant; good choice for massing or mixing with perennials.
Pampas grass *Cortaderia selloana*	Sun	8–12 ft.	Clumping grass with extremely showy, large white plumes in summer. Out of place in most gardens; use as accent or informal screen. Looks great in coastal gardens and withstands salt and wind. Not fully hardy in US.
Ravenna grass *Erianthus ravennae*	Sun	10–15 ft.	Large clump of gray-green leaves topped by silvery plumes in late summer. Not as showy as pampas grass, but more cold-hardy. Use as large accent or informal screen.
River oats *Chasmanthium latifolium*	Sun or partial shade	2–4 ft.	Clumping grass crowned by seed heads that resemble flattened clusters of oats; good textural accent. Grows almost anywhere; self-sows rampantly.
Switch grass *Panicum virgatum*	Full or partial sun	4–5 ft.	Clumping native grass with blue-green leaves that turn red or yellow in fall; airy clouds of pinkish blooms in summer. Takes wet or dry soil. Use as accents or in masses.

Maiden grass

Lindheimer's muhly

Pennisetum

Pampas grass

A. **Spreading by runners,** variegated ribbon grass (*Phalaris arundinacea* 'Picta') forms large clumps of striking foliage.

B. **Lit by the setting sun,** the pink sprays of Gulf muhly grass positively glow in autumn.

C. **High atop graceful foliage,** the reddish flowers of maiden grass appear in late summer and last into winter.

GRASSY GARDENS

Though a single clump of ornamental grass creates a splendid accent, by combining several or even a dozen different types, you can enliven an entire garden. The photographs at left showcase some particularly flamboyant and noteworthy types, illustrating their range of colors and suggesting ways to mix them together or combine them with shrubs and other perennials.

Grasses are often used like shrubs. Some grow only a few inches in height, while others tower 10 to 12 feet tall. They're tough plants and once established tolerate drought. Ornamental grasses are also easy to maintain. They need to be trimmed once a year, usually in late winter, and divided occasionally.

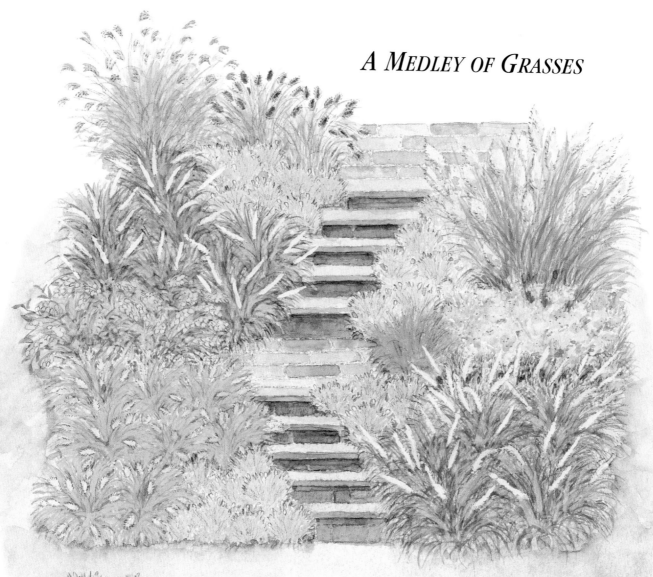

A MEDLEY OF GRASSES

Planting area: 18' × 14'

The Plants

A. LITTLE BLUESTEM
Andropogon scoparius **(7)**

B. RIVER OATS
Chasmanthium latifolium **(6)**

C. COMPACT PAMPAS GRASS
Cortaderia selloana 'Pumila' **(2)**

D. BLUE FESCUE
Festuca ovina 'Glauca' **(36)**

E. JAPANESE SILVER GRASS
Miscanthus sinensis
'Morning Light' **(1)**

F. GULF MUHLY
Muhlenbergia filipes **(3)**

G. LINDHEIMER'S MUHLY
Muhlenbergia lindheimeri **(10)**

H. CHINESE PENNISETUM
Pennisetum alopecuroides
'Moudry' **(5)**

I. ORIENTAL FOUNTAIN GRASS
Pennisetum orientale **(8)**

WILDFLOWERS

More popular than ever, wildflowers appeal to our regional pride. These native plants distinguish the South as a region of grace, beauty, and enormous diversity.

This diversity allows wildflowers to satisfy many landscape situations. For example, reseeding annuals, including calliopsis, Drummond phlox, Indian paintbrush, Indian blanket, and bluebonnets, can be grown in great sweeps in sunny naturalized areas, such as fields, roadsides, hillsides, and informal lawns. The drier and leaner the soil, the better these flowers seem to grow.

Other wildflowers find a good home in traditional perennial borders. Orange coneflower, purple coneflower, and goldenrod are tough, carefree, dependable performers that come back year after year.

Many native flowers prefer the moist, rich soil and dappled shade of a woodland garden. They bloom better beneath limbed-up trees or at the edge of a stand of trees than the center of a thick, dark forest.

Reseeding pink columbines sprout where they will, engulfing this wellhead in a sea of spring bloom.

Favorite woodland wildflowers include blue phlox, Virginia bluebells, and wild columbine. When it comes to making a show with these wildflowers, strength is in numbers. For instance, one wild columbine looks lost; a dozen makes an impact. So plant in sweeps, rather than scattering plants across a wide area.

Some purveyors of wildflower seed mixes would have you believe that anyone can create a beautiful wildflower meadow simply by shaking a can of seeds over the ground. For most Southerners, this is pure hokum. Maintaining an effective wildflower display requires an awful lot of work, including annual tilling and sowing. And the sad fact is, in most areas of the South, the climate is not at all conducive to growing wildflower meadows. We simply get too much rain, which results in weeds and grasses quickly taking over the meadow and choking out the wildflowers. So our advice is, if you want to try a wildflower meadow, make it a small one and be prepared to reseed every year.

A WILDFLOWER SAMPLER

NAME	LIGHT	BLOOM TIME	DESCRIPTION
Bachelor's button *Centaurea cyanus*	Sun	Summer	Annual grown mainly for cut flowers in blue, pink, rose, wine red, or white; also called "cornflower." Easy to grow; reaches 2½ ft. tall.
Blue phlox *Phlox divaricata*	Full sun to light shade	Spring	Blue to purple flowers; spreads by seed; grows 6–12 in. tall; perennial.
Calliopsis *Coreopsis tinctoria*	Sun	Spring	Yellow, orange, maroon, bronze, or burgundy flowers atop wiry stems; grows 1½–3 ft. tall; reseeding annual.
Cardinal flower *Lobelia cardinalis*	Partial to full shade	Summer	Spikes of bright red flowers; attracts hummingbirds; needs moist or wet soil; grows 2–4 ft. high; perennial.
Drummond phlox *Phlox drummondii*	Sun	Summer to fall	Showy clusters of pink, white, rose, salmon, and red flowers; grows 6–18 in. tall; reseeding annual.
Gaura *Gaura lindheimeri*	Sun	Spring to fall	White or pink flowers borne on long, thin stems; self-sows; tolerates drought; grows 2–4 ft. high; perennial.
Goldenrod *Solidago*	Sun	Late summer through fall	Showy yellow flowers; many species; doesn't cause hayfever; grows 2–7 ft.; perennial.
Indian blanket *Gaillardia pulchella*	Sun	Spring to fall	Red, yellow, and maroon daisylike flowers; tolerates poor soil, drought; reseeding annual.
Indian paintbrush *Castilleja indivisa*	Sun	Spring	Showy orange and red flower spikes; thrives in poor, dry soil; reseeding annual.
Joe-Pye weed *Eupatorium purpureum*	Sun to light shade	Late summer and fall	Large clusters of dusty rose flowers; attracts butterflies; grows 3–9 ft. tall; perennial.
Orange coneflower *Rudbeckia fulgida*	Sun to light shade	Summer	Orange-yellow, daisylike blooms; often called "black-eyed Susan"; grows 3–4 ft. tall; perennial.
Swamp sunflower *Helianthus angustifolius*	Sun	Late summer and fall	Showy, bright-yellow, daisylike blooms; tolerates wet or well-drained soil; may be invasive; 5–10 ft. tall; perennial.
Texas bluebonnet *Lupinus texensis*	Sun	Spring	Spikes of blue flowers with white centers that turn red; prefers dry, poor, rocky soil; grows 1 ft. tall; reseeding annual.
Virginia bluebells *Mertensia virginica*	Partial to full shade	Spring	Pink flower buds open to bright blue flowers; needs moist, fertile soil; grows 1–2 ft. tall; perennial.
Wild columbine *Aquilegia canadensis*	Partial to full shade	Spring	Orange-red and yellow, nodding flowers; reseeds; needs moist, fertile soil; grows 1–2 ft. tall; short-lived perennial.
Wild foxglove *Penstemon cobaea*	Sun to light shade	Mid- to late spring	Perennial with showy clusters of tubular flowers in white or lavender with deeper colored throats. Takes regular to little water; grows to 2½ ft. tall.

Bachelor's button

Wild columbine

Gaura

Wild foxglove

TASTE OF THE TROPICS

A mainstay of gardens in the Coastal and Tropical South, tropical and semitropical plants are becoming hot items for gardeners just about every place else. The reasons are obvious. First, these plants revel in our warm, humid climate. Second, many bloom nearly nonstop in warm weather and their flowers are simply spectacular. Third, many offer lush, bold foliage that can serve as an accent or combine with the leaves of other plants to give any garden an exotic look.

In fact, combining different shapes and sizes of leaves can be dramatic and every bit as rewarding as combining different kinds of flowers. Try juxtaposing plants that have large, coarse leaves with those having small, delicate foliage. Or try plants with burgundy or dark green foliage to complement those with light green or variegated leaves.

Don't let the prospect of cold winters keep you from trying tropicals in your garden. Gardeners in the Lower South can often preserve tropicals just by mulching them heavily in autumn. In cases where this won't suffice, you can always grow the plant in a container that you bring indoors for the winter. Saving a banana tree over winter is elementary. Just dig up the bulb in fall, lop off the trunk and leaves, and store the bulb in a cool, dark place indoors. It won't need light, water, or fertilizer until you plant it outside the following spring.

The garden illustrated here shows a luxuriant garden in central Florida awash in tropical and semitropical plants. Don't despair if you can't grow all of them at your home. Select two or three to fill out a border or act as focal points. You'll find your garden to be a lot more interesting.

A TROPICAL COURTYARD

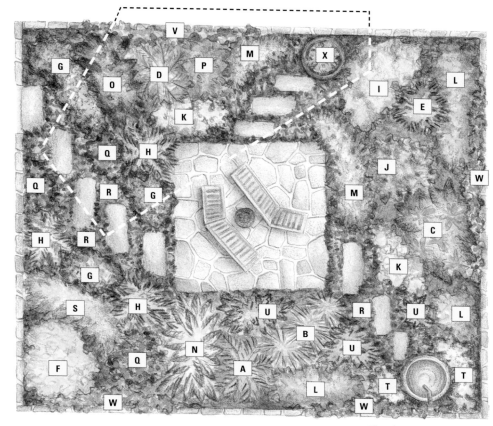

Planting area: 25' × 30'

Illustrated on facing page, dwarf mondo grass, impatiens, and Mexican heather create a lush stage for specimen plants such as sago palm, cannas, silver date palm, and golden bamboo.

The Plants

TREES

A. PINDO PALM
Butia capitata **(1)**

B. MADAGASCAR DRAGON TREE
Dracaena marginata 'Tricolor' **(3)**

C. FLOWERING BANANA
Musa ornata **(1)**

D. SILVER DATE PALM*
Phoenix sylvestris **(1)**

E. CABBAGE PALM
Sabal palmetto **(1)**

F. GOLDEN TRUMPET TREE
Tabebuia chrysotricha **(1)**

SHRUBS

G. MEXICAN HEATHER*
Cuphea hyssopifolia **(5)**

H. SAGO PALM*
Cycas revoluta **(3)**

I. SHOWER OF GOLD*
Galphimia glauca **(2)**

J. CHINESE HIBISCUS
Hibiscus rosa-sinensis 'American Beauty' **(1)**

K. YELLOW SHRIMP PLANT*
Pachystachys lutea **(5)**

L. SHRUBBY YEW PINE
Podocarpus macrophyllus maki **(5)**

PERENNIALS AND ANNUALS

M. LILY-OF-THE-NILE*
Agapanthus 'Peter Pan' **(12)**

N. SHELL GINGER
Alpinia zerumbet 'Variegata' **(2)**

O. CANNA 'RED KING HUMBERT' (2)*

P. HELICONIA PSITTACORUM 'SURINAME SASSY' (1)*

Q. IMPATIENS NEW GUINEA HYBRIDS (6)*

R. DWARF MONDO GRASS*
Ophiopogon japonicus 'Gyoku Ryu' **(18)**

S. COLEUS
Solenostemon scutellarioides 'Alabama Sun' **(4)**

T. PEACE LILY
Spathiphyllum 'Tasson' **(5)**

U. PERSIAN SHIELD
Strobilanthes dyeranus **(4)**

VINES

V. COMMON ALLAMANDA*
Allamanda cathartica **(1)**

W. CREEPING FIG
Ficus pumila **(3)**

CONTAINER

X. GOLDEN BAMBOO*
Phyllostachys aurea **(1)**

Shown in illustration on facing page.

SWEET MEMORIES

More than any other sense, the sense of smell has the power to recall memories of the past. Perhaps this is because olfactory impressions are received by the brain's limbic system, one of its most ancient components that's also associated with emotions. The result is that even a whiff of a certain flower or leaf can instantly transport us in time to when we first encountered the fragrance. Little wonder that fragrant plants have always ranked high among Southern favorites.

When placing fragrant plants in the garden, it seems obvious to choose spots where you are likely to notice the scent. But think also of where you spend particular times of the day. Perhaps you'd like to wake up to the perfume of a gardenia or a sweetshrub growing outside your bedroom window. Sitting in the noontime shade beneath a Southern magnolia in bloom can be heavenly. And what better finish can there be to a day than relaxing in a porch swing and enjoying the sweet smell of nearby four o'clocks?

One caution about using fragrant plants—it's better to plan for a succession of bloom than have every fragrant plant flowering at once. Too many scented plants close together will fight each other and overpower your nose. Either space out blooming times or space out plants.

Don't overlook foliage in this olfactory equation. Many herbs, including rosemary, thyme, lemon balm, and scented geraniums, have aromatic leaves that you'll notice as you lightly brush by. A favorite trick is planting mother-of-thyme (*Thymus praecox arcticus*) between stepping-stones. Every time you tread on the tiny leaves, their aroma envelops you.

A. Every spring is special when wisteria's in bloom. Its fragrant blossoms call you outside to linger beneath the arbor.

B. Clusters of mock orange blooms fill the air with a sweet perfume. The plant's fountainlike form is a graceful addition to any garden.

A TROPICAL COURTYARD

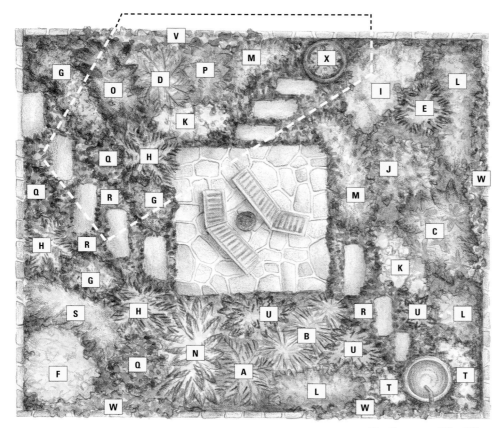

Planting area: 25' × 30'

Illustrated on facing page, dwarf mondo grass, impatiens, and Mexican heather create a lush stage for specimen plants such as sago palm, cannas, silver date palm, and golden bamboo.

The Plants

TREES

A. PINDO PALM
Butia capitata **(1)**

B. MADAGASCAR DRAGON TREE
Dracaena marginata 'Tricolor' **(3)**

C. FLOWERING BANANA
Musa ornata **(1)**

D. SILVER DATE PALM*
Phoenix sylvestris **(1)**

E. CABBAGE PALM
Sabal palmetto **(1)**

F. GOLDEN TRUMPET TREE
Tabebuia chrysotricha **(1)**

SHRUBS

G. MEXICAN HEATHER*
Cuphea hyssopifolia **(5)**

H. SAGO PALM*
Cycas revoluta **(3)**

I. SHOWER OF GOLD*
Galphimia glauca **(2)**

J. CHINESE HIBISCUS
Hibiscus rosa-sinensis
'American Beauty' **(1)**

K. YELLOW SHRIMP PLANT*
Pachystachys lutea **(5)**

L. SHRUBBY YEW PINE
Podocarpus macrophyllus maki **(5)**

PERENNIALS AND ANNUALS

M. LILY-OF-THE-NILE*
Agapanthus 'Peter Pan' **(12)**

N. SHELL GINGER
Alpinia zerumbet
'Variegata' **(2)**

**O. CANNA
'RED KING HUMBERT' (2)***

**P. HELICONIA PSITTACORUM
'SURINAME SASSY' (1)***

**Q. IMPATIENS NEW GUINEA
HYBRIDS (6)***

R. DWARF MONDO GRASS*
Ophiopogon japonicus
'Gyoku Ryu' **(18)**

S. COLEUS
Solenostemon scutellarioides
'Alabama Sun' **(4)**

T. PEACE LILY
Spathiphyllum 'Tasson' **(5)**

U. PERSIAN SHIELD
Strobilanthes dyeranus **(4)**

VINES

V. COMMON ALLAMANDA*
Allamanda cathartica **(1)**

W. CREEPING FIG
Ficus pumila **(3)**

CONTAINER

X. GOLDEN BAMBOO*
Phyllostachys aurea **(1)**

*Shown in illustration on facing page.

SWEET MEMORIES

More than any other sense, the sense of smell has the power to recall memories of the past. Perhaps this is because olfactory impressions are received by the brain's limbic system, one of its most ancient components that's also associated with emotions. The result is that even a whiff of a certain flower or leaf can instantly transport us in time to when we first encountered the fragrance. Little wonder that fragrant plants have always ranked high among Southern favorites.

When placing fragrant plants in the garden, it seems obvious to choose spots where you are likely to notice the scent. But think also of where you spend particular times of the day. Perhaps you'd like to wake up to the perfume of a gardenia or a sweetshrub growing outside your bedroom window. Sitting in the noontime shade beneath a Southern magnolia in bloom can be heavenly. And what better finish can there be to a day than relaxing in a porch swing and enjoying the sweet smell of nearby four o'clocks?

One caution about using fragrant plants—it's better to plan for a succession of bloom than have every fragrant plant flowering at once. Too many scented plants close together will fight each other and overpower your nose. Either space out blooming times or space out plants.

Don't overlook foliage in this olfactory equation. Many herbs, including rosemary, thyme, lemon balm, and scented geraniums, have aromatic leaves that you'll notice as you lightly brush by. A favorite trick is planting mother-of-thyme (*Thymus praecox arcticus*) between stepping-stones. Every time you tread on the tiny leaves, their aroma envelops you.

A. Every spring is special when wisteria's in bloom. Its fragrant blossoms call you outside to linger beneath the arbor.

B. Clusters of mock orange blooms fill the air with a sweet perfume. The plant's fountainlike form is a graceful addition to any garden.

HEAVEN SCENT

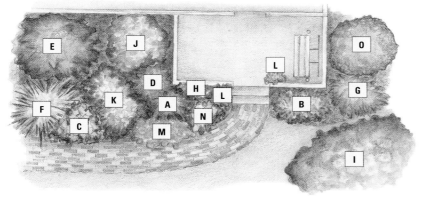

Planting area: 30' × 12'

The Plants

A. GRAND CRINUM
Crinum asiaticum **(1)**

B. WINTER DAPHNE
Daphne odora 'Marginata' **(2)**

C. GARDENIA
Gardenia jasminoides
'Golden Magic' **(1)**

D. COMMON GINGER LILY
Hedychium coronarium **(1)**

E. GOLDEN BUTTERFLY GINGER
Hedychium flavum **(3)**

F. LEMON DAYLILY
Hemerocallis lilio-asphodelus **(6)**

G. FRAGRANT PLANTAIN LILY
Hosta plantaginea **(3)**

H. WOODBINE HONEYSUCKLE
Lonicera periclymenum
'Graham Thomas' **(1)**

I. SOUTHERN MAGNOLIA
Magnolia grandiflora 'St. Mary' **(1)**

J. BANANA SHRUB
Michelia figo **(1)**

K. FOUR O'CLOCK
Mirabilis jalapa (white) **(6)**

L. ROSE-SCENTED GERANIUM
Pelargonium graveolens **(2)**

M. PEPPERMINT-SCENTED GERANIUM
Pelargonium tomentosum **(3)**

N. ROSE
Rosa 'Sun Flare' **(1)**

O. KOREAN SPICE VIBURNUM
Viburnum carlesii **(1)**

ACCENT PLANTS

An accent plant is any plant that stands out because of its color, size, form, structure, or texture of the foliage. The purpose for using it is to call attention to a certain area, add excitement to a low-key border, or serve as a focal point.

Some plants become accents purely as a function of the season. An Exbury azalea dazzles in spring, but retreats into the background once its blooms fade. Elephant's ear *(Colocasia esculenta)* dominates in summer, but dies back with the frost. The green leaves of 'Osakazuki' Japanese maple look ordinary in summer, then transition to a traffic-stopping, incandescent red in autumn. And the smooth, sculptural trunks of crepe myrtle take center stage in winter's slanting sunlight.

When this glorious azalea blooms behind an elegant statue, whose eyes can turn away?

By their very nature, accent plants should be used sparingly. You shouldn't have various accents competing for attention, or the result will be an overplanted cacophony. For example, a pair of handsome planters filled with pink impatiens can do a fine job of calling attention to the front door. But add a banana tree and weeping juniper to the mix and your eye won't know where to go.

When siting these plants, be mindful of calling attention to something that should rightly be played down. For example, telephone poles, traffic signs, and most mailboxes are negative features in a landscape. The last thing you want to do is emphasize them with an assertive grouping of showy plants.

A. Big leaves, big impression. Bursting through mounds of polka-dot plant *(Hypoestes phyllostachya),* the leaves of giant alocasia *(Alocasia macrorrhiza)* command attention.

B. Sudden impact. Some plants, like this Japanese maple, become seasonal accents due to their spectacular autumn foliage. But in summer, when its leaves are green, this tree fades into the background.

ATTRACTING WILDLIFE

Gardens aren't for people alone. Since the Garden of Eden, many home gardens have served as beautiful refuges for birds, butterflies, chipmunks, squirrels, and other wildlife.

Most folks welcome wildlife into their gardens. But attracting critters doesn't mean turning your garden into a wilderness. It can stay as neat and well-ordered as before, only now it sports a few added features. A small pond or waterfall becomes a focal point. An ornamental birdbath, birdhouse, or birdfeeder serves as a charming accent.

Attracting wildlife means supplying three things. The first is food. Hummingbirds and butterflies like nectar-producing flowers, such as lantana, impatiens, and zinnias. Hummers also prefer red, pink, or orange flowers. Larger birds enjoy plants with winter berries, fruits, and seedheads. Squirrels and chipmunks go for seeds and nuts.

The second requirement is water. Water about an inch deep is best for birds and butterflies. (The sound of splashing water attracts more birds.) Of course, frogs, turtles, and fish need deeper water.

The final must for your garden haven is shelter. Overhanging branches out of the reach of cats and dogs provide secure perches for birds. Shrub borders at the edge of the property aid butterflies by buffering the wind. The shrubs also supply hiding places for birds, chipmunks, and toads.

A. Water is an essential element to attracting wildlife to your garden. A shallow pool of water, about an inch deep, is just right for birds and butterflies.

B. Nectar-producing flowers, such as orange-red Mexican sunflowers and fragrant common ginger lilies, are top targets for hummingbirds and butterflies.

C. Thick plant borders give shelter to visiting wildlife, helping them to feel secure. Borders also protect wildlife from predators and the elements.

D. Louisiana irises aren't the only ones that enjoy the deeper water of this backyard pond. So do the frogs, turtles, and fish.

Plants that Attract Wildlife

FOR BUTTERFLY LARVAE

ASTER

BUTTERFLY WEED
Asclepias tuberosa

DILL

JOE-PYE WEED
Eupatorium purpureum

MAYPOP
Passiflora incarnata

PARSLEY

SWEET BAY
Magnolia virginiana

FOR ADULT BUTTERFLIES

BUTTERFLY BUSH
Buddleia

BUTTERFLY WEED
Asclepias tuberosa

COMMON GINGER LILY
Hedychium coronarium

COMMON ZINNIA
Zinnia elegans

COSMOS

FERNLEAF YARROW
Achillea filipendulina

GLOSSY ABELIA
Abelia grandiflora

GOLDENROD (Solidago)

IMPATIENS

JOE-PYE WEED
Eupatorium purpureum

LANTANA

MEXICAN SUNFLOWER
Tithonia rotundifolia

PENTAS (Pentas lanceolata)

SHASTA DAISY
Chrysanthemum maximum

FOR FRUIT AND SEED-EATING BIRDS

CRABAPPLE (Malus)

DOGWOOD (Cornus)

EASTERN RED CEDAR
Juniperus virginiana

ELAEAGNUS

FIRETHORN (Pyracantha)

HOLLY (Ilex)

FOR HUMMINGBIRDS

BEE BALM (Monarda didyma)

CARDINAL FLOWER
Lobelia cardinalis

COMMON GINGER LILY
Hedychium coronarium

IMPATIENS

LANTANA

MEXICAN SUNFLOWER
Tithonia rotundifolia

PENTAS (Pentas lanceolata)

PERENNIAL PHLOX
Phlox paniculata

TIGER LILY
Lilium lancifolium

TRUMPET CREEPER
Campsis

PLANNING FOR FALL

Autumn may well be the South's most pleasant season. It's also among the most colorful. Yet, with the exception of beautyberry *(Callicarpa)*, firethorn *(Pyracantha)*, winged euonymus *(Euonymus alata)*, chrysanthemums, and sasanqua camellias, relatively few plants are grown solely for fall color. It's almost as if plants must earn their keep by igniting at least one other season too.

Fine—many plants meet that criterion, including dogwood (spring blossoms, fall foliage), crabapple (spring flowers, fall and winter fruit), viburnum (spring blooms, fall berries), crepe myrtle (summer flowers, fall foliage), pomegranate (summer flowers, fall foliage and fruit), and oakleaf hydrangea (early summer flowers, fall foliage). And let's not forget ornamental grasses. Many of them combine showy summer or autumn plumes with colorful fall foliage and seedheads that persist through winter.

When planning a fall garden, keep several points in mind. First, try not to place plants with pinkish-red fall foliage (winged euonymus, Bradford pear) next to plants with orange-red leaves (sugar maple, sumac, sassafras, Chinese pistache), as these two colors clash. Second, use green from lawns, ground covers, or evergreen shrubs to set off the autumn colors and make them appear more vibrant.

Finally, remember that bright fall foliage isn't a sure thing in the South. Our most consistent performers include sourwood *(Oxydendrum arboreum)*, hickory *(Carya)*, 'October Glory' red maple *(Acer rubrum* 'October Glory')*, Japanese maple *(Acer palmatum)*, bottlebrush buckeye *(Aesculus parviflora)*, Chinese pistache *(Pistacia chinensis)*, sugar maple *(Acer saccharum)*, sassafras *(Sassafras albidum)*, American beech *(Fagus grandifolia)*, and winged euonymus. If you live in the Coastal or Tropical South where autumn foliage is mainly green, plant cool-weather flowers for fall color—pansies, violas, petunias, sweet alyssum, and pot marigold *(Calendula officinalis)*.

Like fallen stars, radiant leaves of Japanese maple adorn an ornamental cabbage in autumn.

A

B

A. Blazing borders. Dynamic sweeps of pineapple sage *(Salvia elegans)* bathe this garden in scarlet.

B. Don't forget asters when planning your autumn garden. They give you the blues and purples you can't get from that other season staple, chrysanthemums.

C. Bright red berries on this nandina will keep their color through winter, even when harvested for decorations.

D. A tree you can depend on. Even in the most humdrum of autumns, a native hickory will turn brilliant yellow.

E. Mexican bush sage, yellow swamp sunflowers, and red-leaf hibiscus form a striking autumn border at Callaway Gardens in Pine Mountain, Georgia.

THE WINTER GARDEN

When it comes to winter gardens, folks in the Tropical South must wonder what's the big deal. After all, their plants are still green, and many trees and shrubs continue to bloom the same as before. And if people want extra color, they plant winter annuals.

But for everyone else, having winter color *is* a big deal. Southerners hate their gardens to look "dead," even briefly. So we make liberal use of evergreen trees and shrubs to counter the barren look of deciduous plants. This demonstrates the most important rule of winter design—use evergreens to establish the garden's form and "backbone." Then work seasonal interest, provided by flowers, berries, and bark, around this green framework.

Winter flowers mean more than pansies and violas. A surprising number of trees bloom in winter, including saucer magnolia *(Magnolia soulangiana)*, star magnolia *(Magnolia stellata)*, Taiwan

Winter blossoms in this North Carolina border, which features the blooms of lenten rose, mahonia, flowering quince, and heath.

flowering cherry *(Prunus campanulata)*, 'Okame' flowering cherry *(Prunus 'Okame')*, Japanese flowering apricot *(Prunus mume)*, and purple orchid tree *(Bauhinia variegata)*. Winter-blooming shrubs include camellias, wintersweet *(Chimonanthus praecox)*, winter honeysuckle *(Lonicera fragrantissima)*, laurustinus *(Viburnum tinus)*, leatherleaf mahonia *(Mahonia bealei)*, flowering quince *(Chaenomeles)*, and some spiraeas.

Flowers are fleeting, however. For months of winter color, count on berries. Hollies are tops in this regard, from evergreen types to deciduous species, such as possumhaw *(Ilex decidua)* and winterberry *(Ilex verticillata)*. Other "berrynice" plants include crabapple, viburnum, nandina, and hawthorn. And don't overlook beautiful bark. The winter bark of crepe myrtle, Chinese elm *(Ulmus parvifolia)*, eastern red cedar, beech, and birch can be stunning in late afternoon sun.

Can't wait for spring. Flowering quince is so eager to bloom, its blossoms often open in midwinter, after a few mild days have passed.

Look to possumhaw for long-lasting winter color. This deciduous holly bears gleaming orange-red fruits from October to March.

Take a closer look at the bark. Many trees and shrubs, such as this 'Natchez' crepe myrtle, reveal handsome, flaking bark in winter.

A winter winner. Yellowtwig dogwood (*Cornus stolonifera* 'Flaviramea') is showiest in winter, when its leaves drop to reveal its strikingly colored twigs.

Let it snow. One of winter's prettiest sights is a graceful dogwood with every branch, twig, and bud etched in snow. So who needs leaves and flowers?

Leslie Byars Simpson garden,
Mountain Brook, Alabama

FINISHING TOUCHES

A garden's personality doesn't come from plants and structures alone. Much depends on adding finishing touches: an antique olive jar, an old millstone, a mirrored gazing ball, a brightly painted chair, or a collection of hand-made birdhouses. Garden accessories can range from formal and elegant—a Victorian bench and a finely sculpted fountain—to fun and folksy items such as a bottle "tree" or a flock of plastic pink flamingos.

Fortunately, garden ornaments have never been as plentiful or varied as they are today. You can find plant contain-ers, garden furniture, outdoor lighting fixtures, and garden art in mail-order catalogs, garden centers, outdoor gal-leries, flea markets, and garage sales. Even a salvage yard can be a treasure trove of accessories, with old wrought-iron gates, rusted metal sconces, cobble-stones, finials, plaques, sundials, pedestals, and sculptures.

A finishing touch places you in the garden and reflects a mood. So let loose your imagination. Have fun choosing ornaments and experimenting with their placement.

A

CONTAINERS

Potted plants allow you to extend your garden to just about anywhere, but they also work as exclamation points, adding drama and personality to the garden. While you can use almost any container to hold plants, good drainage is a must. The pot should also suit its location. For example, don't plant in terra-cotta pots in the Upper and Middle South unless you plan to bring them in for the winter—otherwise ice will crack them. Protect wooden and other fragile containers from the elements by placing them on a porch or in a sheltered spot. If heavy weight is an issue, such as on a deck or balcony, choose pots made of plastic or other synthetic materials.

When selecting a container, remember that the more ornate the pot, the simpler its contents should be. Visually interesting containers can also be left unplanted to function as pieces of garden art.

B

C

D

A. An old urn filled to the brim with a variety of lemon-scented herbs is both a cook's dream and a gardener's delight.

B. Tucked into a flower border, 'Tricolor' Madagascar dragon tree *(Dracaena marginata)* bursts forth from a handsome concrete container.

C. Create pastel perfection with pink 'Olympia' begonias, salmon 'Polo' petunias, salmon-colored 'Pink Satisfaction' geranium *(Pelargonium)*, 'Tricolor' Madagascar dragon tree, blue fanflower, variegated vinca, and asparagus fern.

D. An old shoeshine box contains pots of artemisia, blue salvia, and dianthus.

E. A tree-form hibiscus, pink 'New Look' pentas, white 'Mermaid' lisianthus, and 'Purple Wave' petunias turn an urn into a garden.

F. Containers with a solid, neutral color work best for displaying colorful plants such as this fancy-leaf geranium.

G. A wire basket lined with sheets of sphagnum peat moss features double-flowered impatiens, sweet alyssum, asparagus fern, variegated ivy, 'Variegata' creeping fig, and spider plant.

H. A mixture of Portland cement, peat moss, sand, and water converts a plastic foam cooler (with drainage holes in the bottom) into a handsome planter.

CONTAINERS FOR SPRING

Spring pots can nestle into a bed of luxuriant foliage or supply needed color to a bare spot in the garden. Bulbs are naturals for spring container plantings, as are cool-season annuals such as pansies planted after the danger of frost has passed. Perennials like blue phlox potted up in the autumn can also be stars of the spring garden, especially when combined with bulbs, annuals, and foliage plants. And what better way to herald spring than with potted green, leafy vegetables such as lettuce, chard, and spinach?

A. For sensational bloom in spring, plant large daffodil and tulip bulbs on a base of gravel in a large pot. Cover with an inch of potting soil, then set in hyacinths and other medium-size bulbs. Extra-large pots may have room for another inch of potting soil and a topping of little bulbs, such as crocuses.

B. Cascades of lettuce in containers will delight both the palate and the eye. Start with cold-tolerant selections, then plant cool-weather types, and, finally, selections that can stand some heat. A splash of color from ornamentals, such as coleuses, or edibles like nasturtiums and herbs, adds sparkle to the plantings.

CONTAINERS FOR SUMMER

Summer is the perfect season for creating lush and varied container plantings. Freely mix sun-loving annuals, perennials, and semitropical plants such as bougainvillea and Chinese hibiscus, choosing some for height, some for texture, and some for a pretty cascade draping the pot. But don't restrict containers to areas with full sun. Shady areas can be brightened with pots filled with combinations of impatiens, caladium, coleus, hosta, astilbe, and liriope.

A. Create an herb garden using a large strawberry pot that rests atop a larger container filled with topsoil. (Potting soil is too spongy for stability.) Fill both pots with rosemary, thyme, parsley, oregano, and other herbs.

B. White flowers, especially fragrant ones, seem to cool down summer heat. This pot contains a white geranium, spice-scented white petunias, vanilla-scented white heliotrope, and white verbena tumbling over the edge. Dusty miller *(Senecio cineraria)* adds a frosty spot of silver.

CONTAINERS FOR AUTUMN

Autumn is the time to compost withered plants, rejuvenate tired ones, and fill pots with seasonal color. Containers of colorful plants are the perfect way to fill gaps in the garden and accent entryways and outdoor living areas. Mixed plantings are prettiest. Use chrysanthemums and ornamental cabbage for the quick mass of color a container needs to become a focal point.

A. A mixture of zebra grass, variegated creeping fig, and ornamental cabbage offer contrast in form, texture, and color. The ribbed pot complements the tall, arching blades of the grass.

B. Vibrant bleeding heart vine is the perfect backdrop for pink and lavender chrysanthemums. When selecting mums, choose complementary shades and flower types. To add even more visual appeal, vary container size and incorporate striking companion plants such as purple heart, pink-striped calatheas, rex begonias, 'Tricolor' Madagascar dragon tree *(Dracaena marginata),* and English ivy.

CONTAINERS FOR WINTER

Splashes of potted color bring a welcome spark of life to your winter garden. If you live in the Lower or Coastal South, many of the plants you select for autumn container gardening, such as ornamental cabbage and kale, will likely survive the winter months. For any Southern climate zone, forcing bulbs to bloom and creating holiday arrangements featuring a green, red, and white theme are other ways to color a winter garden.

A. Seeding window boxes with annual ryegrass keeps them green in winter. The grass grows tall, looking lush and full when so much of the garden is "asleep." Pull out the grass in spring before it dies from the heat.

B. Leyland cypress, blue fescue, and variegated ivy thrive in this tiered container. Confederate jasmine *(Trachelospermum jasminoides)* winds its way up the graceful support.

C. Top-heavy paper whites *(Narcissus tazetta)* can be supported by natural materials such as bamboo and elaeagnus stems or honeysuckle, wisteria, and grape vines. The supports also enhance the overall look of the planting.

WINDOW DRESSINGS

Growing plants in window boxes is no more difficult than gardening in any other type of container. While mass plantings of a single flower can look lovely beneath a window, mixed plantings are usually the showstoppers. Try combining a variety of upright, bushy, and trailing plants in your "windowscape." But make sure all the plants will thrive in the amount of light that the box receives throughout the day.

Window boxes may be wood, plastic, or metal. All should have openings for good drainage. (A plastic or metal liner will protect the box and make planting and maintenance easier.) Attach window boxes and other containers with heavy-duty hardware; if not properly supported, they could fall and cause injury.

A. Unpainted wooden boxes look charmingly rustic but should be made of a rot-resistant wood such as redwood, cedar, teak, or pressure-treated pine.

B. A vine-draped basket displays blue and white cape plumbago, creeping Jenny (*Lysimachia nummularia*), artemisia, rex begonias, and variegated vinca.

C. **Old metal sap buckets** painted and cleverly arranged contain petunias, basil, and the deep purple leaves and stems of a 'Blackie' ornamental sweet potato vine.

D. **Boxwood pyramids,** pink impatiens, and an ivy garland create a formal and festive setting.

Planting a Hayrack

The foundation for a metal hayrack window box is a simple cocoa mat liner. The liner, which feels like a thin doormat and is shaped like a pita bread pocket, holds soil and plants in place.

Purchase hayracks the same width as the windows; hayracks with a weatherproof coating are most durable. When mounting the hayrack, leave about ½ inch between the rack and the wall to prevent moisture buildup, which could damage the siding.

After fitting the cocoa mat liner to the hayrack, fill it with potting soil. As you add plants, the soil will settle, so keep adding soil until it's within an inch of the top of the liner. Leave 3 to 5 inches between plants.

Before selecting plants, think about the colors that will look best against your house. For the maximum impact, choose plants within one color family (perhaps adding a dash of contrasting color), setting tall selections toward the back of the hayrack and short ones toward the front. For year-round eye appeal, replace warm-weather annuals with winter-hardy plants before the first frost.

BIRDBATHS

Come summer, there's nothing so attractive to a bird as a cool dish of clean water. It's the source of a drink and a place for a dip—you might even call it an avian spa.

When choosing a birdbath, consider the setting. A pedestal bath can look lovely at the edge of a flower bed or the end of a lawn. A hanging bath suspended near your home can bring feathered friends close for daily visits. And a few baths placed throughout the garden might attract different birds—mockingbirds in one spot, wrens in another.

Whichever baths you choose, be sure to keep them clean and filled. Once birds discover a reliable source of water, they'll bring their songs and their antics to your garden repeatedly. Even in winter, some birds will rely on the water: They need it for sustenance and for a bracing bath that keeps their feathers clean and fluffed up for maximum warmth.

A. **A cool bath** and purple phlox attract hummingbirds to this cottage garden.

B. **Anything but basic,** this handsome bath doubles as an outdoor sculpture.

C. **A ceramic bath** suspended from a tree limb takes bathing birds to a higher level.

D. **Hostas draw attention** to this wavy concrete bath.

E. **Make your own bath.** This glazed terra-cotta saucer atop a terra-cotta pot makes a simple, inexpensive bath.

F. **A rustic bath** perches on a stand that resembles a moss-covered tree trunk.

G. **It looks like a Roman ruin,** but the top of this column in Washington, D.C., holds water for birds.

C

Birdbath Basics

Shallow water is best. Birds like to wade, but they don't like to swim. Therefore, choose a bath 2 to 3 inches deep, with sides that slope gradually. The ideal diameter is 24 to 36 inches.

Choose the right materials. Stone, concrete, and ceramic make fine birdbaths. If you opt for metal, make it stainless steel for rust resistance. And if you have heavy frost in your area, make sure the bath can handle the cold by adding a heating element to keep the water from freezing or getting too chilly.

Keep the water fresh. Add clean water frequently. If the bath gets dirty or mossy, scrub it with a brush, empty it out, and fill it with fresh water.

Circulate the water. The sound of splashing water attracts birds. You can create a fountain and recirculate the bath's water by adding a small submersible pump with a spray head.

Foil predators. Place elevated birdbaths near trees or shrubs to provide birds with quick escape routes. Place ground-level baths in spots with 10 to 20 feet of open space on all sides. Any less space leaves birds open to cat ambush; any more makes them perfect targets for owls and hawks.

A. **This rustic charmer** makes an ideal "starter home."

B. **A row of rough-hewn cabins** provides rooms for seasonal visitors. An old license plate creates a sturdy roof for the fanciful house in the center.

C. **Moving on up!** This luxury high-rise offers all the modern avian conveniences.

BIRDHOUSES

Food and water bring birds calling. But if you want them to stay a while, you need to provide lodging too.

Before you go shopping or bring out the toolbox, decide what kind of birdhouse you want. Do you want to welcome all bird species or just a few select songbirds? Or will your birdhouse function primarily as a whimsical garden ornament?

Only birds that nest in tree hollows need birdhouses. Small birds like chickadees and nuthatches prefer an entry hole that is 1⅛ inches across. Medium-size birds like swallows need a nest box with a hole of 1½ inches. White-breasted nuthatches need 1¼ inches. Larger birds such as flickers require 2½-inch entry holes.

Bluebirds have very strict building codes. Their houses must be 6 inches wide, 6 inches deep, 9 to 12 inches high, and about 4 feet off the ground with an entry hole 1½ inches wide. The best color? Bright blue. Of course, a house with dimensions to suit a bluebird will likely attract other birds of similar size as well.

Basic Housekeeping

To thwart raccoons and cats, *mount birdhouses atop metal poles or hang them from tree branches.*

Place birdhouses away *from bird feeders (feeding frenzies make nesting birds nervous).*

Face the entry *toward the south or east, but in any case away from prevailing weather and hot afternoon sun.*

Set the birdhouse *on a metal pole fitted with a metal squirrel baffle at least 16 inches wide to protect baby birds from black rat snakes.*

Build with an insulating *material such as 1-inch-thick wood. Thinner materials, such as plastic, ventilate poorly and can get too hot.*

Nest boxes *need to have a side or top that opens the box for cleaning. They also need drain holes in the bottom and ventilation holes high in the sides.*

D. An old tin sign makes a watertight roof for this becoming two-story house.

E. The cathedral may be towering, but the nest box inside its walls is snug and homey.

F. Birds enjoy this deluxe condominium amid a lovely tangle of rose and viburnum.

G. If you listen carefully, you can almost hear the church bells chime.

STONES

Stones seldom show up where you want them. A bushel of baseball-size clunkers in the vegetable bed is no help at all, while that boulder near the impatiens blocks the view of the lilies beyond.

But don't worry. All it takes is some elbow grease (and maybe a backhoe) to put stones where you want them. You can create rock gardens, walls, and steps in a matter of days; build stone benches and sculptures in just a few hours. If your garden lacks stones of any real consequence, consult a local quarry or stone supplier. They can fix you up with everything from gravel and flagstones to massive boulders.

Before you buy, consider your site. Are water-washed granite boulders appropriate to your region? Or might slabs of slate look better? Whatever type of stone you choose, think twice before you act. A 2-ton rock will be with you for a long time.

A. **Chunky boulders,** smooth river stones, and squared-off stone slabs fit right into this gentle slope.

B. **A carpet of moss** gives this boulder a handsome, timeworn appeal.

C. **Flanked by flowers and grasses,** these boulders grace the garden.

Making Friends with Moss

Moss is the garden's patina—a sign of graceful age. Trouble is, it takes many months to grow, and sometimes you just can't wait for that velvety green carpet to develop on your new stones and statues. The solution? This special moss-accelerating formula:

First, stir a fist-size lump of porcelain clay (available at craft shops or ceramic supply companies) into 3 cups of water until the mixture has the consistency of a thick milk shake. Then combine the clay suspension with 1 cup of undiluted liquid fish fertilizer and 1 cup of fresh, shredded moss. Whisk the mixture thoroughly, then paint it on your stones and statues with a brush.

As you paint, remember that moss grows naturally in patches, favors the north side of any object, and takes readily to crevices. If you use this formula in a moist and shady location, you may well have moss in a matter of weeks.

FURNITURE

In a world where free time is scarcer than gardenia blossoms in January, outdoor furniture invites a welcome respite. Tucked away on a terrace or set beneath a tree, a chair or bench invites you to rest a minute, smell the lilies, and let cares slip away.

But which furniture do you choose? Gone are the days when the only choices were a wooden Adirondack or a folding lawn chair. Now there's rustic and formal, manufactured and homemade, wood or metal, stone or brick.

As always, you'll want to consider the garden setting and your objectives. Some benches are easy on the eye but hard on the back. Some chairs are a pleasure to sit in but terribly unattractive. And, yes, some of these pieces are so handsome and comfortable you'll end up bringing them indoors.

A. **Two willow armchairs** create an oasis of calm amid flagstone pavers and flowering plants.

B. **In dappled sunlight** behind a screen of shrubs, this hammock invites long naps and quiet contemplation.

C. **An antique table** and a cozy terrace, protected from rain by a roof, make a perfect setting for outdoor dining.

Hidden Storage

When space is an issue, a storage bench comes in awfully handy. You can place one next to the back door, in the mudroom, or just outside the shed for quick storage of rubber boots, gloves, small tools, hoses, and the like.

A good bench withstands the elements, so galvanized hinges and screws are important. As for wood, consider the stars of rot resistance—cypress, cedar, redwood, or teak. If you choose teak, you won't need marine varnish or an exterior stain. For the other woods, you will. In all cases, brush the bench or spray it with the hose once in a while to remove dust and dirt.

D. **A brick retaining wall** doubles as a comfortable upholstered bench.

E. **Cotton slipcovers** of blue-and-white ticking give this outdoor furniture a finished yet casual look.

GARDEN BENCHES

While we all might enjoy relaxing outdoors, we spend far more time looking at garden benches than we do sitting on them. It makes sense, then, to consider them first as garden ornaments, and place them accordingly.

Keep in mind that the location of a bench should be plausible, accessible, and pleasant. (Next to a path makes sense; in a thicket doesn't.) A bench in the distance can draw visitors through your garden and lead them to a pretty view, while a bench beneath an arbor or a leafy bough *is* the view.

In choosing the type of bench you want, think of the setting and the amount of maintenance the material it's made of requires. Cast iron looks wonderful in old-style gardens but may require occasional painting. Woods such as pine or oak will need a good sealer or periodic paint. Teak, aluminum, stone, and concrete can withstand decades of heavy weather without fuss or bother. And don't forget about benches made of synthetic wicker. This durable material may look and feel like natural wicker, which is less sturdy and better suited to sheltered areas, but it is unaffected by weather and doesn't sag or rot when wet.

Joinery 101

Well-made wooden furniture is distinguished by its joinery—for example, the points at which a chair's legs and arms meet the seat. The photographs at left show three variations of sturdy joinery. Brass hexagonal head bolts and barrel nuts (top) reinforce joints at critical points. Mortise-and-tenon joints held in place with dowels (middle) create a strong bond. Screws and blocking join and reinforce a redwood chair (bottom). If you live in a region with high humidity or near the coast, pay special attention to hardware. Brass, aluminum, or galvanized steel fittings are less likely to rust and leave streaks on the furniture.

A. Fern fronds cast in iron bring leafy beauty to this secluded bench.

B. A stone slab extends from a garden wall and offers a natural resting place.

C. This bright white bench adds Victorian splendor and captures attention.

D. For Southern comfort, try a padded bench of scrollwork iron.

E. Indonesian chairs and bench and a table made from an old boat hatch dress up a simple brick patio.

GARDEN ART

With all due respect to the old masters and postmodern luminaries, you, too, can be an artist in the outdoors. All it takes is an eye for the unusual, a sense of possibility, and maybe an attic full of junk.

Nearly anything, after all, can make its mark in the garden. An old wooden crate can form a handsome container for plants and flowers. Old rakes and hoes can decorate a fence. Bits of ironwork and architectural fragments can edge borders or flank garden paths.

A

Searching for garden art is half the fun. Check rummage sales and salvage yards for sculptural specimens. Mine your own garage for a charming memento such as an old tricycle or wagon. Of course, you may also try outdoor sculpture galleries for statues and fountains, and specialty garden shops for garden ornaments of all types. And don't forget mail-order catalogs. Many offer sundials, birdhouses, wall plaques, and sculpture of all kinds.

The key is choosing art that matches your garden's style. A wooden wagon wheel, upright and partially buried, might make a splendid border for the herb garden, while a winged cherub might look lovely beneath an arbor.

A. This stylized lizard brings bright color to fences and walls.

B. Rust is an asset on this wall-mounted cluster of garden tools. Below the tools, a terra-cotta "pot pal" sculpture rests on a shelf.

C. An iron wheel with "sun rays" radiates across the yard.

D. This cast-iron sculpture greets guests at the edge of a meadow.

E. Classical statuary draws the eye through a series of arbors.

F. Anything goes in this whimsical sculpture of glass, metal, and ceramic.

G. A sundial creates a focal point among the boxwoods and spring flowers.

Display Basics

A successful display of garden art depends on more than just the object itself. Keep in mind the following suggestions when creating your design.

Punctuate your garden. *If your garden lacks a focal point, give it one— a sculpture, statue, fountain, or other object that cannot be ignored. A dark, plain background such as hedges or evergreen shrubs will help the focal point shine; an arbor in front creates an excellent frame for viewing.*

Consider size and scale. *A large sculpture might overwhelm a small garden, while a small piece might get lost in lush foliage. To prevent such problems, place pieces in various parts of the yard until you find spots that suit each perfectly.*

Stick to one style. *A psychedelic sculpture seldom looks good near a classic Grecian urn. So decide which style of art you'll employ, then stick to it. When in doubt, use fewer pieces rather than more. You can always fill the gaps later.*

A. A concrete bunny keeps a steady watch on a garden path.

B. This above-pond statue commands attention in a long, narrow courtyard.

C. An old picture frame, sealed to withstand the weather, prompts a look into the meadow behind.

D. Small cracked tiles and a lot of patience are the foundation for this colorful mosaic compass.

E. A silently crowing rooster greets a perpetual dawn.

F. A concrete fountain draws attention to the creeping strawberry geranium *(Saxifraga stolonifera)* at its base.

G. A metal marsh bird blends into a cluster of ornamental grass near a pool.

A. This painted wooden obelisk towering above the roses immediately catches your eye.

B. An antique iron fence panel creates the illusion of a window into the garden beyond.

C. A terra-cotta architectural piece nestles beside a rustic stone wall.

D. A pair of ornate urns flank a garden gate.

E. This cast-iron weather vane is painted to look like aged copper.

F. Twining vines of a clematis cling to a wrought-iron fixture.

G. An antique angel watches over Lenten roses *(Helleborus orientalis)* in the early morning sunlight.

Living Sculpture

The ultimate melding of the natural and the artificial, topiary is proof that you can sometimes manipulate Mother Nature and get away with it. All you need is a willing plant, a wire form, a pair of sharp shears, and an aptitude for sculpture.

Well, you might need some patience too. It may take a while for English ivy, Asian jasmine, or creeping fig to fill the chicken-wire forms—especially when the forms are as large as the mare and foal above. Then again, a vigorous herb such as rosemary can quickly cover a wire hoop with its fragrant branches. And with an herb, there's a bonus: You can eat the clippings.

PAINT

One of the easiest and most versatile ways to add color to a garden is with paint. You might enliven the scenery with painted chairs, brighten a path with vivid orange paving stones, or paint an entire wall pale pink or robin's egg blue. Color can highlight any area of the garden, such as painted pots tucked into a flower bed or a terrace paved with brightly painted tiles.

Painting an ordinary door or gate a bright color turns it into a focal point.

As with any painting project, it's best to start with sample chips from the paint store. And it's always a good idea to begin by painting just a small portion of your project to gauge the effect. When in doubt, choose one shade lighter. That way, you can easily darken the color or change it completely.

Paint Pointers

To achieve the best finish, paint in fair weather, out of direct sun, after morning dew, and at least two hours before evening dampness arrives.

Prepare the surface by removing dirt, grease, rust, and paint flakes.

For new wood, prime the surface with one or two coats of latex or exterior wood primer. Then paint with flat latex acrylic, vinyl exterior enamel, or house paint in the desired finish.

For plaster and stucco, use exterior latex or acrylic paint. A roller will give a more uniform coverage.

For cast-iron furniture, remove every speck of rust (using steel wool, sanding blocks, or a rust-removing substance will do it); then coat with a rust-resistant paint.

A. **Greens and yellows** above the red brick terrace brighten this shaded area.

B. **"Grape vines"** painted on a stucco wall and wooden shutter add color and texture without taking up space.

C. **Orange paving squares** create an arresting checkerboard pattern in this patio entryway.

D. **Chipped blue and faded red** add rustic charm to this sitting area.

E. **These pots are primed** with nontoxic waterproofing, sealed inside with roofing compound, then painted with exterior latex.

LIGHTING

Lighting the garden allows you to see your creation in a whole new way, emphasizing form, pattern, texture, and shadow. Outdoor lighting serves a practical purpose too: A series of lamps can guide visitors safely along a path, while perimeter lighting can discourage intruders.

Good lighting begins with a plan. Before installing fixtures, think of the effect you want to achieve. Lights near a window can draw the eye outside, effectively enlarging the indoors and easing the transition between home and garden. A light mounted high in a tree can cast dappled "moonlight" on the ground. A single strand of lights placed along an arbor makes any evening a festive occasion.

You can achieve many interesting effects through the creative use of lighting, such as illuminating sculptural tree trunks, spotlighting garden art, and casting plant silhouettes onto walls. In most gardens, low-voltage systems will do the trick. They're easy to install and easy to adjust, and they use less energy than standard-current fixtures.

A. **Well-placed path lights** bring the walkway and both sets of steps into full view.

B. **Lights shine upward** to define leaves and trunks.

C. **This lamppost** adds warm light in the garden and makes a perfect support for the large-flowering clematis 'Henryi'.

Lighting Basics

Some outdoor lights—such as lanterns, path lights, and wall-mounted units—are made to be seen, but most are meant to blend with the background. For this reason, be sure to hide the fixtures as well as you can, and aim them so that the light bulbs are shielded from direct view. The idea is to make your garden—not your lights—the star of the show.

Backlighting gives lacy shrubs a delicate glow.

Path lights can edge walks or shine down from eaves.

Sidelighting dense plants defines shape and detail.

Shadowing casts plant silhouettes against walls.

"Moonlighting" creates soft pools of light.

"Grazing" showcases structure and texture.

Uplighting reveals form and canopy of trees.

Standard Current or Low Voltage?

Outdoor lights can be powered by standard household current or by low-voltage systems. Each method has its advantages and drawbacks.

Standard Current

For large gardens or those still in the planning stage, standard systems work well. These systems tend to last longer than low-voltage systems, and they cast strong light into tall trees. On the other hand, standard systems tend to be more expensive, more difficult to move, and harder to aim and conceal.

The installation alone can be daunting. You'll need to get a building permit, wire all circuits through ground-fault circuit interrupters, and encase all wires in rigid conduit—unless you bury them at least 18 inches deep.

Low Voltage

For smaller areas or established gardens that you don't want to upset with lots of digging, consider a low-voltage system. These lights, which use transformers that reduce household current to 12 volts, consume less energy and are easier to install than standard fixtures. They're also safer, more portable, and easier to aim. On the downside, the number of lamps that can be attached to one transformer is limited. Always choose high-quality metal fixtures. They cost more than plastic fixtures but last longer and look much better.

A. A tin lantern filled with a string of clear Christmas lights gives a soft glow to the courtyard.

B. This pear-shaped lantern, surrounded by clematis blooms, adds warm light to the garden.

C. A simple terra-cotta pot creates an excellent shield for this indoor uplight.

CANDLES

There's something alluring about a candle flame. It dances and flickers, sparkles and glimmers, and glows with a warmth unmatched by science. Perhaps this is why we switch off the lights whenever we can and relax in the primitive pleasures of firelight.

Before setting out those candles, however, keep in mind a few basics. First, nearly any candle will smoke or drip if it's placed in a draft. So shield it inside a paper sack with sand in the bottom or in a hurricane lamp, a glass jar, or even a tin can with artfully punched holes in the sides. Next, locate candles where they're not likely to be accidentally knocked over, come into contact with loose clothing, or damage nearby plants with their heat.

A. **A hanging candelabra** casts soft light for intimate outdoor dining.

B. **A "candle" sconce** mounted to a wood fence keeps the vigil light burning.

C. **Hurricane lanterns** atop these posts protect the candles from breezes.

D. **Votive candles** supported by metal "stems" highlight window plantings and can be enjoyed from indoors.

MATERIALS AND TECHNIQUES

We've said it before, but it bears repeating—when creating a garden, put in the structures first. But unless you're a carpenter or stone mason, this may raise a host of disconcerting questions. Should I use cedar or pressure-treated pine for the deck? What kind of stain preserves wood the longest? How deep should I set my fence posts? Should I install porcelain or ceramic tiles?

This chapter answers these and many other questions. It also provides step-by-step instructions for popular garden projects such as building a deck, putting up a fence, laying bricks, mixing and pouring concrete, installing a pond, making stepping-stones, and constructing a stacked-stone wall.

Should you do the work yourself? That depends on your level of expertise. Remember, doing it yourself is satisfying and costs less only if you can do it right. Don't hesitate to call in a professional if you feel you're in over your head.

LUMBER

Many landscaping projects begin with lumber, including decks, fences, steps, and raised beds. In the following pages you'll find an overview of the lumber products required for most garden construction projects, along with the fasteners and finishes you'll also need. Step-by-step directions illustrate the most common outdoor wooden construction projects, among them an attached deck (see pages 326–327), a basic board fence (see pages 328–329), and a freestanding arbor (see pages 330–331).

Lumberyard tools and materials

Because wood comes in so many sizes, species, and grades, a visit to a lumberyard can be a daunting experience for the beginner. Busy salespeople may not be very helpful if you are unfamiliar with basic building terminology, so it's a good idea to make a list of the things you'll need for your projects *before* asking an employee for help.

SOFTWOOD OR HARDWOOD? Lumber is divided into these two broad categories, which refer to the origin of the wood. Softwoods come from conifers, hardwoods from deciduous trees.

As a rule, softwoods are much less expensive, easier to tool, and more readily available than hardwoods. In fact, nearly all outdoor construction is done with softwoods. However, many lumberyards now stock more economical offerings of hardwoods, such as mahogany.

SPECIES. All woods have different properties. Cypress and cedar, for instance, are both attractive woods with a natural resistance to decay. They are good choices for deck planking and seating, lath roofing, and railings. But because these woods are too costly for use as structural members or for features that will be painted, save them for areas where appearance matters. Substitute less expensive softwoods or pressure-treated lumber for the understructure.

LUMBER GRADES. Wood is sorted and graded at a lumber mill according to several factors: natural growth characteristics (such as knots), defects resulting from milling errors, and commercial drying and preserving techniques that affect each piece's strength, durability, and appearance. Generally, a stamp on each piece of lumber tells you its moisture content and its grade and species mark, as well as the mill that produced it and the grading agency (often SPIB, Southern Pine Inspection Bureau).

In general, the higher the grade, the more expensive the wood. One of the best ways to save money on an outdoor structure is to identify the most appropriate grade (not necessarily the highest grade) for each element.

Structural lumber and timbers are rated for strength. The most common grading system includes the grades Select Structural, No. 1, No. 2, and No. 3. For premium strength, choose Select Structural. Often, lumberyards sell a mix of grades called No. 2 and Better. Other grading systems used for some lumber (typically 2 by 4s) classify wood as Construction, Standard, and Utility, or as a mixture of grades called Standard and Better.

Cedar grades you are likely to see, starting with the highest quality, are Architect Clear, Custom Clear, Architect Knotty, and Custom Knotty. These grades don't indicate if wood is heartwood or sapwood but that distinction affects the price. Because heartwood is more durable, it is also more expensive.

BUYING LUMBER. Lumber is divided into categories according to size: *dimension lumber,* which is from 2 to 4 inches thick and at least 2 inches wide; *timbers,* heavy structural lumber at least 5 inches thick; and *boards,* which are normally not more than 1 inch thick and 4 to 12 inches wide.

Lumber is sold either by the *lineal foot* or by the *board foot.* The lineal foot, commonly used for small orders, considers only the length of a piece of wood. So, for

Lumber is available in a variety of sizes to perform specific tasks. Cedar and pressure-treated pine are commonly used in the South. Some boards come with finished or decorative ends.

example, twenty 2 by 4s, 8 feet long, would be the same as 160 lineal feet of 2 by 4s.

The board foot is the most common unit for volume orders. A piece of wood 1 inch thick, 12 inches wide, and 12 inches long equals one board foot. To compute board feet, use this formula:

Thickness (in inches) × width (in feet) × length (in feet). So a 1 by 6, 10 feet long, would be computed as follows:

1 inch × ½ foot (6 inches) × 10 feet = 5 board feet. When you place an order at a lumberyard, you must give the exact dimensions of the lumber you need.

MOISTURE CONTENT. Lumber is either air-dried in stacks or kiln-dried to a certain percentage moisture content, which dramatically affects the wood's shrinkage, ability to hold nails, and other important properties. Damp wood is more likely to split, warp, or cup as it dries. S-GRN designates "green" (unseasoned) lumber with a moisture content of 20% or more; S-DRY means the moisture content is 19% or less; MC 15 is dried to a moisture content of 15% or less. Pressure-treated wood often has a high moisture content (below).

NOMINAL SIZES. Remember that a "2 by 4" does not actually measure 2 by 4 inches. Its *nominal size* is designated before it is dried and surface-planed; the finished size is actually 1½ by 3½ inches. A nominal 4 by 4 is 3½ by 3½ inches.

Rough lumber is usually closer to the nominal size because it is wetter and has not been surface-planed. If your measurements are critical, be sure to check the actual dimensions of any lumber you are considering before you decide to buy it.

DEFECTS. Lumber is subject to a number of defects due to weathering and milling errors. To check, lift each piece and look down the face and edges for any defects. The most common problems are knots, or cupping and bowing—warps and hollows on the board. Such defects can affect both the appearance and the usefulness of wood. For example, a large knot can seriously weaken a structural member, such as a deck joist. In addition, be on the lookout for problems such as rotting, staining, splits, and missing wood or untrimmed bark along the edges or corners of the piece, called wane. Also look for insect holes and reservoirs of sap, or pitch.

Pressure-treated Lumber

It makes a lot of sense in the South to use pressure-treated wood, especially pine, for outdoor building projects. Treated lumber lasts longer than untreated wood. Although there have been concerns about the chemicals added during the treatment process, treated wood is generally safe for outdoor construction. However, these chemicals (usually CCA—chromated copper arsenate) call for a few precautions. Here are some basic guidelines:

Avoid buying pieces of lumber with crystallized chemicals or residue on the surface.

To keep chips and dust out of your eyes, wear safety glasses or a plastic face shield when cutting or sanding pressure-treated wood. For further protection against dust, wear a disposable dust mask, especially when sanding.

If you've been handling pressure-treated wood, wash your hands with soap and water to remove any dust or chemical residue. Shower after you've finished work for the day, and wash your work clothes separately.

Never burn scraps of treated lumber, because the smoke and ashes could contain chemicals.

Although it isn't widely available, lumber that has been kiln-dried both before and after treatment contains much less of the water that is used in the treatment process. This lumber, marked KDAT, is more expensive than other pressure-treated wood, but it is drier, lighter, more stable, easier to cut, and less likely to release chemical-laden moisture when worked.

Taming a slope. Built of 6 × 6 pressure-treated pine timbers, this retaining wall creates usable gardening space in a steeply sloping backyard. The zigzag shape makes the wall visually interesting and more structurally sound.

FASTENERS AND HARDWARE

Nails, screws, and metal framing connectors are essential for outdoor projects. After all, without them it would be difficult to hold anything together.

NAILS. Use hot-dipped galvanized, aluminum, or stainless steel nails for outdoor construction because they resist rust. Common and box nails are similar, but the former have a thicker shank. This makes them more difficult to drive, but increases their holding power. Both types are sold in boxes (weighing 1, 5, or 50 pounds) or loose in bins. Standard nail sizes are given in "pennies" (penny is abbreviated as "d," from the Latin *denarius*). The higher the penny number, the longer the nail. Equivalents in inches for the most common nails are as follows:

4d = 1½ in. 6d = 2 in. 8d = 2½ in. 10d = 3 in. 16d = 3½ in. 20d = 4 in.

Choose nails that have a length two or three times the thickness of the material through which you will be nailing. Most decking, fence, and overhead framing should be secured with 8d and 16d nails.

DECK SCREWS. Although they're more expensive than nails, galvanized deck screws have several advantages: They don't pop up as readily, their coating is less likely to be damaged during installation, and using them eliminates hammer dents in your decking. Moreover, they are surprisingly easy to drive into soft woods, such as cypress and cedar, especially if you use an electric drill or screw gun with an adjustable clutch and a Phillips screwdriver tip. Screws are not

rated for shear (or hanging) strength, so use nails, lag screws, or bolts to fasten heavy members such as joists to beams. The heavy-duty lag screw, or bolt, has a square or hexagonal head that you tighten with a wrench or a ratchet and socket.

For decks, choose screws that are long enough to penetrate joists at least as deep as the decking is thick (for 2-by-4 or 2-by-6 decking, buy 3-inch screws).

FRAMING CONNECTORS. The photo at right shows several framing connectors. Galvanized metal connectors can help prevent lumber splits caused by toenailing two boards together. Be sure to attach connectors with the fasteners specified by the manufacturer.

To eliminate visible fasteners, deck clips can be nailed to the sides of decking lumber and secured to joists. In addition to remaining hidden between the deck boards, these clips also elevate the boards slightly off the joist, discouraging the rot that wood-to-wood contact may breed. Unfortunately, the clips are more expensive to buy and more time-consuming to install than nails or screws.

BOLTS. For heavy-duty fastening, choose bolts. Most are zinc-plated steel, but aluminum and brass ones are also available. You need to pre-drill holes for the bolts and then secure them with nuts. Machine bolts have square or hexagonal heads that must be tightened with a wrench. Carriage bolts have self-anchoring heads that dig into the wood as you tighten the nut. To secure wooden ledgers to masonry walls, use expanding anchor bolts.

Bolts are classified by diameter (⅛ to 1 inch) and length (⅜ inch and up). To give the nut a firm bite, select a bolt ½ to 1 inch longer than the combined thicknesses of the pieces to be joined.

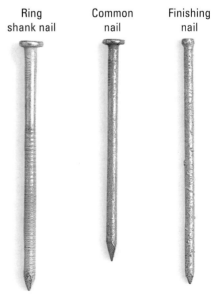

| Ring shank nail | Common nail | Finishing nail |

Framing connectors and hardware, clockwise from top right: post anchors, deck post tie, strengthening straps, rigid tie corner, joist hangers, rigid flat tie, and decorative post tops.

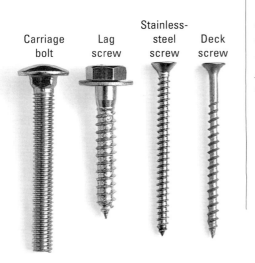

Carriage bolt	Lag screw	Stainless-steel screw	Deck screw

Wood Finishes

Structural elements that go into the ground or are embedded in concrete do not require a finish. But to protect other parts of a structure and to preserve its beauty, apply a water repellent, a semitransparent stain, or a solid-color stain.

Finishes change a wood's color or tone and may mask its grain and texture. Whatever product you choose, try it on a sample board first to be sure you like the appearance. Always read labels: Some products should not be applied over new wood; others may require a sealer first.

Water repellents, also known as water sealers, help prevent decking and other exposed wood from warping and cracking. Clear sealers don't color wood but they allow it to gradually fade to gray; some types come in slightly tinted versions. Clear stains don't block ultraviolet light, which can damage exposed wood as much or more than water.

Don't use clear-surface finishes such as spar varnish or polyurethane on outdoor lumber. In addition to their high price, they wear quickly and are very hard to renew.

Semitransparent stains contain enough pigment to tint the wood's surface with just one coat, while permitting the natural grain to show through. They are available in both water- and oil-base versions. In addition to traditional grays and wood tones, you'll find products for "reviving" a deck's color or for dressing up pressure-treated wood.

Solid-color coverings include both deck stains and deck paint. The stains are essentially paints; their heavy pigments cover wood grain completely. Usually, any paint color can be mixed into this base. Solid stains offer good protection from ultraviolet rays. A word of caution: Don't choose stains or paints intended for house siding; they won't last.

Shown here, from top to bottom, are: unfinished wood, clear water sealer, tinted oil-base repellent, semitransparent gray stain, and red solid-color stain.

BUILDING A LOW-LEVEL DECK

A low-level, house-attached deck is a project well within the scope of most do-it-yourselfers. Before you begin, review the advice given on pages 158–161 and check your local building codes. This type of deck can be completed in a few weekends' time, but it's a job for at least two people.

Think ahead about benches or other built-in features that may need to be integrated with the deck's framing. Be sure the completed deck will be at least 1 inch below adjacent access doors. If you're planning a freestanding deck, substitute an extra beam and posts for the ledger shown; extra bracing at the corners may also be necessary.

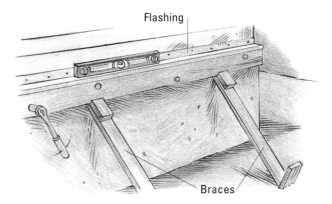

1. Determine the position of the ledger and prop it into place with 2 × 4 blocks or braces. Drill staggered holes for lag screws every 16 inches, then fasten ledger in place, making sure it is level. To prevent rot, either space the ledger off the wall with blocks or washers, or add metal flashing, as shown.

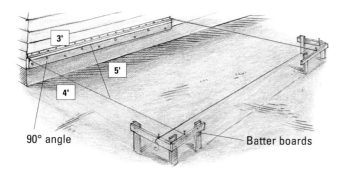

2. Batter boards mark height of deck; build them at outside corners, level with the ledger top. To mark deck edges, string mason's line from batter boards to ledger. Corners must be square; determine using the "3-4-5" triangle method shown.

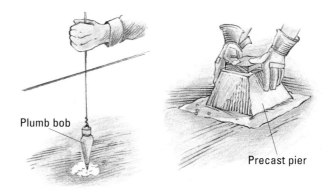

3. Dangle a plumb bob from mason's lines to mark footings. Dig holes to depths required by code; add gravel, then fill with concrete (see page 329). Push piers into the concrete, level their tops, and let concrete set overnight.

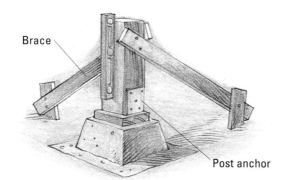

4. Unless piers have integral post anchors, add them now. Measure and cut posts—for this design, a joist's depth below the top of ledger. Check plumb on two sides of each post, temporarily brace each in place, and fasten to piers.

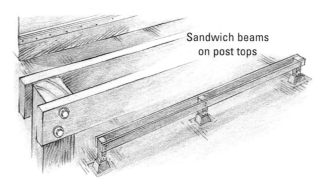

5. Position 2-by beams on each side of post tops, as shown. After leveling them with post tops, clamp them in place. Drill staggered holes, then fasten each beam to posts with bolts or lag screws.

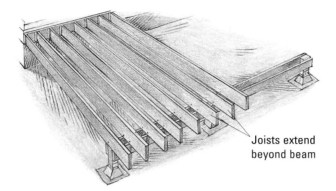

Joists extend
beyond beam

6. Position joists at predetermined span intervals and secure to ledger with framing connectors, as shown. Set them atop beams and toenail in place. Brace joists with spacers at open ends and, if required, at midspan. Add posts for any railings or benches, or an overhead anchored to deck framing.

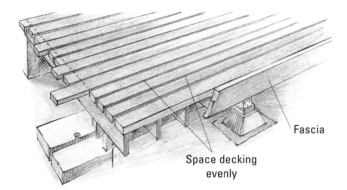

Fascia

Space decking
evenly

7. Align decking boards atop joists, staggering joints (if any). Space boards, leaving about 3/16 inch—or the thickness of a 16d nail—for drainage. Fasten decking to joists with 16d common nails or deck screws. Trim edges with circular saw.

4 × 4 post

8. Finish decking ends and edges as desired with fascia boards or other trim. If you're planning benches, planters, steps, or railings that aren't tied directly to substructure, add them now.

Decking Patterns

One of your first decisions when designing a deck is what kind of decking pattern you'd like; this pattern may affect how the deck's substructure is built. For a house-attached deck similar to the one shown, it's often simplest to run decking boards parallel to the house wall. Generally, more complex decking patterns call for smaller joist spans and a more complicated substructure.

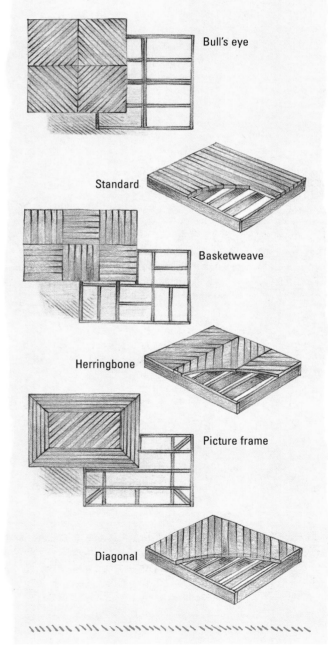

Bull's eye

Standard

Basketweave

Herringbone

Picture frame

Diagonal

BUILDING A BOARD FENCE

In general, fence-building is a straightforward task. The hardest part is sinking the posts; use a posthole digger or rent a power auger to make the job easier. The procedure outlined here is a good one for putting up a basic board fence.

Before you set a post or pound a nail, check your local building and zoning codes, as they may influence style, material, setback, and other requirements. Then tackle the building stages: plotting the fence, installing posts, and finally adding rails and siding.

For fences from 3 to 6 feet tall, plan to set posts at least 2 feet deep—12 inches deeper for end and gate posts. For taller fences, the rule of thumb for post depth is one-third the post length. You can either dig postholes to a uniform depth or cut the posts once they are in the ground. Once the posts are installed, the rest of the job is easy, especially when you have one or two helpers.

If you're planning to hang a gate, too, see pages 182–183 for construction and design pointers.

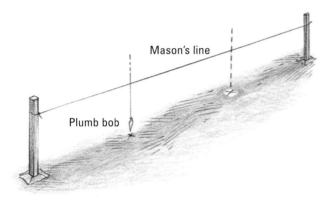

1. First, mark each end or corner post location with a stake. Run mason's line between the stakes, as shown. With chalk, mark remaining post locations on the line. Using a level or plumb bob, transfer each mark to the ground and drive in additional stakes. Then dig holes 6 inches deeper than post depth, making them 2½ to 3 times the post's diameter.

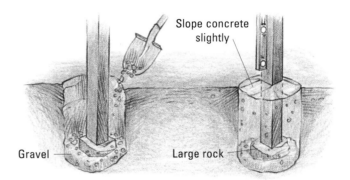

2. Place a rock at the base of each hole and add 4 to 6 inches of gravel. Place a post in a hole and shovel in concrete, tamping it down with a broomstick or capped steel pipe. Adjust the post for plumb with a level. Continue filling until the concrete extends 1 or 2 inches above ground level, and slope it away from the post to divert water.

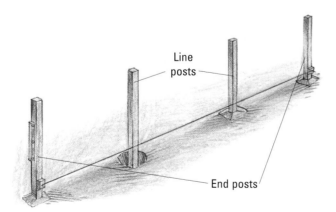

3. To align posts, first position two end or corner posts so their faces are parallel, then plumb them and set them permanently. Use spacer blocks and a mason's line to locate line posts, spacing each a block's thickness from the line. After setting posts in fresh concrete, you have about 20 minutes to align them before concrete hardens. Let cure for 2 days.

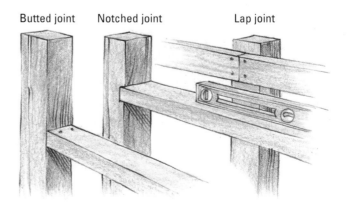

4. Brush on wood preservative where rails and posts will meet. Then fasten one end of each rail; check level with a helper and secure the other end. You can butt them against the post and toenail them, notch them in (cut notches before installing posts), or lap them over the sides or top of each post. If making lap joints, plan to span at least three posts for strength.

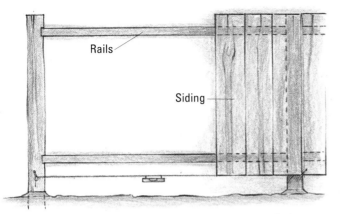

Rails

Siding

5. Cut siding boards to the same length. Stretch and level a line from post to post to mark the bottom of the siding. Check the first board for plumb, then secure it to rails with galvanized nails three times as long as the board's thickness. Add additional boards, checking alignment as you go.

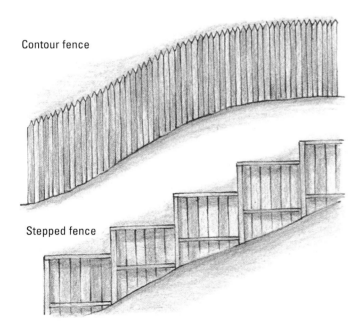

Contour fence

Stepped fence

6. On a hillside, post-and-rail and solid fences with pickets or grape stakes make good contour fences. Board, louver, basketweave, and panel styles work better for stepped fences, which are more difficult to build. For both kinds, make sure that the bottoms of boards 6 inches or wider are cut to follow the contour of the hillside; otherwise, gaps will remain.

Planting Posts

When building an outdoor structure with posts, you'll likely use concrete to keep those posts firmly anchored in the ground. Start by digging a hole that is three times the post diameter (for example, 12 inches for a 4 × 4 post). For maximum stability, plan to sink a full third of the post into the ground. Dig down an additional 6 inches to allow for a layer of coarse gravel at the bottom, which will help water drain away from the base of the post.

For the strongest construction, undercut the posthole slightly so the diameter at the bottom is slightly larger than at the top. Use a section of post to tamp the bottom and sides of the hole. After dumping gravel in the hole, insert the post, centering it in the hole. Check that the post is exactly vertical with a level, then temporarily brace it in position.

Finish up by mixing the concrete and pouring it in the hole. Tamp with a metal rod to eliminate air bubbles. Slope the top of the concrete so water will drain away. Before removing the braces, allow the concrete to cure completely. A sheet of plastic placed over the concrete will prevent it drying out too fast.

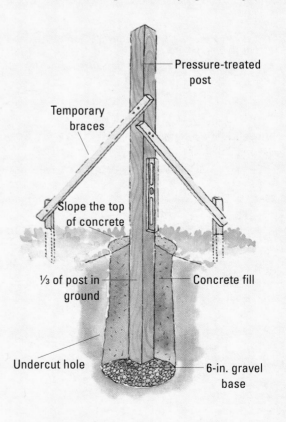

Pressure-treated post

Temporary braces

Slope the top of concrete

⅓ of post in ground

Concrete fill

Undercut hole

6-in. gravel base

BUILDING AN ARBOR

Building an arbor is similar to building a deck, although you'll probably spend a lot more time on a ladder. These illustrations outline the sequence for erecting a freestanding arbor; for construction details on a house-attached arbor, see the facing page. An arbor is essentially horizontal members atop vertical ones; for design ideas, refer to pages 150–157.

If your arbor will span an existing patio, you can set the posts on footings and piers located outside the edge of the patio, or break through the existing paving, dig holes, and pour new concrete footings (and, if necessary, add piers). If you're planning to install a new concrete patio, then you can pour footings and paving at the same time, embedding the post anchors in the wet concrete.

1. Precut posts to length (or run a level line and cut them later). Set posts in anchors embedded in concrete footing or atop precast piers. Hold each post vertical and nail anchor to it.

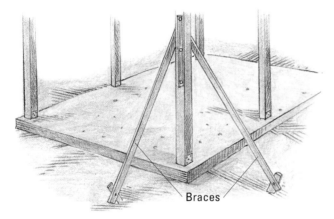

Braces

2. Continue to put up posts, plumbing each post with level on two adjacent sides. Secure each in position with temporary braces nailed to wooden stakes that are driven into ground.

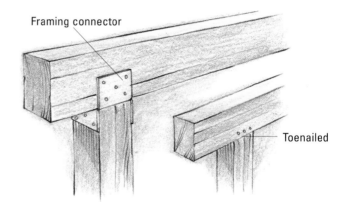

Framing connector

Toenailed

3. With a helper, position a beam on top of posts. Check that posts are vertical and beam is level (adjust, if necessary, with shims); then secure beam to posts.

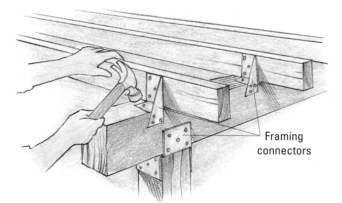

Framing connectors

4. Set and space rafters on top of beams and secure them with framing connectors (shown) or by toenailing to beams. For extra strength, install bracing between posts and beams.

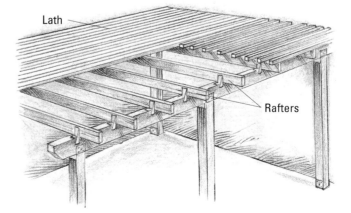

Lath

Rafters

5. Cover rafters with lath, either 1 × 2s or 2 × 2s. Space the lath for plant support or to achieve a specific amount of shade (see facing page).

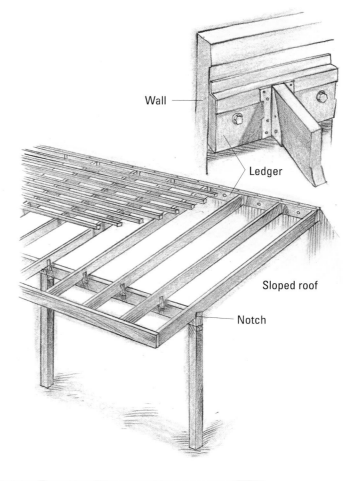

Wall

Ledger

Sloped roof

Notch

Arbor alternatives

Although most arbors employ the same basic components (posts, beams, rafters or joists, and some type of roofing), there are many different ways to assemble them. Each, however, must conform to spans determined by local building codes. So be sure to check them before you start to build.

To attach an arbor to your house, you will need to install a ledger, much like a deck ledger (see page 326). Usually made from a 2 by 4 or a 2 by 6, the ledger is typically attached with lag screws—either to wall studs, to second-story floor framing, or to the roof. If the house wall is brick or stone, however, you'll need to drill holes and install expanding anchors to bolt the ledger in place.

Rafters can be set on top of the ledger or hung from it with anchors, joist hangers, or rafter hangers. If your arbor's roof will be flat, simply square up rafter ends. Sloped rafters, however, require angled cuts at each end, plus a notch (as shown at right) where rafters cross the beam.

You can also opt for a solid roofing material such as shingles, siding, or even asphalt. If you leave the structure uncovered, treating it with a preservative or other finish can add years to its life.

Designing for Shade

How shady your arbor is depends in large part on how you arrange the rafters or lath on top. For example, running the rafters east-west provides midday shade. But if you plan on enjoying the arbor more in the early mornings and late afternoons, run these top boards north-south.

How you attach the top boards to the arbor also affects shade. If you stand 1 by 2s or 1 by 3s on edge, they will give little shade at midday when the sun is overhead, but plenty of shade in morning and afternoon when the sun is at an angle. Lay them flat and the result will be exactly the opposite.

On the pitched roof, pictured at right, pieces of 2-by-2 lattice, spaced 2 inches apart, were laid atop the rafters. Because they're angled by the pitch of the roof, they create an even greater surface area to block the sun. This arbor provides not only midday shade, but also lots of shade during the afternoon, except for a brief period when the angle of the sun matches the angle of the lattice pieces.

Use these ideas as general guidelines. Which design is better for you depends on where you live, the side of the house the arbor is located on, the shape and size of the arbor, and other factors. You might want to experiment with the placement of a few top boards before attaching them permanently to the structure.

MASONRY

Gravel and crushed rock come in many sizes and colors. Counterclockwise from top right: pea gravel, crushed limestone, crushed brick, marble chips, broken slate.

This section will guide you through the world of masonry materials and explain the basic techniques for building paths, patios, and walls. Although some stonework requires years of training, these simple masonry projects can be successfully completed by a do-it-yourselfer. The key is to proceed with patience.

However, you should seek advice from your local building department or garden supplier about the best concrete mix, brick types, or base treatment for use in your climate and soil. Speak with your neighbors about the materials they have successfully used in their gardens, and browse through local offerings of stone and paving products before buying— new items constantly appear.

Stone is particularly appealing because it is a natural material, and most types are very durable. But the availability of stone types, shapes, sizes, and colors varies by locale, and its primary drawback is that it can cost up to five times as much as concrete or brick. Geography dictates price: The farther you live from the quarry, the more you'll have to pay. Some dealers sell stone by the cubic yard, which simplifies ordering; others sell it by the ton. Most suppliers can help you calculate how much you need based on a square-foot estimate.

STONES FOR PAVING. Many stones are precut in square or rectangular shapes; these are fairly uniform in thickness and easy to lay in a grid pattern. Others, however, come in more random widths and thicknesses.

Granite and marble are both valued for their hardness and durability. Although marble is a beautiful choice for formal settings, it is too expensive for most garden construction. Sandstone, limestone, and other sedimentary stones are popular choices; they are more porous than other types and usually have a chalky or gritty texture. Slate, a fine-grained metamorphic rock that is dense and smooth, is also an excellent choice for paving.

Flat flagstones and cut stone tiles are ideal for formal settings. Technically, flagstone is any flat stone that is either naturally thin or split from rock that cleaves easily. It blends well with plants and ponds or other water features. Furthermore, flagstone is one of the few paving materials that can be set directly on stable soil. You can also lay it in mortar (see page 344). However, outdoor furniture and objects with wheels sometimes get caught on its irregular surface. Also, some types of flagstone become dirty easily and are difficult to clean.

Available stone varies from one region to another but may include limestone, slate, marble, granite, and a variety of native stone.

Fieldstone, river rock, and pebbles are less expensive than flagstone or cut tiles. These water-worn or glacier-ground stones produce rustic, uneven pavings that make up in charm what they may lack in smoothness underfoot. Smaller stones and pebbles, for example, can be set or seeded into concrete; cobblestones can be laid in concrete or on tamped earth to cover an entire surface; or narrow mosaic panels of very small stone can be used to break up an expanse of concrete or brick (see page 338).

For economy, good drainage, and a more casual look, don't forget gravel or crushed rock, both of which can provide material for garden paving. Gravel is collected or mined from natural deposits; crushed rock is mechanically fractured and graded to a uniform size. Frequently, gravels are named after the regions where they were quarried.

When choosing a gravel, consider color, sheen, texture, and size. Take home samples as you would paint chips. Keep in mind that gravel color, like paint color, looks more intense when spread over a large area, and that it can change color considerably when wet.

STONES FOR WALLS. There are two broad classes of stonework that work well for walls: rubble (untrimmed) and ashlar (trimmed). In addition, partially trimmed pieces such as cobblestones can create attractive effects.

The stones used in rubble walls are often rounded from glacial or water action; examples (often igneous in origin) include granite and basalt river rock and fieldstone. Since they can be difficult to cut, it's usually easier to search for rocks that are the size you need. Rubblestone is frequently the cheapest kind available.

Fully trimmed ashlar stone is almost as easy to lay as brick. The flat surfaces and limited range of sizes make formal coursing possible and require less mortar than for rubble-work. Ashlar stone is usually sedimentary in origin; the most commonly available types are bluestone and limestone. When a tougher igneous stone, such as granite, is cut and trimmed for ashlar masonry, you are going to have to pay quite a bit more money.

Better than the Real Thing

As an alternative to real stone, which can be costly and hard to find in large sizes, consider "stones" made of concrete. With the proper reinforcement, concrete stones can be made as big as needed; varying their shapes and sizes gives the stones a completely realistic look. But because they're poured to uniform thickness, concrete stones make a more stable paving surface than natural stone.

Concrete stones are typically formed within a grid of wooden forms atop a 2-inch sand base. Steel reinforces (when constructing large stones) are set in place, then the concrete is poured. The stonelike surface comes from pressing a textured, rubber mat onto the surface of the wet concrete. After the concrete has dried and the forms are removed, the stones are chipped around the edges for a rough, irregular appearance that mimics real stone. The last step is to add penetrating concrete stains. These come in a variety of colors, making it easy to blend artificial stones with their natural cousins in the landscape.

If you'd like something like this in your yard, contact a landscape architect or concrete contractor. Mention that you don't really want the real thing—sometimes fake is better. For a do-it-yourself version of these stones, see page 339.

BRICK

Of the bewildering variety of bricks available, only two basic kinds are used for most garden construction: rough-textured common brick and smoother-surfaced face brick.

Most garden paving is done with common brick. People like its familiar, warm color and texture, and it has the advantage of being less expensive than face brick. Common brick is more porous than face brick and less uniform in size and color (bricks may vary up to ¼ inch in length).

Face brick, with its sand-finished, glazed surface, is not as widely available as common brick. More often used for facing buildings than for garden projects, this brick can also be used to make elegant formal walls, attractive accents, edgings, header courses, stair nosings, and raised beds—all projects where its smoothness won't present a safety hazard.

Used brick has uneven surfaces and streaks of old mortar that can look very attractive in an informal pavement. Imitation-used, or "rustic," brick costs about the same as genuine used brick and is easier to find; it is also more consistent in quality than most of the older brick.

Low-density firebrick, blond-colored and porous, is tailor-made for built-in barbecues and outdoor fireplaces. It provides interesting accents but doesn't wear as well as common brick.

The standard brick is about 8 by 4 by 2⅜ inches thick. "Paver" bricks, which are solid and made to use underfoot, are roughly half the thickness of standard bricks. "True," or "mortarless," pavers are a standard 4 by 8 inches (plus or minus ⅛ inch) and can be invaluable for laying a complex pattern with tightly butted joints. To calculate the quantities of brick you'll need for a project, visit a building supplier first, with your measuring tape in hand.

All outdoor bricks are graded according to their ability to withstand weathering. If you live in a region where it regularly freezes and thaws, buy only bricks graded SW, which indicates the brick will not crack when subject to changing weather conditions.

A display of brick includes rough common bricks in various colors, smoother face bricks for accents and edgings, bullnose types (with rounded ends) for stairs and to cap walls, used or imitation-used bricks, and precut bricks (such as the triangle, above left) for patterns.

Precast pavers allow you to experiment with designs and shapes, and many imitate tile, brick, or concrete. An assortment is shown here, including those that interlock with puzzlelike shapes, stepping-stones, and turf blocks.

Concrete Pavers

Available in many sizes, colors, and textures, concrete pavers are no longer limited to 12-inch squares. And because they are easy to install, pavers are an ideal material for do-it-yourself masonry projects.

A simple square can form part of a grid or even a gentle arc. Squares or rectangles can butt together to create broad, unbroken surfaces, or they can be spaced apart and surrounded with grass, a ground cover, or gravel.

Interlocking pavers fit together like puzzle pieces. They are made of very dense concrete that is mechanically pressure-formed. Laid in sand with closed (butted) joints, they create a surface that is more rigid than brick. No paver can tip out of alignment without taking several of its neighbors with it, and the surface remains intact even under substantial loads. Some interlocking shapes are proprietary, available at only a few outlets or direct from distributors. Check the Yellow Pages under Concrete Products.

Modern cobblestone blocks are very popular for casual gardens; butt them tightly together and then sweep sand or soil between the irregular edges.

Turf blocks, which leave spaces for grass to grow through, are designed to carry light traffic while retaining and protecting a lawn or ground cover. In theory, these systems allow you to create grassy patios and driveways or side-yard access routes that stand up to wear.

Cast concrete "bricks," available in classic terracotta red as well as imitation-used or antique styles, have become increasingly popular as substitutes for the real thing because, in many areas, they're significantly less expensive. However, it's rare that they truly duplicate the warm look of aged brick.

Some landscape professionals cast their own pavers in custom shapes, textures, and colors: adobe, stone, and imitation tile, for example. You can also make forms and pour your own pavers, but they won't be as strong as standard pressure-formed units.

TILE

Both ceramic and porcelain tiles are popular for flooring and steps. Porcelain works better outdoors in areas with cold winters, because it won't chip in freezing weather.

Once you've chosen the type of tile, your next decision is whether to use glazed or unglazed tile. Glaze is a hard finish, usually colored, applied to the surface of a tile before its final firing. Most bright, colorful tiles are glazed. Unfortunately, unless a special grit is added to the surface of glazed tile, it can be slippery when wet, so for outdoor use choose unglazed tiles for paving and reserve the glazed ones for occasional accents, edgings, or raised planting beds.

Most outdoor tile, whether glazed or unglazed, falls into one of three categories: pavers, quarry tile, or synthetic stone.

Pavers are made by pouring clay into wooden or metal molds, drying or curing the tiles, and then firing them. They usually have a grainy, handcrafted look. Perhaps the best-known hand-molded

pavers are Saltillo tiles (named for the city in Mexico where they are made). Pavers are not recommended for use outdoors in cool, wet climates, as mildew and moss are likely to become problems.

Quarry tiles are denser and more regular in shape than pavers. They come in natural shades of yellow, brown, and red, and are available with rounded edges and with varied finishes. These tiles are made by squeezing clay into forms under great pressure, then firing them until they are very hard.

Synthetic stone is now being developed by tile manufacturers impressed by the increasing popularity of real stone. These tiles, which mimic the look of granite, limestone, or sandstone, generally have enough surface bite to be safely used on patios and are often cheaper and lighter than the real thing. You can also buy concrete imitations of paver tiles; unlike concrete pavers (see page 335), these should be installed on a rigid mortar bed.

Varied and versatile, tiles serve a number of purposes. Painted tiles, like the ones shown above, can adorn steps, walls, pool surrounds, and outdoor eating areas. Quarry, ceramic, and porcelain tiles (below) come in many sizes and are mainly used for flooring.

Sealer for tile

Some unglazed tiles are sealed at the factory; those that aren't should be coated with a penetrating sealer that allows the tile to "breathe" after installation. A sealer may darken a tile's surface or give it a shiny appearance, so you should try it first on an extra piece of tile. Some sealers require more maintenance than others. Ask your tile dealer to recommend the product most appropriate for your situation.

A. **Small tiles** can be used to create elaborate patterns, adding elegance to the garden.

B. **Though expensive,** slate is durable, comes in a number of colors, and provides secure footing.

Create a Mosaic Paver

A path of handmade mosaic pavers created from pieces of tile or pottery can add special charm and a very personal touch to your garden, especially if the pieces have fond associations for you. Perhaps you've broken a favorite dish or pottery piece, or maybe you have colorful tiles left over from a remodeling project. By recycling them, you can create a little pathway of several pavers or use a single one as an accent.

For each stepping-stone you want to make, start with a ready-made concrete paver purchased at a building or garden center. (Also buy grout and tile adhesive from a building center or tile store.) To start with, keep your design simple and use a limited palette of colors, loosely sketching it on the paver.

Protect your eyes with goggles and wear rubber gloves for this part of the project. In a heavy-duty, zip-top plastic bag, seal up a whole tile or large pottery piece. With a hammer, gently break up the tiles and pottery into pieces of an appropriate size.

Apply tile adhesive to the back of the pieces and place them on the paver, following your design (top). Make sure you allow sufficient space between pieces to apply grout, and let the layout dry for the amount of time specified by the adhesive manufacturer.

In a small, disposable container, mix the tile grout to a thick consistency (follow the package directions). Wearing rubber gloves, press the grout evenly into the spaces between the pieces (middle). The grout should be flush with the outer edge of the stone all around.

After the grout has dried for 10 minutes, wipe off any excess with a damp sponge, but don't remove too much grout. Shine the tile with a towel and let it dry for 24 hours. If you wish, you can then apply an outdoor sealer. Now you're ready to position your paver in the garden.

CONCRETE

Though sometimes disparaged as cold and forbidding, poured—or, more accurately, cast—concrete can be more varied in appearance than brick. Used with well-made forms, it can conform to almost any shape. Furthermore, it can be lightly smoothed or heavily brushed, surfaced with handsome pebbles, swirled or scored, tinted or painted, patterned, or molded to resemble another material. And if you eventually get tired of the concrete surface you have chosen, you can use it as a foundation for a new pavement of brick, stone, or tile set in mortar.

Concrete does have certain disadvantages. In some situations, it can seem harsh, hot, glaring, or simply boring. And if smoothly troweled, concrete can become slick when wet. Moreover, once its dry ingredients are combined with water, you have to work quickly before the mix hardens. A mistake could require an extensive and perhaps costly redo.

Concrete paving is usually given some surface treatment, both to upgrade its appearance and to improve traction. For example, you can spray it with a hose jet or sandblast it to uncover the aggregate, or you can embed colorful pebbles and stone in it. These finishes, known as exposed aggregate, are probably the most common contemporary paving surfaces used for terraces and walkways.

Stamped concrete can have sufficient texture to give good traction even on steps.

Other ways to modify a standard steel-troweled concrete surface include color dusting, staining, masking, acid washing, and salt finishing. Concrete can also be stamped and tinted to resemble stone, tile, or brick. The patterns simulate either butted joints or open ones, which can then be grouted to look like masonry units.

The standard slab for pathways and patios should be 4 inches thick. In addition, allow for a 4- to 8-inch base in most areas (in frost-free areas, 2 inches is sufficient).

Forms for concrete are built in the same way as for wood edgings. For standard paving, you will need 2 by 4s on edge for forms and 12-inch 1 by 3s or 2 by 2s for stakes. If you leave the lumber in place as permanent edgings and dividers, use rot-resistant cedar or pressure-treated lumber. For curved forms, choose either tempered hardboard, plywood, or, if they will be permanent, metal edgings.

To prevent buckling and cracking, reinforce a concrete area more than 8 feet square with 6-inch-square welded wire mesh; install it after the forms are ready (see pages 348–349). If you're not sure whether your slab will need this reinforcement, consult your building department or a landscape architect or contractor.

Concrete with flair. This courtyard floor is a series of individually formed concrete squares; beach pebbles set in mortar fill the gaps between squares.

Offset rectangular concrete forms this walkway in Winter Park, Florida. The surface was "antiqued" with a rock salt finish, leaving irregular pits in the surface.

Stamping wet concrete created a textured pattern for this patio. The best stamps are made of flexible material that covers the concrete in sections.

Weighty facts about concrete

Although many people think concrete is just "cement," it is actually a combination of portland cement, sand, aggregate (usually gravel), and water. The cement, which is a complex, finely ground material, undergoes a chemical reaction when mixed with water, and becomes a kind of "glue" that binds everything together. It also gives the finished product its hardness. The sand and aggregate act as fillers and control shrinkage.

Buying bagged, dry, ready-mixed concrete is expensive but convenient, especially for small jobs. The standard 90-pound bag makes ⅔ cubic foot of concrete, enough to fill one posthole or to cover a 16-inch-square area 4 inches deep.

If your project is fairly large, order materials in bulk and mix them yourself, either by hand or with a power mixer. For small projects hand-mixing is less complicated, but it requires significant exertion. Large forms that must be filled in a single pour will warrant a power mixer, which can be rented.

Use this formula for regular concrete (the proportions are by volume):

1 part cement	2¾ parts aggregate
2½ parts sand	½ part water

Some dealers also supply trailers containing about 1 cubic yard of wet, ready-mixed concrete (about enough for an 8- by 10-foot patio). These trailers have either a revolving drum that mixes the concrete or a simple metal box into which the concrete is placed. Both types are designed to be hauled by car.

For a large patio, plan to have a commercial transit-mix truck deliver enough concrete to allow you to finish your project in a single pour. To locate concrete plants, look in the Yellow Pages under Concrete, Ready Mixed.

Molded Concrete

To create the look of stones by using concrete, you can dig holes or build shaped wooden forms and fill them with concrete. The resulting pads—with planting spaces in between—can be textured, smoothed, or seeded with aggregate. Commercial forms are also available, as shown below.

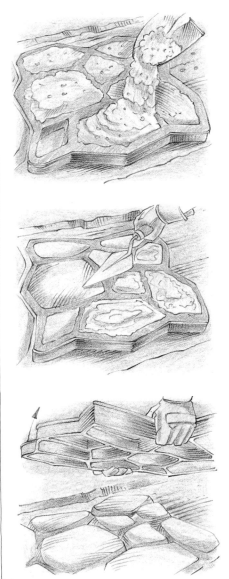

Plastic forms can be used to form a path of concrete "flagstone." Place the form on a clean, level surface (top); use a trowel to fill the mold with concrete (center), and smooth the top. When the concrete can hold its shape, remove the mold (bottom).

339

RECYCLED MATERIALS

A "recycled" garden doesn't necessarily mean one that features old bottles and broken concrete. In fact, incorporating used materials into your garden has several practical advantages. First, it's generally less expensive to re-use materials than to buy new ones. You get a lot of bang for your buck by turning would-be castoffs into a striking pathway or arbor. Second, recycled materials often produce unique results that are laden with character. You're not likely to see the duplicate you've built from recycled products in anybody else's yard. And, finally, by putting materials destined for a landfill to good use, you are doing your bit to protect the environment.

There are many common building materials that lend themselves to re-use in the garden. Salvaged and remilled lumber or "barn wood" can frame arbors. Broken concrete can be used for retaining walls and raised beds. Stones and bricks from torn-down walls can be crafted into new walkways and patios. Scrap metal can roof a shed. Old reinforcing bar can be twisted into decorative trellises and arbors. Even rusty watering cans, barrels, and jugs can be born again as fountains. Keep an eye on nearby remodeling projects—and flea markets—to see what leftover materials spark your imagination.

High-tech recycled materials are also available. One of the most surprising materials for landscaping, for example, is a lumber look-alike made from recycled plastic. It can be used as timbers for framing beds or as step risers. Much of this plastic stock is high-density polyethylene recycled from bottles that once held milk and liquid detergents. Large timbers are formed by injection molding— shooting the hot plastic into a mold. Smaller ones are formed by extruding hot plastic from a mold. Then the boards and timbers are textured and colored so they resemble wood, or pigmented to look painted.

Other manufacturers make fireproof thermoplastic shingles from cast-off computers, or combine landfill-bound wood with waste plastic to produce a weatherproof composite wood in common wood sizes. Though not meant for structural purposes, wood-plastic composite can be used for decking, railings, and fencing. It can be painted or stained, and has the additional advantage of being cool underfoot and splinter-free.

Naturally, when using recycled materials, it's important to make sure they'll stand up to the job for which they're chosen. Be especially careful with old brick, for example. While used bricks are valued for their beauty, unless you know how the bricks were originally used, they may not be the best choice for building a terrace or garden wall. Salvaged bricks frequently come from the interior walls of buildings, and are not durable enough for exterior use in some climates. When these soft bricks (sometimes called salmons because of their light-pink color) are exposed to weather or sudden changes in temperature, they often flake, crack, or break.

Likewise, salvaged wood from old buildings shouldn't be used for structural purposes unless you are absolutely sure that it is strong enough and free from rot or insect damage. If in doubt, consult a contractor or carpenter.

Rugged and virtually maintenance-free wood composite material was used to frame this water-view deck.

A. **Newly installed,** this walk looks as if it's been around for years thanks to old sandstone pavers from another location.

B. **Salvaged bricks** have been laid into this path. Old mortar on the brick gives an aged look.

C. **Broken concrete edgings** from a demolished driveway form a handsome boundary between lawn and border.

D. **Scrap lumber and rusted tin** salvaged from a nearby farm create this rustic archway at the base of the stairs.

LAYING BRICKS IN SAND

With careful preparation and installation, a brick-in-sand path or patio can prove as durable as bricks set in mortar. In addition, if you decide to change the surface later, you need chip out only one brick to remove the rest intact.

Typically, a bed of 1½- to 2-inch-thick sand or rock fines (a mix of grain sizes) is prepared and the bricks are laid with closed joints. You'll need a 4- to 8-inch gravel base anywhere that drainage is poor or where the ground freezes in winter.

To hold both the bricks and sand firmly in place, build permanent edgings around the perimeter (see page 346). Install the edgings first; they serve as good leveling guides for preparing and laying the bricks. If you have a lot of cutting to do, or you want to create curved edgings or complex angles, rent a brick saw from a masonry supplier or tool rental outlet (follow the supplier's directions to the letter; you'll need to wear goggles, heavy gloves, and possibly ear protection).

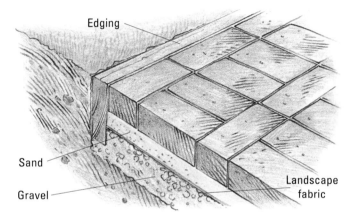

1. This typical brick-in-sand patio includes a gravel bed, a layer of landscape fabric, packed sand, and rigid edgings, which hold the bricks in place. Install edgings first.

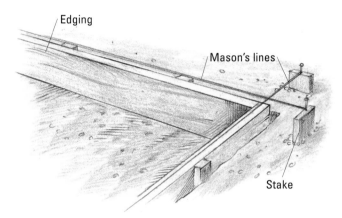

2. String mason's lines from stakes to serve as guides, first to mark edgings at the desired level and slope. Later, edgings can serve as a reference for leveling sand and bricks.

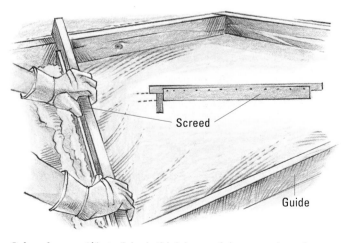

3. Lay down a 1½- to 2-inch-thick layer of dampened sand and level it with a bladed screed, as shown. If necessary, use a temporary guide on which to rest one end of the screed.

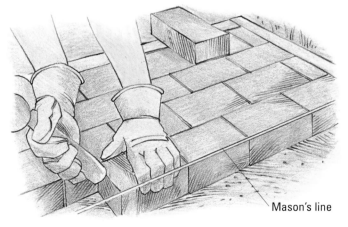

4. Another mason's line will help align courses. Begin at one corner; lay bricks tightly against one another, tapping each into place with a hand sledge or mallet. Check level frequently.

Concrete pavers can also be laid in sand much like bricks. With interlocking pavers, alignment between the units is almost automatic. After laying these units, it's best to make several passes with a power-plate vibrator to settle them. You can probably rent a vibrator locally; if not, you can use a heavy drum roller instead. Then spread damp, fine sand over the surface; when it dries, sweep it into the paver joints. Additional passes with either vibrator or roller will help lock the pavers together.

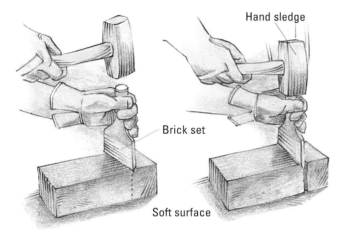

5. To cut bricks, score a line on all four sides (left); make the cut with one sharp blow (right). To cut angles, "nibble" at the waste area in several passes, a little at a time.

6. Throw fine sand over finished pavement, let dry for a few hours, and then sweep it with a stiff broom into joints. Spray lightly with water, so that the sand settles completely.

Brick in Stone

When choosing a brick pattern (also known as a bond), consider how hard it's going to be to lay it. Some bonds require not only accuracy but also a lot of brick cutting. The patterns shown below are among the most popular; the jack-on-jack and running bonds are the simplest to lay.

Jack-on-jack

Running bond

Basket weave

Half basket

Herringbone

Pinwheel

LAYING MASONRY IN MORTAR

The instructions here are for laying a flagstone path, but you can apply them to any masonry unit—ceramic tile, brick, or broken concrete—that you want to set in mortar. Remember that for a path, you must allow a minimum slope for drainage: 1 inch per 10 feet of run or ¼ inch per foot from side to side. This means that the path should have a slight crown in the center.

For the most permanent masonry surface, set stones, bricks, or tiles in a mortar bed over concrete that is at least 3 inches thick. If it is an existing concrete slab, it must be clean and in good condition. Ask a concrete dealer whether you need to use a bonding agent to ensure that the mortar will adhere to an existing or new concrete surface.

Mixing mortar

Mortar recipes vary according to their intended use, but the ingredients are usually the same: cement, sand, possibly lime (or fireclay), and water. Either make your own or buy more expensive ready-to-mix mortar. To build a wall, you will need to make a mix consisting of 1 part portland cement, ½ part hydrated lime or fireclay, and 6 parts sand. This mixture is much like Type N, sold for general use. In contrast, a typical mortar for paving and most other below-grade installations contains only 1 part portland cement and 3 parts sand.

Small amounts of mortar can easily be mixed by hand, but mortar can be caustic, so wear gloves when you work with it.

1. Dry-fit all stones, trimming if necessary. Mix mortar just stiff enough to support the stones. Spread the mortar 1 inch deep, covering enough space to lay one or two stones at a time. Furrow the mortar with a trowel.

2. Set each stone in place, bedding it with a rubber mallet, and checking for level. If a stone isn't level, lift it up and scoop out or add mortar as needed. Clean stones with a wet cloth as you work.

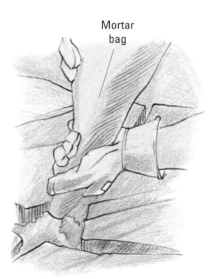

Mortar bag

3. Let the mortar set for 24 hours, then fill in joints between stones with the same mortar mix (plus an optional ½ to 1 part fireclay for workability, but no lime). A mortar bag will keep mortar off stones that could stain.

Carefully measure the sand, cement, and lime into a wheel-barrow or similar container. Use a hoe to thoroughly mix the dry ingredients and form them into a pile. Make a depression in the center of the dry mix and pour some water into it. Mix, then repeat the process. When ready for use, mortar should have a smooth, uniform, granular consistency; it should also spread well and adhere to vertical surfaces (important when building a wall) but not "smear" the face of your work, which can happen when the mortar is too watery. Add water gradually until these conditions are met. Make only enough mortar to last a few hours; any more is likely to be wasted.

Trimming stone

Because most flagstones are irregular, you'll probably need to trim some pieces before setting them. You can keep this chore to a minimum, however, by carefully dry-fitting a design.

Wear gloves and safety glasses for even small trimming jobs. Chip off pieces with a mason's hammer or brick set and hand sledge. To make a major cut, use the adjacent stone as a guide and proceed with a brick set and sledge, as shown at right. It is often difficult to keep a stone from splitting or shattering beyond the cut line, so have some extra stone on hand.

TRIMMING STONE

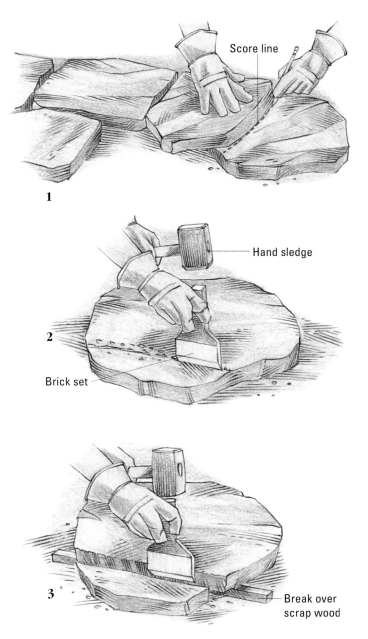

To cut flagstone, lay one block over its neighbor and trace its outline **(1)**. Then score a groove in the stone to be cut **(2)**. Finally, prop up the stone and split it with a sharp blow **(3)**.

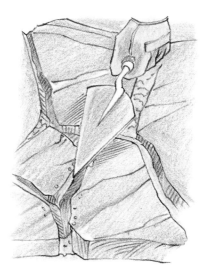

4. If stone is a nonstaining type, you can work grout across stones and into joints with a wet sponge. No matter how the grout is applied, use a mason's trowel to smooth the joints.

INSTALLING A GRAVEL PATH

Gravel—either smooth river rock or the more stable crushed rock—makes a low-cost, fast-draining path that suits a wide variety of informal and formal garden styles. It's also an easy project for most homeowners. The first step in laying a gravel path is to install edgings to hold the loose material in place. Then secure some landscape fabric to discourage weeds. Gravel surfaces tend to shift when walked on, but the movement will be minimized if you underlay the gravel with a compacted base of crushed rock or sand. This will also help with drainage.

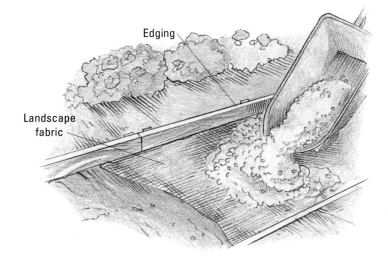

1. Install edgings first, then put down landscape fabric or plastic sheeting to protect against weeds. Pour fine crushed stone or sand over the site, taking care not to dislodge the liner.

2. Rake the base material evenly over the path until it is a uniform 1-inch thickness. As you rake, wet the material with a fine spray.

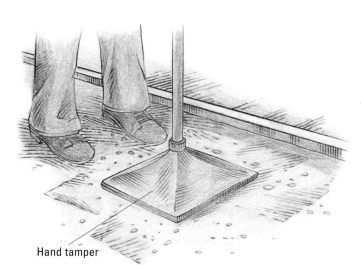

3. Using a drum roller or hand tamper, pass over the wet base several times, packing it down firmly. This firm base aids drainage and helps keep the topcoat from shifting underfoot.

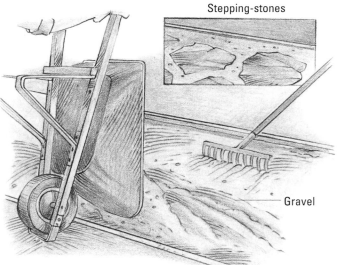

4. Spread the gravel at least 2 inches thick and rake it evenly over the base. If desired, place stepping-stones on the base so that their tops protrude slightly above the surrounding gravel.

A look at edgings

What do walks, patios, lawns, and garden beds have in common? They all need edging to keep them in place. Edging is especially important when working with loose materials, such as gravel, or when setting bricks in sand. It also serves to visually define a surface.

Several tried and true edging options are illustrated here. Probably the simplest is a shallow trench, filled with mulch, that separates a lawn and garden beds. Wooden edging is also popular though it doesn't work well with curves. Most gardeners use 2-by-4 or 2-by-6 lumber, but you can also use 4-by-4 or 6-by-6 materials.

Another effective edging material is poured concrete. It is excellent for constructing curved edging, serving as a footing for mortared masonry units, or installing flush with the ground. Bricks also establish a neat, precise edge. Set them directly in firm soil—horizontally, vertically, or even at an angle (but don't expect them to last forever). And a random edging of uncut stone makes a perfect edging for a path in a rustic or naturalistic garden.

Manufactured plastic or aluminum edgings are functional but not especially attractive. These strips secure bricks or concrete pavers below finished paving height; they can be concealed with soil, sod, or plants. Flexible sections are convenient for tight curves.

For curbing paved areas, an edging is often installed after the base has been prepared and before the setting bed and paving are laid. String mason's lines around the perimeter, not only to mark the exact borders of the paving, but also to designate the outside top border of the edging. To achieve the correct edging height, you'll probably need to dig narrow trenches under the lines.

A. A crisp, cut edge defines this garden bed, but you'll need to use a sharp edger or spade to keep the grass in check.

B. Cast concrete edging is attractive and easy to install, but it's expensive and doesn't lend itself to smooth curves.

C. Brick edging is highly effective at keeping lawns at bay. When set low, it serves as a mowing strip, too.

D. Metal strips are inexpensive, easy to install, and very durable. The flexibility is useful for curving beds and borders.

POURING A CONCRETE SLAB

The key to successfully pouring a concrete path or patio lies in preparation. This entails grading (to level any irregularities that are in the soil) and formwork (building the wooden outlines for the concrete). Lay out stakes and mason's lines to mark the outline of the slab, allowing for at least a 1-inch drop for each 10 feet away from the house for drainage. If the exposed soil is soft, wet it and then tamp it firmly.

Wooden, steel, or copper dividers can be permanent partitions; they also serve as control joints to prevent cracking and help break up the job into several manageable pours.

Be sure to add any required reinforcement to formwork before pouring. Check local building codes; usually, 6-inch-square welded wire mesh is the best choice for pavings.

See page 339 for information on concrete. Pour large areas in sections and be sure to have helpers on hand to assist with hauling and spreading the wet concrete. Wear gloves to protect your hands from the concrete's caustic ingredients and rubber boots if you have to walk on the wet mix.

1. For rough grading, dig deep enough to allow for 4 inches of concrete plus 2 to 8 inches of gravel. Construct forms from 2 × 4s secured to 12-inch stakes, placing the form tops at finished slab height. Add welded wire mesh for reinforcement.

2. Begin pouring concrete at one end of form while a helper spreads it with a hoe. Work concrete up against form and tamp it into corners, but don't press it down too hard. A splashboard or ramp lets you pour the concrete where you want.

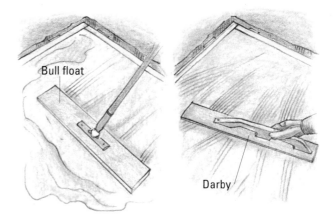

3. With a helper, move a 2-×-4 screed across the form to level concrete, using a rapid zigzag, sawing motion. A third person can shovel concrete into any hollows.

4. Initial floating smooths down high spots and fills small hollows left after screeding. As shown, use a darby for small jobs and a bull float with an extension handle for larger slabs.

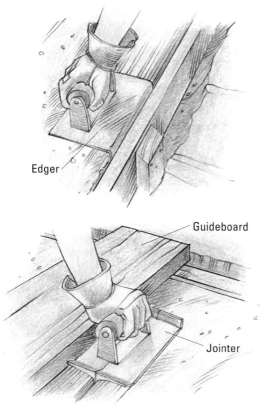

Edger

Guideboard

Jointer

5. Run the edge of a trowel between concrete and form. Then run an edger back and forth to create a smooth, curved edge (top). Make control joints every 10 feet with a jointer (bottom).

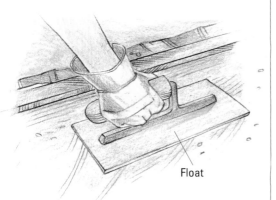

Float

6. Before the surface stiffens, give it a final floating with a wooden float. For a smoother surface, follow with a steel trowel. For a nonskid surface, drag a broom lightly across the concrete, without overlapping strokes.

Pouring a Footing

You must provide a garden wall with a solid base, or footing. Very low walls (no more than 12 inches) and dry-stone walls (see page 350) may only require a leveled trench or a rubble base; but other walls require a footing fashioned from concrete that is twice as wide and at least as deep as the wall's thickness. In cold-weather areas, extend the footing below the frost line. Add 6 inches to the trench depth for a bottom layer of gravel.

If you need to pour a post footing for a deck, fence, or arbor, see page 329. Use bags of ready-mixed concrete for these small jobs.

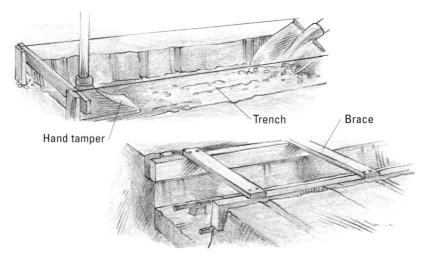

Hand tamper

Trench

Brace

1. Prepare a base for the footing by leveling and tamping the bottom of the trench and adding a 6-inch layer of gravel (top). Trenches in very firm soil may serve as forms; otherwise, build forms with 2-by lumber, stakes, and braces (bottom). Set any required reinforcing bars on a layer of broken bricks or other rubble.

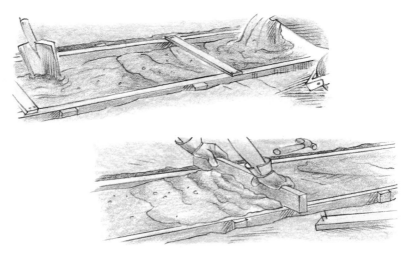

2. Pour concrete (top) and insert any vertical reinforcing bars required by building codes. Screed concrete level with tops of forms (bottom). Cover with a plastic sheet, leave to cure for 2 days, then remove the forms and begin to build the wall.

BUILDING A DRY-STONE WALL

A precise fit is essential to building a stone wall. Because the wall is built without mortar, its stability depends on the weight and friction of one stone upon another. The finished structure should appear to be a unit rather than just a pile of rocks.

Use the largest stones for the foundation course. Reserve long ones for "bond" stones that run completely through one side of the wall to the other. Set aside broad, flat stones to cap the top of the wall. As you lay the stones, you can place soil and plants in the unmortared spaces.

Most dry-stone walls slope inward on both surfaces; this tilting of the faces is called batter and helps secure the wall. To check your work, make a batter gauge by taping together a 2-by-4 board, a scrap block, and a carpenter's level (below).

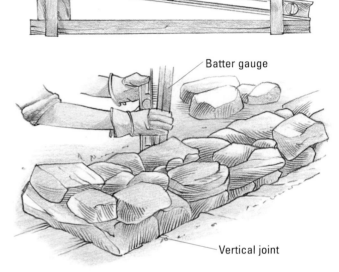

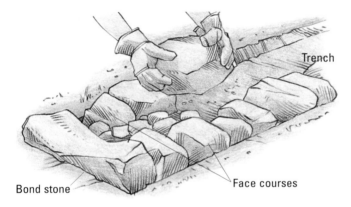

1. Lay foundation stones in a trench about 6 inches deep. First, place a bond stone (one as deep as the wall) at one end; then position the two face courses at both edges of the trench. Choose whole, well-shaped stones for the face courses. Fill in the space between face courses with tightly packed rubble.

2. Lay stones atop the first course, staggering vertical joints. Select stones that fit together solidly and tilt the stones of each face inward toward one another. Use a batter gauge on faces and ends of the wall to check the tilt. Place bond stones every 5 to 10 square feet to tie the wall together.

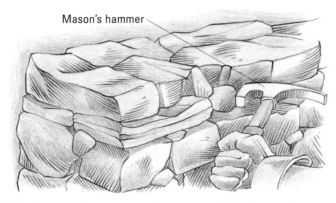

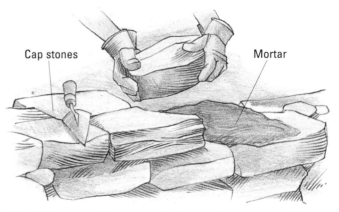

3. Continue to add courses, staggering vertical joints and maintaining the inward slope, so that gravity and the friction of the stones set one upon another will help hold the wall together. Gently tap small stones into any gaps with a mason's hammer.

4. Finish the top with as many flat, broad stones as possible. If you live in an area that experiences frost, mortar the cap as shown. Don't rake (indent) these joints; level them flush with a piece of scrap wood to prevent water from collecting.

Retaining walls

If your home sits on a sloping lot or a hillside, a retaining wall may be needed to hold back the earth and prevent erosion. Homeowners have a choice of three basic wall-building materials—wood, stone, or concrete. Now a number of new modular masonry systems have been developed with the owner-builder in mind (see below). These proprietary systems come with complete instructions for installation.

Simple wood or masonry retaining walls, less than 3 feet high and on a gentle slope with stable soil, can be built by a do-it-yourselfer. But it's a good idea to consult your local building department. Most communities call for a building permit for any retaining wall. They may also require a soil analysis in any area suspected of being unstable.

In general, it's best to site your retaining wall so it results in the least possible disruption of the natural slope, but even so, extensive cutting and filling may be needed. The hill can be held back with a single wall or a series of low retaining walls that form terraces. Though terracing is less risky, both methods disturb the hill and should be designed by an engineer. If space permits, the safest approach is not to disturb the slope at all, but to build the wall on the level ground closer to the foot of the slope and fill in behind it.

In any case, the retaining wall should rest on cut or undisturbed ground, never on fill. Planning for drainage is also essential. Usually, you'll need a gravel backfill to collect water that dams up behind the wall. Water in the gravel bed can be drained off through weep holes in the base of the wall or through a drain pipe that channels the water into a storm sewer or other disposal area.

Slope is cut away and excess earth is moved downhill. Retaining wall now holds back long, level terrace.

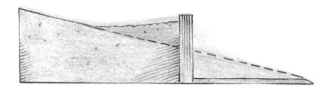

Earth is cut away and moved behind tall retaining wall. Result is level ground below; high, level slope behind.

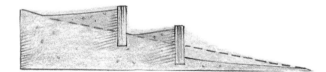

Total wall height is divided between two terraces, resulting in a series of level beds.

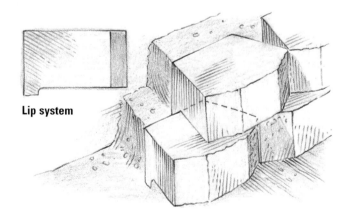

Lip system

For low retaining walls or small raised planters, modular masonry systems are available in various styles and weights. Most use cast "lips" (left) or interlocking pins to establish

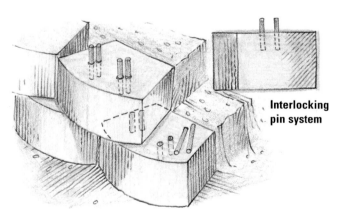

Interlocking pin system

the setback and resist outward pushing forces. Fiberglass or steel pins drop through holes in upper blocks and stop in grooves on units below, joining each to two beneath (right).

BUILDING A RAISED BED

Some of the most frustrating problems facing gardeners—including poor soil and bad drainage—can be solved by simply raising your garden above the ground. An easy-to-build raised bed makes it possible for plants to thrive where soil is compacted, wildlife is hungry, or the growing season is short. And if you need easy access to your plants, due to a disability or simply to eliminate back-bending labor, you can sit on the edge of the bed and garden in comfort.

For drainage, break up the soil underneath the bed and then fill the bed with the best soil you can; you can place plants closer together in good soil, making a small area more productive. Line the bottom of the bed with wire screening to keep out pests, or fit it with a PVC framework for bird netting.

If the bed is more than 4 feet wide, it will be difficult to reach the middle from either side. If the sides will double as benches, build the frame 18 to 24 inches high.

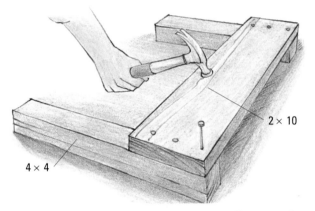

1. Orient a rectangular bed from north to south. For a 4 × 10 foot bed, first nail short sides of 2 × 10s to 3-foot-high 4 × 4 corner posts. Use rot-resistant lumber and galvanized nails.

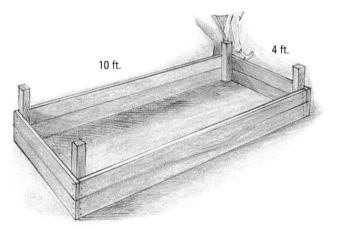

2. Flip over structure and nail 10-foot lengths to corner posts. For added strength, install wooden bracing or metal L-straps. Work on level ground so that bed is as square as possible.

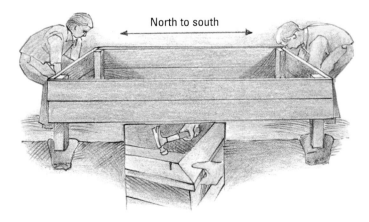

3. Set bed right side up and insert corner posts into predug foot-deep holes. Level if necessary. Cap the top with surfaced cedar 2 × 6s, with ends cut at a 45-degree angle (inset).

4. Place 3 to 4 inches of new soil in the bottom of the bed and mix it into the ground to aid drainage. This 20-inch-deep bed holds about 2½ cubic yards of soil.

Vegetables, herbs, and flowers thrive inside raised beds filled with rich soil. These beds are pressure-treated 2 × 10s, faced with cedar siding to match the house. Their 4-foot width means they're easy to reach into from all sides.

Back-bending work can be eliminated if you just raise the garden high enough. This raised bed brings flowers and vegetables within easy reach. The extra depth also improves drainage and provides more room for roots to grow.

Easy-access Gardening

Gardening with a disability isn't always easy, especially if you need to maneuver a wheelchair through tight spaces. But thoughtful planning to improve access can make the job a joy rather than a chore.

Raised beds *can accommodate both flowers and edible plants. To put gardening chores within easy reach of a wheelchair, the beds should be about 16 inches tall and no more than 4 feet wide; they can be linear or U-shaped, with the opening in the U just wide enough for a chair.*

Paved paths, *about 4 feet wide, can allow a chair to turn, maneuver, and glide easily. Ideally, the paths should be extensions of a paved patio at the rear of the house and a porch or terrace at the front. If the house site is higher than the garden, a wide, gently sloping ramp can angle off a back deck.*

Hinged trellises *can be lowered to tend or gather crops such as peas and tomatoes.*

An automatic irrigation system *eliminates the need for routine watering. See pages 358–361 for options.*

Railings *for walks and ramps should be sunk in concrete footings for extra support.*

Special tools *are available with extra-long handles to reach into beds from a chair.*

Mulch *— with fabric or loose materials — reduces the need for frequent weeding.*

Plant for low maintenance. *Choose trees that don't shed a lot of litter, opt for a smaller lawn — or no lawn at all — and choose plants that don't require frequent pruning or pest and disease control.*

STEP-BUILDING BASICS

Rustic steps in a sloping garden path can vary widely in dimension. But if designing formal steps for a porch, deck, or walk, you must adhere to certain proportions.

The flat part of a step is the tread; the vertical element is the riser. Ideally, the depth of the tread plus twice the riser height should equal 25 to 27 inches. Based on an average length of stride, the ideal outdoor step should have a 6-inch-high riser and a 15-inch-deep tread, but riser and tread dimensions can vary. Risers should be no lower than 5 inches and no higher than 8 inches; tread depth should never be less than 11 inches. The overall riser-tread relationship should remain the same. All the risers and treads in any one flight of steps should be uniform in size (see page 179).

Plan on a minimum width of 2 feet for utility steps and 4 feet for most others. If you want two people to be able to walk abreast, allow 5 feet.

Rarely do steps fit exactly into a slope. More than likely, you will have to cut and fill the slope to accommodate the steps. If your slope is too steep for even 8-inch risers, remember that steps need not run straight up and down. Landings and switchbacks make the distance longer but the climb gentler.

Timber steps

In addition to the step layouts shown here, you can build simple but rugged steps using 6-by-6 pressure-treated timbers. To begin, excavate the site and tamp the soil in the tread area firmly. Lay the timbers on the soil, then drill a hole near both ends of each tie or timber. With a small sledgehammer, drive either $\frac{1}{2}$-inch galvanized steel pipes or $\frac{3}{4}$-inch reinforcing bars through the holes into the ground.

Or, for extra support, pour small concrete footings and set anchor bolts in the slightly stiffened concrete. When the concrete has set (after about two days), secure the ties to the footings with the bolts.

Once the tie or timber risers are in place, fill the tread spaces behind them with concrete, brick-in-sand paving, gravel, grass, or another material.

Stone steps

The easiest way to construct stone steps is without mortar, but it does call for fairly large and heavy stones—20 inches deep, 2 feet wide, and 6 to 8 inches thick. These steps work particularly well for informal areas of the garden or where foot traffic isn't high.

Starting at the downhill end of the slope, excavate a hole for the first stone and spread 2 inches of sand in the bottom. (If your soil drains poorly, put 4 inches of tamped gravel beneath the sand.) Wet and tamp the sand, then lay the stone on the sand and twist it until it is level and firmly embedded, with its surface about 2 inches above grade.

With the first stone securely in place, repeat the process working up the slope; where the slope is steep, overlap the stones a few inches for stability. For extra strength, spread a 1-inch layer of mortar at the back of the lower step, to bond the steps where they meet.

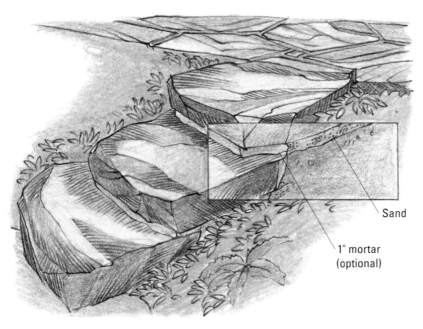

Sand

1" mortar (optional)

Wooden stairs

Formal wooden steps are best for a low-level deck or for easy access to a doorway. Make stringers from 2 by 10s or 2 by 12s. If the steps are more than 4 feet wide, a third stringer will be needed in the middle.

Use galvanized bolts or metal joist hangers to secure stringers to a deck beam or joist; if you're running stringers off stucco siding or another masonry surface, hang them on a ledger, as shown. Note that when bolts are used, the first tread is below the surface of the interior floor or deck; when joist hangers are the fasteners, however, the first tread must be level with the floor.

To avoid rotting out the stringers at the bottom, attach them to wooden nailing blocks anchored in a concrete footing. Build risers and treads from 2-by material cut to width; treads should overlap the risers below and may hang over slightly.

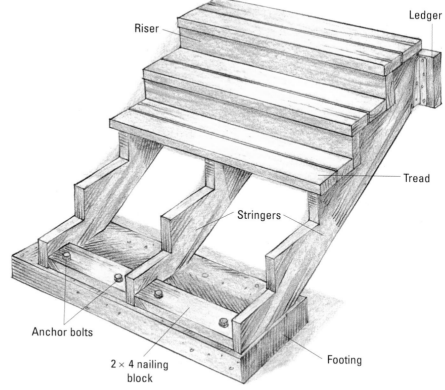

Riser

Ledger

Tread

Stringers

Anchor bolts

2 × 4 nailing block

Footing

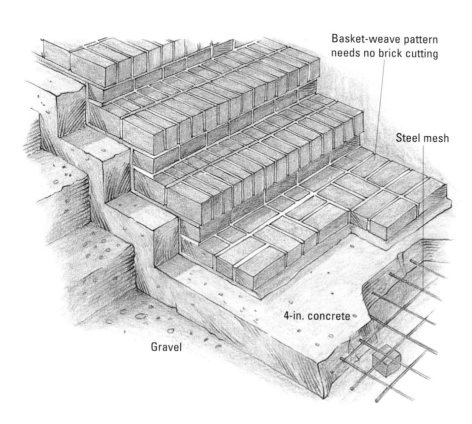

Basket-weave pattern needs no brick cutting

Steel mesh

4-in. concrete

Gravel

Masonry steps

Steps can be built entirely of concrete or, for a finished look, the concrete can be used as a base for mortared bricks.

First, form rough steps in the earth. Allow space for at least a 6-inch gravel setting bed and a 4-inch thickness of concrete on both treads and risers. (In cold climates you will need 6 to 8 inches of concrete, plus a footing that is sunk below the frost line.) Add the thickness of the bricks to tread-and-riser dimensions. Tamp filled areas thoroughly.

With 2-inch-thick lumber, build forms like those shown on page 348. Lay the gravel bed, keeping it 4 inches back from the front of the steps; you will pour the concrete thicker at that potentially weak point. Reinforce the concrete with 6-inch-square welded wire mesh.

Pour and screed the concrete as for a poured concrete footing. To make treads more weather safe, broom the wet concrete to roughen its surface, then cure as for a concrete footing (see page 349).

INSTALLING A GARDEN POND

With either a flexible plastic or rubber pond liner and a bit of elbow grease, even a beginner can fashion an average-size garden pond in a single weekend, though the surrounding plants will take somewhat longer to establish.

A liner can take almost any shape, even accommodating curves and undulations. You can also weld together two or more pieces of liner with solvent cement, or have the supplier do it for you.

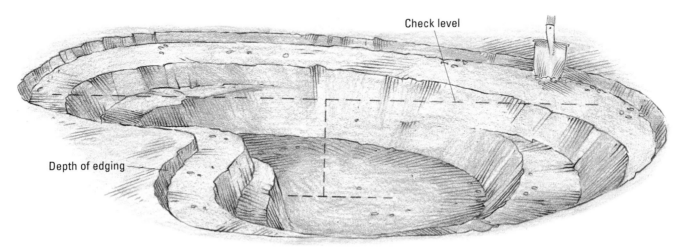

1. Mark the pond's outline with a hose or a length of rope. Dig all around the outline with a sharp spade; remove any sod and keep it in a shady spot for later patching. Excavate the hole to the desired depth and width, plus 2 inches all around for a layer of sand. Dig down to the thickness of any edging material. Check level carefully, using a straight board to bridge the rim.

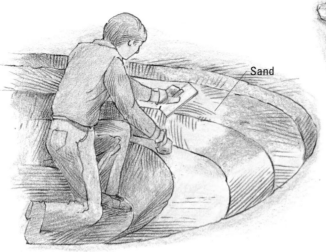

2. Next, remove all protruding roots and rocks and fill any holes with soil. Pack a 2-inch layer of clean, damp sand into the excavation. Smooth the sand with a board or a concrete float.

3. Open up the liner and let it soften in the sun. Then spread it over the hole, evening up the overlap all around. Place heavy stones or bricks around the perimeter to weigh it down, then slowly begin to fill the pond with water.

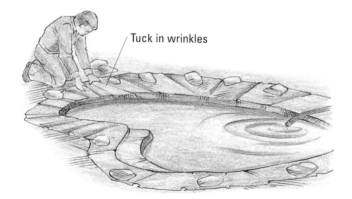

Tuck in wrinkles

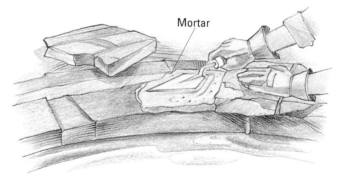

Mortar

4. Continue filling, tucking in wrinkles all around; as required, fold pleats at hard corners (they won't be visible when the pool is filled). You can wade into the pool to tuck in the lining, but the water's weight will make it fit the contours of the hole.

5. When the pond is full, add overhanging edging. Lay flagstones or brick in a thin bed of mortar. Bring the liner up behind the edging, then trim the liner. Drain the pool and refill it with fresh water.

Fountains and Falls

Water in motion, whether gently spilling, gurgling, or energetically tumbling, is always enchanting. Both fountains and waterfalls help bring the sparkle and the musical sounds of falling water into the garden.

Surprisingly, fountains can be simple to create. A wooden planter box, a metal basin, or a large pot, for example, can easily be converted into a small fountain. Just coat the inside of a wooden container or an unglazed pot with asphalt emulsion or epoxy paint, or use a flexible liner. Then drop in a submersible pump with a riser pipe and add water (in shallow water, a few rocks can conceal the pump).

For larger holding pools, many designers prefer precast rigid fiberglass or reinforced concrete. A wall fountain's raised holding pool is often concrete or concrete block, covered with plaster or faced with brick, tile, or stone above the water line. A submersible pump and water pipes can be combined to add a fountain to an existing wall. An electrical switch, perhaps

located indoors, controls the pump-driven flow; a ball or 3-way valve allows alteration of the flow, depending on your taste. To automatically replace water lost through evaporation, hook up a float valve to the water supply line. A drain is also handy.

Waterfalls pose some unique design considerations. The major technical concern is waterproofing. Before plunging into construction, determine which pump, pipes, and other plumbing hardware you'll need to provide the desired flow. For a waterproof channel, use either a flexible liner, free-form concrete, a fiberglass shell or series of splash pans, or a combination of the above.

If you opt for a liner, position waterfall rocks carefully, making sure not to damage or displace the liner. Once the basic structure is complete, secure secondary stones and add loose rocks or pebbles to provide visual accents or to form a ripple pattern. Only creative experimentation will reveal the most pleasing sights and sounds.

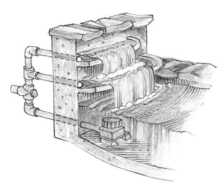

A formal wall fountain combines a raised holding pool, masonry wall, and decorative spill shelves. Water tumbles from pipe outlets to spill shelves to a holding pool; a submersible pump sends it back around again.

Waterfall design calls for a watertight channel, natural-looking stones, and adequate camouflage for plumbing parts. Flexible liner is the simplest channel option; stone placement conceals liner.

GARDEN WATERING SYSTEMS

An irrigation system should fit the lay of your land and the arrangement of your plants. But you should also choose a system that doesn't demand more time than you have to spend in the garden. Choose wisely and watering becomes a leisurely and rewarding process, producing healthy, attractive plants. Choose poorly and watering becomes a dreaded task, an obligation that takes away from the joys of gardening. Worse, a poorly designed irrigation system results in unhealthy plants and wasted water.

A wealth of equipment—from micro-sprinklers to automatic timers to soil moisture sensors—can help you water your garden efficiently, even when you're busy or out of town.

The most common irrigation devices are pictured on these pages; for step-by-step instructions on installing drip and sprinkler systems, see pages 360–361.

Hoses

A hose can make watering your garden easy or difficult. Unreinforced vinyl hoses are inexpensive and lightweight, but they are also the least durable and most prone to kinking. Reinforced vinyl hoses are less likely to kink and lightweight—important if you have to move the hose around a lot. Rubber hoses, which have dull surfaces, are the heaviest and toughest types. They kink in hot weather but work well in cold weather. Reinforced rubber-vinyl hoses are flexible, kink resistant, moderately heavy, and durable.

Hoses are sold by length and have various inside diameters ($\frac{1}{2}$-inch, $\frac{5}{8}$-inch, and $\frac{3}{4}$-inch hoses are common). Though the difference in hose diameter may seem slight, the water volume each carries varies greatly. If you have low water pressure or if you must run your hose uphill, you'll need all the pressure and flow you can get. You

should choose the hose with the largest diameter and the shortest length that is practical for the situation.

Hose-end sprinklers

These come in a variety of forms, from impulse sprinklers that can cover hundreds of square feet to small bubblers ideal for watering shrubs or containers. Choose models with a spray pattern that matches the areas you'll be watering. If you have clay soil or sloping ground that is slow to absorb water, select models that steadily apply low volumes of water over long periods to avoid wasteful runoff.

The downside of hose-end sprinklers is that you have to move them around by hand to cover large areas. They also deliver water unevenly; some areas get wetter than others. To get an idea of how much and how evenly your sprinklers apply water, place five identical, straight-sided cups randomly in the

A. Drip hose with factory-drilled holes lets water slowly drizzle out.

B. Water from emitter line spreads slowly through soil to moisten plant roots.

C. Porous polyvinyl tubing soaks soil at high pressure; at low pressure, water seeps.

D. Delivery tubes for irrigation systems range from (left to right) $\frac{1}{2}$-inch-diameter tube, spaghetti tube, and two soaker tubes.

E. Other components of an irrigation system include (left to right) emitters, mini-sprinklers, and connection to the water source and timer, including a Y-shaped filter and pressure regulator.

F. This hose is a reinforced type that can bend without kinking.

D

E

coverage area. Run the sprinklers for 15 or 30 minutes, then measure the water accumulated in each cup. Those cups nearest and farthest from the sprinkler will probably have the least water. In any case, both the amount of water and the unevenness of the distribution will give you an idea of how long to run the sprinklers (use timers so you don't forget the sprinklers are on) and how to move them so that patterns overlap and all the plants are watered evenly.

Soaker hoses

One of the simplest and least expensive ways to water plants is with soaker hoses. Unlike sprinklers or a complete drip irrigation system, they attach to hose bibs quickly with little fuss.

Of the two types of soaker hoses available, one applies a fine spray, the other small droplets. Both are generally sold in 50- and 100-foot lengths.

Perforated plastic emits streams of water from uniform holes drilled along one side. The hose can be used face down, so water goes directly into the soil, or turned up for broader coverage. Output depends on pressure. This type of soaker hose is very useful for irrigating narrow areas of lawn or bedding plants, or around the bases of trees that need slow, deep irrigation.

Ooze tubing or "leaky hose" is made from recycled tires. The water seeps out of tiny pores. It requires a filter in the nozzle to prevent clogging, and applies water slowly—as little as 4 gallons per minute per 100-foot length. If you don't use a pressure regulator, turn on the water until it seeps out of the pores. If you see pinhole sprays, reduce the pressure.

You can use ooze tubing to water large beds. Run it out in rows spaced 2 to 3 feet apart. To keep it from being an eyesore, cover it with mulch or bury it 2 to 6 inches deep.

Drip irrigation

For many situations, drip irrigation is the most efficient way to get water down to the roots. Drip irrigation applies water slowly so it can be absorbed without runoff. Because the water is applied directly where it is needed, it uses less water and results in fewer weeds.

Even though a drip irrigation system may look intimidating, it is easy to install, even for a beginner. The key is good planning and design. Start your design with a detailed drawing of the garden, including the positions and spacing of plants. Learn the water needs of your plants. Are they drought tolerant or do they need frequent irrigation? If you are starting a new garden, group the plants according to their water needs.

Rough out your plan on paper, and take it to an irrigation contractor for some expert help with the design and installation of your system.

Sprinkler systems

Traditionally used for watering lawns, underground pipe systems with risers for sprinkler heads are the best way to water medium-size to large lawns and low-growing ground covers. Drip irrigation, however, is a better choice for trees, shrubs, perennials, annuals, and vegetables. With a good electronic controller, both kinds of systems can be run automatically.

The basic components of a rigid-pipe system are shown on page 360. You may need to divide your sprinkler system into several circuits, each serving only part of the lawn or garden and operated by its own valve. Then you can water each circuit separately, as you need it. Established shrubs, for instance, may call for once-per-week watering; lawns may require a daily soak.

Automated irrigation

An automatic sprinkler system is the most efficient way to water. Manufacturers now offer a dazzling array of equipment that can make those systems work even better.

TIMERS. Electronic timers are more complicated but more reliable than mechanical timers (see page 361).

Controllers capable of daily multiple cycles reduce runoff, which happens if water is applied faster than the soil can absorb it. If you have this problem, set a repeat cycle to operate the sprinklers for 10 or 15 minutes at, for example, 4, 5, and 6 A.M.

Dual- or multiple-program controllers let you water a lawn on a more frequent schedule than that needed for ground covers, shrubs, and trees.

SPRINKLERS. New low-precipitation-rate nozzles reduce runoff, improve spray uniformity, and allow a large area to be irrigated at one time. They are particularly useful on sloping ground or on soil that absorbs water slowly.

F

INSTALLING WATERING SYSTEMS

The information given on the previous pages will help you choose the best system for your garden. These pages show how to install the two main types of irrigation systems—sprinkler and drip.

Most systems can be attached to an existing water supply pipe (1-inch diameter or larger is best). Because drip systems require only low water volume and pressure, you may be able to connect a drip system to a convenient outdoor faucet; instructions from the supplier or manufacturer can help you determine if this simple solution will work for you. You will want to pick out some possible locations to place your valves. Consider how to conceal them and, if your system will be automated, where you can put an electricity-powered timer and control box. Make sure you have a map of your system so you can easily locate broken pipes or clogged valves.

No matter how you connect your system to the water supply, you will need proper filter, pressure regulator, and backflow devices. Filters ensure that emitters don't clog. Pressure regulators prevent too much water pressure from building up in the system and possibly popping the emitter heads off the supply lines. Backflow devices, often required by law, prevent irrigation water from backing into the home water supply.

Whether or not your irrigation system is automated, check it often for broken or clogged sprinklers or drip emitters.

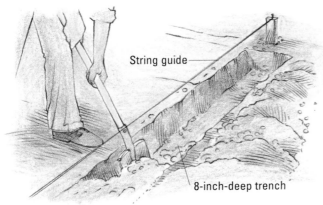

1. Sprinkler system must be laid underground. First, dig 8-inch-deep trenches for pipes. To keep trench lines straight, run string between two stakes.

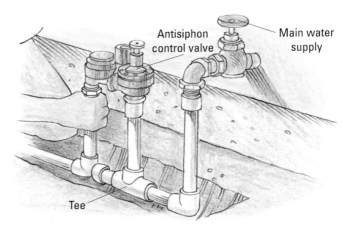

2. Connect pipes to the water supply pipe, then attach control valve (with built-in antisiphon valve) at least 6 inches above ground. Use thick-walled, ¾-inch PVC pipe.

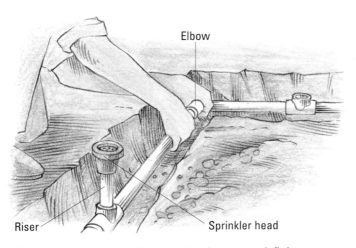

3. Assemble pipes from the control valve outward, fitting risers and sprinkler heads to elbows, tees, and side outlets. Joints may screw together or require PVC solvent cement.

4. Flush out pipes with heads removed. Then fill in trenches, mounding loose soil along center of trench. Tamp the soil firmly with a hand tamper. Avoid striking the sprinkler heads.

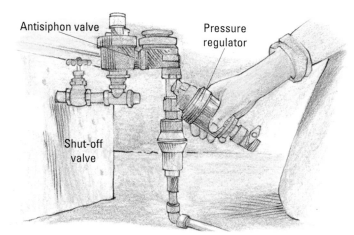

1. Drip irrigation system assembly starts with connecting the control valve, filter, and pressure regulator to the water supply line (for hose-end system, use a hose bib).

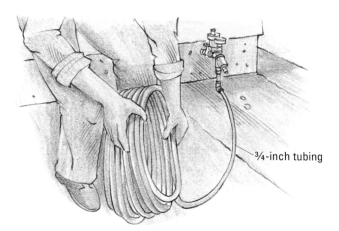

2. Connect ¾-inch flexible polyvinyl tubing and lay out main lines on the surface of the soil or in shallow trenches. For a more sturdy system, use buried PVC pipe for main lines.

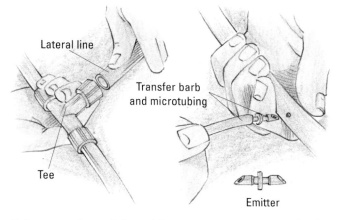

3. Lay out and attach lateral lines using tee connectors (left). Many kinds hold tubing without cement. Attach end caps, then insert emitters or transfer barbs for microtubing (right).

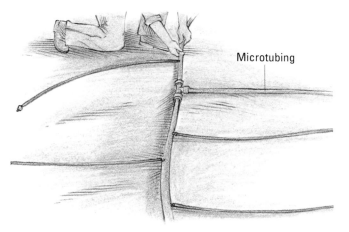

4. Flush system to ensure that all emitters work properly. Cover the lines with a thin layer of mulch, if desired, but leave the emitters and microtubing above ground.

Timers

To water your garden, or parts of it, for a set amount of time, install an electric-powered or manual timer. Both types can be set up to run a drip system, sprinkler system, or any common watering device such as a sprinkler.

More-expensive electric or electronic timers are either battery-powered or may require an electric outlet. You can buy types with various controls, ranging from very complex to pretty straightforward. Some can be set for both several irrigation circuits and for alternating watering times. A word of caution: If you have a professional install the system for you, make sure to get directions

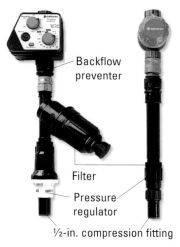

on how to reset the controls (if, for instance, you have a power failure that wipes out the timer's settings).

Manual timers are not as convenient as automatic types—you need to actually walk out to the garden and turn them on—but they are less prone to breakage and have automatic shut-off valves to ensure that your garden doesn't become completely soaked.

Timers are installed between the faucet and any other system components, including backflow preventers, filters, and pressure regulators.

WORKING SAFELY

Although we don't think of the garden as a hazardous place, any time you pick up a tool, climb a ladder, or start moving around heavy materials, you can injure yourself—or someone else. If you are planning to carry out any of the outdoor construction shown in the previous pages, follow the guidelines given here.

Safety accessories and clothing

Many masonry projects call for safety precautions. To protect yourself from flying particles of dust or rock when cutting stone or brick, wear safety goggles or a full face mask. Look for comfortably fitting, fog-free types made of scratch-resistant, shatterproof plastic. Dry portland cement irritates the

eyes, nose, and mouth, so wear a dust mask when mixing concrete. Wet concrete and mortar irritate the skin, so wear heavy rubber gloves and tuck your sleeves into them. Also wear rubber boots if you must walk in the concrete to finish it off. Wash your skin thoroughly with water if wet mortar or concrete contacts it.

When working with lumber, protect your hands from splinters with all-leather or leather-reinforced cotton work gloves. If sanding wood, wear a disposable painter's mask. For work with solvents, finishes, or adhesives, wear disposable rubber or plastic gloves.

Working safely with power tools

Portable power tools can cause injuries in an instant. Handle these tools with respect and follow some basic safety precautions.

꙰ Read the owner's manual before using any tool.

꙰ When operating a power tool, minimize interruptions or distractions. If possible, block off the work area to keep visitors away—especially children and pets.

꙰ Never wear loose-fitting clothing or jewelry that could catch in a tool. If you have long hair, tie it back.

꙰ Never use a power tool if you are tired or under the influence of alcohol or drugs.

꙰ Before you plug in a tool, check that safety devices such as guards are in good working order. Also tighten any clamping mechanisms on the tool to ensure that the blade or bit is securely installed. Set up any necessary supports or clamps for securing the work.

꙰ Ensure that your hands and body—and power cord— are well away from a tool's blade or bit.

꙰ Never stand on a wet surface when using a power tool that is plugged into an electrical outlet, unless the outlet is GFCI protected (see opposite page).

꙰ Never cut wet wood. If you can't avoid cutting warped boards or knots, watch for kickback—when the tool lurches back out of the wood.

꙰ Make sure any lumber you are sawing or drilling does not contain fasteners.

꙰ If a blade or bit jams in a piece of wood, turn off and unplug the tool before trying to extricate it. To keep your balance, don't reach too far with the tool; move closer to it and keep a stable footing.

꙰ Always allow the bit or blade to stop on its own before setting down the tool.

꙰ Unplug a tool before servicing or adjusting it, and after you have finished using it.

꙰ Follow the manufacturer's specifications to lubricate and clean power tools, and make sure all blades and bits are sharp and undamaged.

꙰ If you are using a rented concrete mixer, never reach into the rotating drum with your hands or tools. Keep well away from the moving parts.

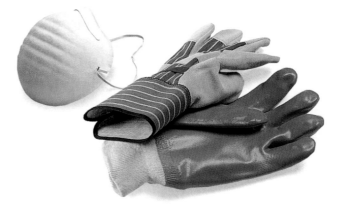

Working safely with electricity

Tools powered by electricity are essential for most outdoor construction projects. But unless a drill, circular saw, or other power tool is double-insulated, it must be properly grounded or it can give a serious shock. Double-insulated tools should be clearly marked (the plug will have only two prongs). When you are working in a damp area or outdoors, a ground fault circuit interrupter (GFCI) is essential.

When working outside, you will probably need to use an extension cord for your tools. Use the shortest extension cord possible (long cords can overheat, causing a fire hazard), and make sure it's rated for outdoor use. The longer the cord, the less amperage it will deliver, which means less power gets to the tool's motor. Look for the nameplate on the tool that contains its amperage requirement. Avoid crimping the cord; don't run it through a door that will be continually opened and closed.

A main disconnect allows you to shut down your entire electrical system whenever you need to change a fuse or in case of an emergency. If you need to work on an outdoor switch, circuit, or outlet, you'll need to shut off power to a branch circuit. *Never* work on a live electrical circuit. Two typical disconnects are shown at right. Familiarize yourself with them before you start to work.

TWO DISCONNECTS

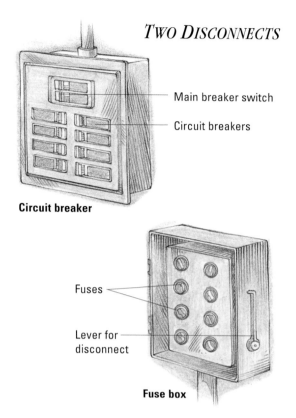

Main breaker switch

Circuit breakers

Circuit breaker

Fuses

Lever for disconnect

Fuse box

To lift heavy objects, spread your feet a comfortable width apart. Then bend your knees and, keeping your back straight, pick up the object—never bend at the waist or you could injure your back. If an object is very heavy, get help.

When working on a ladder, wear sturdy shoes with good traction. Overlap the sections of an extension ladder by three or four rungs and tie the top of the ladder to a stable object. Haul up your equipment using a rope and bucket, as shown.

Katherine Owens residence
Mountain Brook, Alabama

GARDEN MAKEOVERS

It never fails. Guide someone through a beautiful garden, then show them a "before" photo of the original site. The first word they always say is "Wow!"

As you look at the makeovers on the following pages, you'll be saying "wow" a lot. We've gathered some remarkable before-and-after garden stories from many areas of the South to show what great work your neighbors have done. Budgets for these types of projects can range from very large to quite modest. But if your neighbors can do it, so can you.

These makeovers cover a wide range of subjects, such as creating a welcoming entry, solving parking problems, detailing a deck, making a small space seem larger, updating a pool, and planting a new home's first garden.

In each case, note that success depended on attending to structures first and plantings last, based on a comprehensive step-by-step plan.

BEFORE

KEEPING IT SIMPLE

Simple doesn't have to mean unimaginative. When faced with redoing this front yard in Bethesda, Maryland, garden designer Jim Sines of Garden Gate Landscaping, Silver Spring, Maryland, focused on design fundamentals to create a welcoming entryway that is both striking and easy to maintain.

A wide bluestone landing at the curb gives guests room to step out of their cars in comfort. River birches, surrounded by liriope, help screen the house from the street. To give the garden evergreen structure, Sines planted spreading English yews on either side of the doorway. These plants are perfect for growing underneath low windows because they need little trimming or maintenance.

"I try to keep the number of different plants in a foundation planting to a minimum," he says. "It gives you a simpler, cleaner, and neater look." It also makes it easy to combine plants that enjoy similar growing conditions.

Because the paving and ground cover replaced much of the original lawn, maintenance of the yard takes mere minutes. About the only chore the owners face is keeping the small flower bed across from the seating area stocked with annual color.

BEFORE

THE MAKEOVER

PROBLEM *Hedges from the curb to the front door made guests feel like they were on a runway.*

SOLUTION *The new bluestone landing and walk bordered by low plantings give guests plenty of room for a comfortable stroll to the front door.*

PROBLEM *The large lawn required hours of maintenance each week.*

SOLUTION *River birches and ground cover add interest to the lawn and minimize its maintenance.*

MAKEOVER FEATURES

A. River birches provide cooling shade and add texture and color in the garden with their handsome, flaking bark. Glossy green leaves backed with silvery green flutter gently in a breeze.

B. Lush sweeps of liriope beneath river birches frame the front garden. A new bluestone walk and landing at the curb welcome guests and lead them to the front entry.

C. Outdoor seating areas are usually in the backyard. This one is right up front, inviting visitors to linger and admire the flowers.

NEW LIFE FOR AN OLD POOL

When this swimming pool was built about 30 years ago, its primary purpose was to channel the energy of growing children. But when the children grew up, the owners asked Dallas landscape architect Harold Leidner to update the old pool and make it a part of the garden.

One of the first things Leidner did was darken the water by adding green marble dust to the sides and bottom of the pool. The darker color makes the water appear deeper and the pool more natural. Then he removed the exposed-aggregate surround and brought the lawn nearly to the edge of the pool, using bluestone coping to separate the grass from the water. Next he replaced the diving board with a waterfall that spills over large stones into the pool. To tie in the waterfall with the pool's new look, he massed large ferns and evergreen shrubs in back of the stones. This gave the look he wanted and the appearance of a higher grade behind the pool.

Leidner replaced the original exposed-aggregate terrace that connected the house to the pool with a larger stone terrace. Three broad, curving steps lead guests from the terrace past the pool by way of a bluestone walk. The stones are set without mortar and spaced so that ribbons of grass grow between them, underscoring the lush, natural look of the garden.

THE MAKEOVER

PROBLEM *Bright pool water looked unnatural.*

SOLUTION *Darkened bottom and sides make the pool appear deeper and more natural.*

PROBLEM *Exposed-aggregate pool surround looked dated.*

SOLUTION *Replacing the surround with bluestone coping and planting grass to its edge update the look.*

PROBLEM *The diving board wasn't needed.*

SOLUTION *A waterfall creates a soothing replacement.*

PROBLEM *The old terrace matched the dated pool surround.*

SOLUTION *A new, larger bluestone terrace and walk tie in the pool with the house.*

BEFORE

A. **A bluestone walkway** leads from the new terrace past the swimming pool. Lush ferns, perfect companions for water features, visually soften the pool's border.

B. **Massed plantings** at the edge of the swimming pool help tie it in with the garden. Although the pool is perfectly round, the stone waterfall gives it a more natural, free-form shape.

C. **Stones and plantings** that extend over the water help integrate the garden with the swimming pool.

AFFORDABLE CHANGE

Many homeowners think that redoing a front yard requires the wealth of Fort Knox, but this house in Tuscaloosa, Alabama, demonstrates how you can make big improvements on a small budget.

The family enjoyed spending time on the front porch, but the yard didn't create the sense of intimacy and welcome they wanted. Barton's Nursery created a plan that offered both and was simple and economical.

A pair of large boxwoods flanking the front door visually overpowered the porch and called too much attention to the steeply pitched roof and high gable above the entry. Replacing them with multistemmed crepe myrtles solved both problems. Now the focus is on the front door instead of the gable. And while the crepe myrtles provide separation between the porch and the yard, you can still see between the trunks to the house behind them.

The lawn needed some work too. It fell off sharply to the right beside the porch, focusing attention on the side yard. So additional soil was brought in to level the corner. Now beds of evergreens and ground cover wrap the lawn and porch. The lawn has an attractive curved shape, and the new plantings foster the feeling of intimacy that the owners wanted.

As a finishing touch, the old concrete walk was surfaced with handsome brick pavers that match those on the porch.

A

THE MAKEOVER

PROBLEM Massive boxwoods dwarfed the front porch and drew too much attention to the high gable above the entry.

SOLUTION Crepe myrtles focus attention on the front door without blocking views of the house and porch.

PROBLEM The front yard dropped off sharply and called attention to the side yard.

SOLUTION Leveling that corner of the yard allows space for plantings and focuses attention on the front yard.

BEFORE

A. **Removing the two large boxwoods** from the entry opened up the front of the house, making it more inviting. The lawn area is small, but its shape and placement showcase planting areas and walkway.

B. **A screen of evergreen shrubs** gives a sense of privacy and coziness. Ground covers add a layer of lushness while enhancing the view of the front porch.

THE LONG AND SHORT OF IT

Architect Bill Edwards admits that living in a split-level home was at the bottom of the list of things he thought he would do. When he and his family moved in, a front yard update rose to the top of his priority list. To give the house a more contemporary look, Bill teamed up with Atlanta landscape architect Dan Franklin.

They worked to shorten the long appearance of the house by breaking up horizontal lines and introducing vertical lines wherever they could. "It's like trying to dress when you're overweight," Bill explains. "You do everything vertically that you can." Wooden panels and molding underneath the windows and the addition of long shutters give a more vertical feel to the one-story side of the house. Adding heftier columns and moving them to the corners of the porch kept it from looking as long, and framed the front entry.

To eliminate the line between the light siding and dark brick on the two-story wing, they painted the wood on the house a dark color. Tall shutters added to this wing also mask the split levels. "Pulling those windows up aligned them with the main floor and kept the small windows above almost like transoms," says Bill.

As for the landscape, a long line of shrubs near the foundation made the house seem to sink. Franklin broke up the line and used lower plantings such as hollies and ground covers to make the house appear taller. He rearranged many of the existing shrubs to help Bill stay on budget.

BEFORE

THE MAKEOVER

PROBLEM *Short windows accentuated the house's horizontal lines.*

SOLUTION *Windows visually lengthened with panels. Shutters also add a more vertical look.*

PROBLEM *A long line of shrubs along the foundation gave the house the appearance of sinking.*

SOLUTION *Lower foundation plantings make the house appear taller.*

PROBLEM *Four posts in a row masked the entry and made the porch appear longer.*

SOLUTION *New post columns on porch corners emphasize the entrance.*

MAKEOVER FEATURES

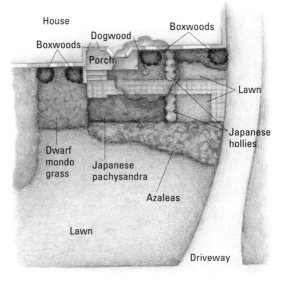

A. New post columns open up the front porch and make it appear wider. The upright trunk of a dogwood reinforces the strong vertical lines of the columns and shutters, adding a feeling of height to the one-story section of the house.

B. Painting the house siding a darker color reduces the contrast between the wood and dark brick. The darker paint also helps the house blend with the surrounding garden.

C. Azalea shrubs formerly massed against the house foundation now form a bold sweep of color highlighted by the lawn. Rearranging existing plants rather than buying new ones helped to reduce makeover costs.

REMADE FOR THE SHADE

The owners of this home wanted it all—a nice lawn, lush plantings, and little maintenance. But deep shade prevented the lawn from thriving. Removing several pine trees helped, but the edges of the yard were still too shady for grass, and the bare front bank facing the street began to erode.

Landscape architect Charles Sowell offered the owners several solutions. He recommended leveling most of the yard and locating the lawn in the center, where the yard receives the most sun. Along the shadier edges of the property, easy-to-grow evergreens, such as dwarf yaupons, Satsuki Hybrid azaleas, and 'Dwarf Burford' hollies, make themselves at home in sweeping shrub beds. A carpet of big blue liriope covering the bank helps frame the lawn and control erosion. Just as important, planting ground cover instead of grass eliminates the need to mow the steep slope.

The now softly curving lawn acts as a living stage, accentuating the house and garden. Its small size and lack of sharp angles allow the owners to cut it in a few minutes. Pruning the shrubs takes only an hour or two once a year.

THE MAKEOVER

PROBLEM *Too many trees shading the yard limited growth of lawn grass.*

SOLUTION *Removal of pine trees brings sunshine into the center of the yard where a lush lawn grows.*

PROBLEM *A shapeless front yard detracted from the home's appearance.*

SOLUTION *A softly curving lawn ringed with ground cover and shrubs frames the house.*

PROBLEM *The steep bank in front was eroding.*

SOLUTION *Adding a carpet of liriope ground cover controls erosion and eliminates the need for mowing.*

BEFORE

A. Low-maintenance planting beds include hollies, Satsuki Hybrid azaleas, and oakleaf hydrangeas. These plants thrive in shade and don't need extensive pruning. A layer of mulch keeps down the weeds.

B. Pretty as a putting green, this zoysia lawn is in perfect scale with the house. Low-maintenance, shade-tolerant liriope borders the lawn in front. The clusters of blue or purple liriope flowers are a bonus in summer.

A New Sense of Order

When the owner of this San Antonio, Texas, home called landscape designer Jodie Collins, she had spring fever and wanted to begin planting right away. Construction projects on the house were complete, but the heavy equipment and debris had left the yard a mess. "She was ready for plants that weekend," Collins says. "But there's a natural order you should follow."

The owner's wish list included increased privacy, a low-maintenance yard, an array of colorful plants, and a small lawn that would serve as an overflow area for entertaining. First Collins drew up a plan. Then he trimmed trees, cut back leggy shrubs, and removed plants that weren't worth keeping. Next he added soil to form a berm at the front of the property for privacy. But he still wasn't ready to begin planting.

He knew that he shouldn't tackle the landscape until other projects such as the new driveway and irrigation system were finished. Supplying the irrigation contractor with a planting plan helped tailor the new sprinkler system to match the designer's proposed landscape.

Once the driveway and irrigation system were in place, it was time to plant trees, shrubs, and ground covers. Annuals and sod went in last. Ten months after planting, the owner had a lush landscape that looked as if it had been in place for years.

THE MAKEOVER

PROBLEM *The owner wanted to plant right away.*

SOLUTION *A planting plan came first.*

PROBLEM *Busy street was visible from the front door.*

SOLUTION *A berm out front adds privacy.*

PROBLEM *Entertaining area was too small.*

SOLUTION *Lawn design creates an overflow area for entertaining.*

BEFORE

A. **A zigzag path to the front door** invites visitors to slow down and enjoy the garden. Stepping pads made of hand-molded tiles from Saltillo, Mexico, match the home's floors, creating an easy flow from house to garden.

B. **Beds of lush plantings** slope down to a bright green St. Augustine lawn. A well-planned irrigation system keeps the correct amount of water flowing to the lawn and garden beds.

C. **Native limestone** edges a raised bed for shrubs, flowers, and ground covers and accentuates the graceful curves of the lawn. The mulched area between the stones and the lawn makes for easy mowing.

CLEARING THE WAY

Visiting this Washington, D.C., home was like going through an obstacle course. To get from the street to the front door, you had to navigate around the end of a large brick wall, squeeze past a car, then traverse the parking area. What's worse, once you made it to the terrace, which doubled as extra parking space, you looked out onto a hodgepodge of garden features that didn't fit together.

Garden designers Tom Mannion and Louise Kane charted a new, less roundabout course for the garden. First they separated the entryway and parking areas. Now an entry gate, wide enough for two people, clearly marks an outdoor foyer. A brick wall and a cedar fence screen the foyer and garden from the now separate parking area. Taking advantage of a slight slope away from the house, the designers divided the terrace area into two level tiers connected by stone pavers at one end and wooden steps at the other. The first tier, a deck, is easily accessed from the house. The second and lower level, a flagstone terrace, accommodates dining and entertaining.

The small fish pond nestled next to the deck also received a makeover. Mannion and Kane reset the coping, giving it an overhang that casts a shadow on the water. Painting the inside of the pond black gives the illusion of depth. Water plants such as dwarf papyrus mask the edges of the pool.

Large native stones that lead from the pond and the terrace to a side yard below replace the old railroad-tie steps. The uneven stones create a pleasant woodland path in the garden.

BEFORE

A. **A large entry gate** opens onto an outdoor foyer that leads to the two-level terrace, front door, and garden.

B. **The clean lines and neutral colors** of the deck, terrace, and steps create a simple yet elegant setting for the garden.

C. **Native stone steps** look as if they had tumbled into place naturally. Lush borders complete the image of a woodland path.

D. **Renovating the fish pond** included adding new coping and painting the pond's interior black, giving the water a natural look.

MAKEOVER FEATURES

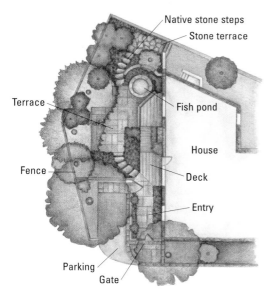

Native stone steps
Stone terrace
Terrace
Fish pond
Fence
House
Deck
Entry
Parking
Gate

BACK IN STYLE

When board-and-batten siding was the rage, Jackson, Mississippi, landscape architect Carter Brown included it on the ranch-style house he designed for his family. Years later, he looked at the house and declared, "Gosh almighty, it's dated." He came up with a simple makeover plan.

First he covered the front of the house with stucco. Using this material, he added a stylized, contemporary frame around the existing windows. He also replaced the old board-and-batten fence in the entry courtyard with new concrete block walls covered with the same stucco material as the house.

Carter decided to leave the courtyard, which is entered near the front door, in its original design. The small pond and plantings in this tranquil retreat can be viewed through windows in the foyer, living room, and dining room.

The entryway planting also escaped major changes. A large loquat still anchors one side of the entryway while a bed of Asian star jasmine carpets the ground beneath the front windows. A beautiful pink crepe myrtle, the most notable planting addition, complements the new house color and acts as a focal point, framing the entrance.

THE MAKEOVER

PROBLEM *Board-and-batten siding made the house look dated.*

SOLUTION *A stucco finish gives the house a more contemporary look.*

PROBLEM *Long, skinny windows looked plain and uninteresting.*

SOLUTION *Elaborate molding treatments dress up the windows.*

PROBLEM *The front door receded in shadow under the eaves.*

SOLUTION *A multistemmed crepe myrtle focuses attention on the front door.*

BEFORE

A. The play of shadows on a new stucco wall enhances the peaceful mood of the courtyard, entered near the front door.

B. A fresh new look for the house includes muted colors for the walls and trim, new window framing, sweeps of shrubs and evergreen ground covers, and a single crepe myrtle used as a focal point.

NEW WALK, NEW LOOK

Openness and privacy may seem opposites, but this house in Greensboro, North Carolina, proves you can have both. The owners relied on landscape designer Chip Callaway to come up with a plan that provided an open, welcoming entryway without sacrificing privacy. Before, visitors had no direct way to get from the street to the front door. Callaway designed

a handsome bluestone walk and a front terrace that open up the front yard and guide visitors to the entry in style.

The shallow lot made the house look like it was near the curb. Callaway couldn't move the house or the street, so he did the next best thing—he faked it. "One of the tricks I use when dealing with a shallow space is to slice it up into sections," he says. A series of garden sections between house and street creates the illusion of depth.

Now the yard consists of three distinct sections. The first begins at the street side. A stacked stone wall backed by a sweep of English ivy divides the yard from the street. River birches flanking the walk frame the view of the house and add a feeling of privacy. The second section is a thick green carpet of lawn with a pleasing curved shape. The third section makes up the front entry. Here, a low stone wall designed for seating encloses the new semicircular terrace and helps to make the house seem farther away from the street.

THE MAKEOVER

PROBLEM *No access available from the street to the front doors.*

SOLUTION *The new bluestone walk and terrace greet visitors and guide them to the entry.*

PROBLEM *A shallow lot made the house look too close to the street.*

SOLUTION *Dividing the yard into garden sections gives the appearance of depth.*

BEFORE

A. This low stone wall encloses the front terrace, defining a privacy zone at the entry. Drifts of foolproof impatiens blur the edge between wall and lawn.

B. A pleasant stroll from street to house begins when visitors pass between a pair of river birches planted in ivy beds. On the new walk, visitors cross a graceful sweep of lawn before arriving at the entry terrace.

STARTING FROM SCRATCH

A brand-new home often comes with a landscape that consists of a minimum number of plants. The owners of this new home in Watkinsville, Georgia, took one look at the flat lawn and tiny plants and knew they needed professional advice.

Horticulturist Ron Deal sketched a rough plan to direct the couple's do-it-yourself efforts. He designed a simple retaining wall to separate the lawn area by the street from a smaller planting area three steps down. Truckloads of soil were brought in to create this multilevel garden.

One of the best ways to avoid the look of a new house dropped onto a blank landscape is to plant a tree that gets big fast. A river birch planted beside the garage quickly grew higher than the roof, and the tree's leafy canopy provides needed shade. The owners' next priority was privacy. A quick-growing chaste tree, spreading English yews, and yaupon hollies planted on a berm give privacy and frame the view of the house.

Low-maintenance plants stand out against the light stucco house. The bright green leaves of 'Goldmound' spiraeas contrast with a bed of 'Crimson Pygmy' Japanese barberries. Lavender spikes crown the chaste tree each summer, while evergreen wax myrtles and Zabel cherry laurels provide interest through the seasons.

THE MAKEOVER

PROBLEM New house dominated the property.

SOLUTION A river birch planted by the garage gives height to the landscape.

PROBLEM No privacy.

SOLUTION Trees and shrubs planted on a berm screen unwanted views.

PROBLEM Lawn was boring and flat.

SOLUTION Multilevel yard with lively color adds interest.

BEFORE

A. At the corner of the garage, a narrow river of lawn grass flows between curved planting beds.

B. Colorful trees and shrubs screen the house from the street. Steps between the chaste tree and Indian hawthorns lead to a narrow lower lawn.

MAKEOVER FEATURES

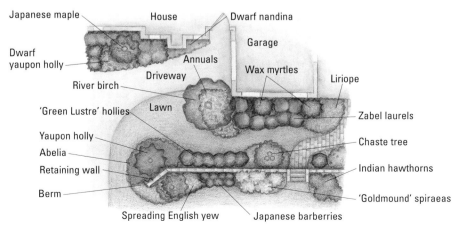

Japanese maple

House

Dwarf nandina

Garage

Dwarf yaupon holly

Annuals

Wax myrtles

Liriope

Driveway

River birch

'Green Lustre' hollies

Lawn

Zabel laurels

Yaupon holly

Chaste tree

Abelia

Indian hawthorns

Retaining wall

'Goldmound' spiraeas

Berm

Spreading English yew

Japanese barberries

NOT BIGGER, JUST BETTER

Before, a cookie-cutter deck was tacked onto the back of this house without regard to usefulness or style. Instead of tearing it down and starting over, the owners transformed the deck into something special.

Because the surface of the deck is only about a foot above the ground, safety rails weren't necessary. Removing the old railing instantly opened up the area, making the deck seem twice as large. Backless benches added to two sides of the deck provide seating without taking up precious floor space. They also prevent people from stepping off the deck into the planting areas below.

Next, the owners built a generous step that wraps around one corner. The step makes the deck seem larger and improves the flow of foot traffic into the backyard. Using a solid-color stain over the entire surface of the deck helps integrate the new benches and step with the rest of the structure. A simple pavers-on-sand patio at the base of the step increases the outdoor living area.

To tone down the wide two-story chimney, the owners added an awning crafted from shutters and mounted it on the outside chimney wall. Placed at a height of about 8 feet, the awning takes attention away from the tall chimney and gives the deck the people-size dimensions of a room. Decorative iron mounted below the awning completes the look. A new light fixture and plenty of potted plants enhance the feeling of coziness.

THE MAKEOVER

PROBLEM *Prefabricated rails made the deck seem smaller.*

SOLUTION *Removing the rails visually enlarges the deck.*

PROBLEM *The small deck was cramped with lots of furniture.*

SOLUTION *Backless benches along two sides add seating without taking up floor space.*

PROBLEM *A wide two-story chimney overpowered the deck.*

SOLUTION *Hanging an awning with accessories on the exterior takes attention away from the chimney.*

BEFORE

A. To divert attention from a chimney cased in siding, the owners placed a homemade table in front of the chimney and added decorative iron and an awning made from shutters.

B. Widening the steps and replacing an old railing with backless benches makes this deck feel spacious. An adjacent paver-on-sand patio provides plenty of extra seating.

FRONT YARD REFRESHER

When Greg McDonnell saw this humble bungalow in Mobile, Alabama, he knew he had found a house with great potential. But realizing that potential required a complete face-lift for both the house and the front yard.

Greg removed the 16-inch brick columns supporting the porch roof because they were out of scale with the house. In their place, six wooden posts boxed with 1-by-6s wrap the corners. He then tore out the broken concrete walk and laid a wider entry using old bricks. A few simple details, such as painting the house in contemporary colors, replacing the plain front door with a leaded-glass door, and adding a pediment window and additional trim, made the front of the house much more appealing.

Next, Greg turned his attention to the garden. He replaced the narrow strip of grass between the sidewalk and the street with panels of brick and planting areas filled with crepe myrtles and autumn ferns. "Looking through these crepe myrtle trunks gives the illusion that the house is farther away and that the front garden is bigger than it really is," he says.

When the weather is warm, caladiums and impatiens thrive in front of the dwarf camellias planted around the foundation. In the cool months, pansies, sweet Williams, and flowering cabbage and kale make an appealing combination.

THE MAKEOVER

PROBLEM *Brick columns looked massive on the small front porch.*

SOLUTION *Simple wooden post columns are more in scale with the house.*

PROBLEM *A narrow strip of grass between sidewalk and street made the front yard look small.*

SOLUTION *Replacing the grass strip with brick paving and planting areas complements the new brick walk and creates a larger-looking front yard.*

PROBLEM *Sparse plantings made the front yard uninviting.*

SOLUTION *Light-colored foliage and seasonal displays of bloom add inviting color and a welcoming touch.*

BEFORE

A. Potted sago palms and colorful mounds of impatiens and caladiums highlight the brick walk and focus attention on the inviting front entry.

B. A flowering arch of crepe myrtle branches frames the entryway and completes the transition from street to door. Autumn ferns beneath the trees look delicate but are actually quite tough. Their evergreen fronds provide year-round interest.

A TURN FOR THE BETTER

Solving a common parking problem yielded an unexpected benefit—a secret garden right in the front yard. Before, a narrow driveway ran straight into the garage under the house. Drivers who pulled in couldn't turn their cars around and had to slowly back out into traffic.

To remedy this parking dilemma, Atlanta landscape architect Bill Smith cut into the slope in front of the house and added a turnaround and guest parking area. At the head of the turnaround, a brick landing ties together the new retaining walls and brick steps. Smith also dyed the concrete in the driveway light gray to complement the house and reduce glare.

A small flower bed visible from the front door turns this utilitarian space into a hidden garden. The garden sits at the head of the parking area and near the foot of the porch steps, about 4 feet below the front lawn. Only the 'New Dawn' climbing roses peeking over the retaining wall from the garden hint of this space from the street. A Chippendale bench in front of the wall repeats the detail of the porch railing and provides a focal point for the garden. A strong "backbone" of evergreen shrubs planted above the retaining walls keeps the area green even in winter.

THE MAKEOVER

PROBLEM THE NARROW DRIVEWAY DIDN'T PROVIDE A PLACE FOR GUESTS TO PARK OR TURN THEIR CARS AROUND.

SOLUTION A NEW PARKING AREA AND TURNAROUND MEANS GUESTS NO LONGER HAVE TO BACK OUT OF THE DRIVEWAY INTO TRAFFIC.

BEFORE

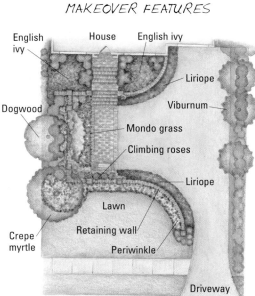

MAKEOVER FEATURES

English ivy — House — English ivy — Liriope — Viburnum — Dogwood — Mondo grass — Climbing roses — Liriope — Lawn — Retaining wall — Crepe myrtle — Periwinkle — Driveway

A. A spacious entryway made from a sloping front yard creates a parking area and multilevel garden.

B. The inspiring view from the front door includes a stylish bench and private flower garden.

NO MORE WASTED SPACE

Narrow, walk-through spaces that usually house trash cans, side yards often go unnoticed and unattended. This courtyard in Columbia, South Carolina, proves that this "wasted" space can be wonderful.

The owners felt that the side yard was an ideal spot for a patio and a fountain. But they questioned where to place them and how to handle the grade change between front and backyard. Landscape architect George Betsill helped them with placing the 12-foot-square patio and 3-foot-square fountain. To adjust for the grade change, he placed a step just outside the gated entrance of the side yard and used a knee-high brick wall to separate the new courtyard garden from the courtyard in the back. A 7-foot, pierced-top brick wall encloses the courtyard at the property line.

For plantings, the owners chose a color scheme based on white and blue. 'Nikko Blue', 'Sister Theresa', oakleaf, and variegated lace cap hydrangeas contribute a long season of blue and white blooms. Shade-loving hostas, ferns, coleuses, and Lenten roses *(Helleborus orientalis)* add their luxuriant foliage to the garden. Layers of vines add texture in narrow planting beds, and creeping fig cushions the walls. A Japanese maple anchors one corner of the courtyard.

An antique olive-jar-turned-fountain adds the crowning touch to this charming courtyard. Smooth sheets of water spill over its sides into a small pool, mimicking the sounds of a trickling stream.

THE MAKEOVER

PROBLEM THE SIDE YARD WAS NEGLECTED SPACE.

SOLUTION ADDING A PATIO AND A FOUNTAIN TURNS THE SPACE INTO A PRIVATE RETREAT.

PROBLEM VIEW TO THE NEIGHBOR'S YARD WAS MUCH TOO OPEN.

SOLUTION A 7-FOOT-HIGH BRICK WALL OFFERS ENCLOSURE AND PRIVACY.

PROBLEM BLANK BRICK WALLS LOOKED STARK AND IMPOSING.

SOLUTION CLIMBING VINES SOFTEN THE WALLS' APPEARANCE.

PROBLEM THE PROPERTY GRADE CHANGED BETWEEN THE FRONT AND BACKYARD.

SOLUTION A STEP JUST OUTSIDE THE ENTRANCE OF THE SIDE YARD CREATES A TRANSITION.

BEFORE

A. **Vibrant with color and texture,** a shady corner creates the perfect environment for ferns, hostas, hardy orchids, violets, and Lenten roses. Layers of vines add a feeling of depth to the garden.

B. **A bronze frog** stands guard at the entrance of this peaceful retreat, where lush hydrangeas bloom against walls textured with creeping fig. An elegant fountain anchors the new brick terrace.

C. **Antique wrought-iron gates** invite you into the courtyard, where mounds of foliage spill onto the walk. Large-leafed plants such as elephant's ears and cast-iron plants add a lush, tropical feel.

A BRIGHT NEW START

Imagine house-hunting one weekend and driving by this home as it used to look. You likely wouldn't have even slowed the car. But a few inexpensive changes gave this dull, homely front yard and entryway a bright new beginning.

The original awning was too low and obscured the door. Replacing it with a bubble awning made of jet black canvas increased the front door's prominence and helped tone down the high, blank gable. Then the owner painted the door a different color than the steps and added a new brass knocker, kick plate, and mail slot.

A lattice trellis on one side of the door helps to balance the asymmetrical facade. Small spacers keep the lattice from touching its black backing, leaving enough room for vines to twine through.

Next, the owner installed a landing at the foot of the steps. Eighteen-inch-square concrete pads were set atop a bed of crushed limestone. Staining every other square black creates a striking checkerboard pattern.

A simple planting adds color and minimizes maintenance. After pruning the existing overgrown nandinas in a stair-step fashion, the owner framed the entryway with 'Helleri' Japanese hollies, ornamental grasses, Southern shield ferns *(Thelypteris kunthii),* and a mixture of colorful annuals and perennials. A new 'Natchez' crepe myrtle gives privacy to the triple front window.

THE MAKEOVER

PROBLEM *The original awning was low and hid the top of the door, creating a somber look.*

SOLUTION *A jet black bubble awning above the overhang of the house adds style and highlights the door.*

PROBLEM *An asymmetrical facade gave the house an unbalanced look.*

SOLUTION *A lattice trellis on one side of the off-center door restores balance.*

PROBLEM *Existing nandinas planted in front of the house were overgrown and unattractive.*

SOLUTION *The nandinas were pruned and became part of the low-maintenance plantings that frame the entry.*

BEFORE

A. **A new bubble awning** adds impact to the entry. Below it, bush daisies *(Euryops pectinatus)* planted in pots supply early summer color.

B. **Bold strokes of black** in the awning and the checkerboard landing draw the eye and balance each other. Potted marigolds, Joe-Pye weed *(Eupatorium purpureum)*, and lantanas replace the bush daisies in early fall.

PERSONALITY PLUS

Dressing up the front porch and installing some new plants turned this Birmingham, Alabama, house from a yawner into a charmer. Breathing new life into the landscape was a priority, but work on the house needed to be done first. Completing construction before planting avoided damage to the garden from equipment.

To update the porch, the owners replaced spindly wrought-iron trim with new wooden columns and handrails. Painting them bright white brings the entry to life. Black shutters add detail to the plain porch window. A lattice panel screens the view of the two-story house next door and still allows breezes to pass through. Leaving a 30-by-30-inch open frame in the lattice cleverly focuses attention on the crepe myrtle planted beside the porch.

The owners shaped the lawn to direct attention toward the newly remodeled porch and away from the driveway. Rows of plants across the foundation were replaced with curving beds that follow the shape of the lawn. Removing one of the existing maple trees opened up the view of the house and made it easier to mow the lawn. Lusterleaf hollies screen the view of the neighbor's driveway.

THE MAKEOVER

PROBLEM *Spindly wrought-iron trim dated the porch.*

SOLUTION *New painted wood columns and handrails add personality, and focus attention on the entry.*

PROBLEM *A two-story house next door overwhelmed the porch.*

SOLUTION *A lattice panel screens the view yet allows breezes onto the porch.*

PROBLEM *Driveways visually dominated and hemmed in the yard.*

SOLUTION *Lusterleaf hollies block views of the neighbor's driveway; curved edges keep focus on the pleasing shape of the front yard and away from the home's driveway.*

BEFORE

MAKEOVER FEATURES

Crepe myrtle
Lattice
House
Porch
Japanese hollies
Ferns
Dogwood
Neighbor's driveway
Melampodiums
Lusterleaf hollies
Bench
Maple
Black-eyed Susans
Driveway
Lawn

A. Curved planting beds direct attention toward the porch. Drifts of hostas, Southern shield ferns, liriopes, and oakleaf hydrangeas thrive in the shade of a dogwood.

B. White handrails tie in the front yard and walkway with the porch. A lush zoysia lawn showcases the curved walk and planting beds. A bench at the edge of the lawn offers a cool place to sit.

A CHARMING REDESIGN

When landscape architect Diane Dunaway looked at this back-yard in Decatur, Georgia, she envisioned a design in the shape of a four-leaf clover. Her inspiration transformed a barren backyard into a relaxing spot to entertain or simply unwind.

The new clover-shaped terrace is a private nook, separated from neighbors by a fence and screened from the drive by two yaupon hollies that will grow into small gray-barked trees.

One "leaf" or arc of the terrace provides footing for a generous swing. With night lighting and outdoor stereo speakers nearby, the swing is a perfect place to start or end the day. Another arc leads through a pair of yaupon hollies to the back door. Even though you can see between the slender trunks, the hollies give a sense of separation that makes the area feel secluded. A third arc curves toward the house and creates a spot for a favorite chair as well as a generous planting bed for evergreen shrubs and seasonal flowers. Impatiens edge the terrace in bright and cheery colors throughout the summer.

While the first three arcs have a raised brick edging, the edge of the fourth arc is paved even with the lawn and invites a stroll.

THE MAKEOVER

PROBLEM BACKYARD DIDN'T OFFER A COMFORTABLE PLACE TO RELAX.

SOLUTION A CLOVER-SHAPED TERRACE CREATES A GARDEN "ROOM" TO ENJOY.

PROBLEM NOTHING SEPARATED THE DRIVE FROM THE LAWN.

SOLUTION YAUPON HOLLIES SCREEN THE DRIVE FROM THE NEW TERRACE.

PROBLEM SPARSE, DRAB PLANTINGS DIDN'T OFFER SEASONAL COLOR.

SOLUTION BEDS FLANKING THE TERRACE ACCOMMODATE LUSH EVERGREENS AND COLORFUL ANNUALS AND PERENNIALS.

BEFORE

This airy yet secluded terrace with its three-seat swing, comfortable chairs, and beds filled with evergreen shrubs and impatiens offers a great place to relax. The owners consider it another room of the house—perhaps their favorite.

FIRST THINGS FIRST

The new owners of this South Carolina island home loved the established neighborhood, quiet cul-de-sac, and harbor view. But the dated look of the house and garden didn't fit their personal style. They asked landscape architect Robert Chesnut for help.

His advice to the owners: "Embark on construction first and do the planting second. Reversing the process can waste money. A window might become a door—then you've got to redo the whole garden."

The first change involved increasing the pitch of the roof. Originally, the low roof had a squatty 1970s look. Elevating it improved the home's proportions, and enlarging the chimney added to the improved visual balance of the architecture.

Next, Chesnut rearranged the windows and doors to take advantage of the waterfront views. He replaced the double front doors with a single one framed by floor-to-ceiling windows. His design also called for the removal of an interior wall just beyond the windows. "Now the minute you walk in, you look all the way through the house to an incredible harbor view," he says. Covering the original wood siding with stucco instantly updated the entire facade.

Improving the garden was the last step. Hardy, easy-to-grow plants such as tree-form wax myrtles, dwarf Indian hawthorns, and azaleas keep the planting simple. An evergreen wisteria twining up the columns of the portico adds a finishing touch to both yard and house.

THE MAKEOVER

PROBLEM A SQUATTY ROOF DATED THE HOUSE.

SOLUTION INCREASING THE PITCH OF THE ROOF GIVES THE HOUSE A MORE CONTEMPORARY LOOK.

PROBLEM WINDOWS AND DOORS DIDN'T TAKE ADVANTAGE OF THE VIEW.

SOLUTION REARRANGING WINDOWS AND DOORS AND REMOVING AN INTERIOR WALL OPENS UP THE VIEW OF THE WATER.

PROBLEM VERTICAL WOOD SIDING MADE THE HOUSE LOOK DATED.

SOLUTION COVERING THE SIDING WITH STUCCO CREATES AN UP-TO-DATE LOOK.

BEFORE

Removing an interior wall and adding large windows on each side of the front door focuses the viewer's eye in the middle of the house and right at the entry. Low shrubs blur the edges of the walkway without blocking the view. Their deep green color offers a striking contrast with the soft ocean green color of the house.

A COMPLETE TURNAROUND

This home's narrow driveway made it impossible to turn a car around once you pulled in. Moving one car into the driveway usually meant having to move another. And there wasn't any off-street parking. Guests had to hike up the driveway and use a sunken stone walk to reach the front door. The owners needed a driveway that was functional, convenient, and attractive. They also wanted to update the home's entryway.

To get a feel for the amount of space needed for the parking court, they pulled a van in the yard and marked the dimensions before excavating the area. The space measures 30 by 30 feet and allows plenty of room for parking, stepping in and out of the car, and turning the car around. A stacked-stone retaining wall separates the area from the front yard and repeats the stone used on the home's foundation. A new front walk and steps are also made of stone. Using salvaged stones for these new structures makes them look as if they have always been there.

Flower beds framing the walk put on a show of seasonal color. In fall, pansies and sweet Williams fill out the beds. In spring, pink impatiens, trailing torenia, and caladiums provide a cool color scheme. Ferns tumble over the walk's edge.

The owners improved the porch by replacing a small square column with a large round one that adds weight to the entry. They painted the front door a rich dark green to make it stand out. Squatty urns lining the steps and brimming with flowers add a welcoming mix of color.

BEFORE

THE MAKEOVER

PROBLEM *No room for turning cars around or for guest parking.*

SOLUTION *New turnaround space is also a parking court.*

PROBLEM *Loose stones made old walk untidy and unsafe.*

SOLUTION *New steps and walk are attractive and provide safe footing.*

PROBLEM *Lack of color made landscape drab and unappealing.*

SOLUTION *New flower beds bordering the walk and containers on the steps are filled with annuals for color.*

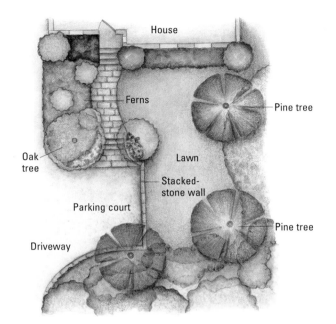

MAKEOVER FEATURES

House

Ferns

Pine tree

Oak tree

Lawn

Stacked-stone wall

Parking court

Pine tree

Driveway

A. A dry stacked-stone retaining wall separates the parking area from the front yard. The wall provides many places where plants can be tucked into its crevices, adding color and texture to the stone wall.

B. A new walk and steps lead visitors from the parking area to the front door. Ferns, impatiens, caladiums, and silver variegated Japanese sedges add to the warm welcome.

C. A spacious new parking court gives people enough space to turn cars around and avoid backing out into the street.

SUBJECT INDEX

Page references in **bold type** indicate main entries, including photographs and illustrations. Page references in *italics* indicate other photographs or illustrations.

PLANT INDEX

Page references in *italics* indicate photographs.

DESIGN CREDITS

Sharon Abroms-McHale
Atlanta, Georgia

Clay Adams
Fairhope, Alabama

John Adams
Ocala, Florida

Allen and Julia Anderson
Poplarville, Mississippi

Clare Ashby
Tulsa, Oklahoma

Barton's Nursery
Tuscaloosa, Alabama

Judy Beatty
Birmingham, Alabama

Caroline Benson
Leeds Creek, Maryland

George Betsill
Columbia, South Carolina

Kurt Bluemel
Baldwin, Maryland

Blue Moon Gardens
Chandler, Texas

Carrington Brown
Richmond, Virginia

Carter Brown
Jackson, Mississippi

Naud Burnett
Dallas, Texas

Christian Busk
Naples, Florida

Chip Callaway
Greensboro, North Carolina

Bruce Cavey
Gainesville, Florida

Robert C. Chesnut
Charleston, South Carolina

Christopher Glenn, Inc.
Homewood, Alabama

Jodie Collins
San Antonio, Texas

Alex and Vicki Cureton
Tallahassee, Florida

Walter Dahlberg
Lambert's
Dallas, Texas

Preston Dalrymple
Richmond, Virginia

Hugh and Mary Palmer Dargan
Atlanta, Georgia

Richard Dawson and Lawrence Estes
Houston, Texas

Ron Deal
Watkinsville, Georgia

David Dempsey, Garden Works
Atlanta, Georgia

Greg Duke
Andalusia, Alabama

Diane Dunaway
Atlanta, Georgia

Warren Edwards
Oklahoma City, Oklahoma

Edmund Ely
Louisville, Kentucky

Paul Fields
Lambert's
Dallas, Texas

Rosa Finsley
Cedar Hill, Texas

Kay Flory
Grottoes, Virginia

Peggy Ford
Manakin-Sabot, Virginia

Dan Franklin
Atlanta, Georgia

Rene Fransen
New Orleans, Louisiana

Charles Freeman
St. Louis, Missouri

Rodney Fulcher
Abilene, Texas

Ryan Gainey
Atlanta, Georgia

George Gambrill
Birmingham, Alabama

Greg Garcia
Athens, Georgia

Garden Gate Landscaping
Silver Spring, Maryland

Charlotte Goodwyn
Montgomery, Alabama

Phil Graham
St. Petersburg, Florida

The Greenery
Hilton Head Island, South Carolina

Ken Hall and Rick Enge
Winter Park, Florida

Susan Hall
Miami, Florida

Steve Harrell
Brandon, Mississippi

Bob Hartwig
Jacksonville, Florida

Bill Henkel
Lexington, Kentucky

Phyllis Herring
Camden, South Carolina

Wayne Hester
Birmingham, Alabama

Missy Hodapp
New Orleans, Louisiana

Michael Hopping
Port Allen, Louisiana

John James
Orange, Virginia

Norman Kent Johnson
Birmingham, Alabama

Tom Kauffmann
Tulsa, Oklahoma

Tom Keith
Greenville, South Carolina

Jan Kirsch
Bozman, Maryland

Ruthie Lacey
Columbia, South Carolina

Mary LaLone
Blacksburg, Virginia

William Leathers
Orlando, Florida

Harold Leidner
Dallas, Texas

Terry Lewis
San Antonio, Texas

Jack Lieber
Ft. Lauderdale, Florida

Jane MacLeish
Washington, D.C.

Catherine Mahan
Baltimore, Maryland

Emily Major
Mountain Brook, Alabama

Tom Mannion
Arlington, Virginia

Douglas Martin
Richmond, Virginia

J.D. Martin
Arbor Engineering
Greenville, South Carolina

Robert Marvin
Walterboro, South Carolina

Greg McDonnell
Mobile, Alabama

Patty Merson and Herman Weis
Atlanta, Georgia

Andy Moore
Lexington, Kentucky

Paul Moore
Nashville, Tennessee

Don Morris and Harry White
San Antonio, Texas

Bill Nance
Huntsville, Alabama

Wolfgang Oehme
Baltimore, Maryland

Ben Page
Nashville, Tennessee

Frances Parker
Beaufort, South Carolina

Dabney Peeples
Easley, South Carolina

Michael Perry
Winter Park, Florida

Karin Purvis
Greenville, South Carolina

Felder Rushing
Jackson, Mississippi

Dan Sears
Raleigh, North Carolina

Jeremy Smearman
Atlanta, Georgia

Bill Smith
Atlanta, Georgia

Charles Sowell
Birmingham, Alabama

Elissa Steeves
Blacksburg, Virginia

Jimmy and Becky Stewart
Atlanta, Georgia

Hal Stringer
Waco, Texas

Liz Tedder
Newnan, Georgia

Barbie Thomas
Louisville, Kentucky

John Troy
San Antonio, Texas

Carolyn Tynes
Birmingham, Alabama

Nancy Volkman
College Station, Texas

Philip Watson
Fredericksburg, Virginia

Wade Weaver
Johnstown, Pennsylvania

William Welch
College Station, Texas

Shelia Wertimer
Charleston, South Carolina

Lindie Wilson—restored Elizabeth
Lawrence garden
Charlotte, North Carolina

Fritz Woehle
Birmingham, Alabama

Kerry Wood
Birmingham, Alabama

Kevin Young
Atlanta, Georgia

Mary Zahl
Birmingham, Alabama

Donald and Tommy Zimlich
Mobile, Alabama

Brian Zimmerman
Charlotte, North Carolina

ACKNOWLEDGMENTS

Our thanks to the following for their contributions to this book:
National Soil Survey Center Staff, 1999. Soil Reaction in the Southern United States. USDA-Natural Resources Conservation Service. National Survey Center, Lincoln, Nebraska. Digital map product.

Our thanks to the following for allowing us to show their merchandise in this book:
Lyngso Garden Materials, Nightscaping by Loran, Smith & Hawken, Trex, Inc.

PHOTOGRAPHY CREDITS

For pages with four or fewer photographs, each image has been identified by its position on the page: Left (L), center (C), or right (R); top (T), middle (M), or bottom (B). On other pages, photographs are identified by their position in the grid (shown right).

L	LC	RC	R
1	1	1	1
2			
3			
4			

Arena Roses: 232 C3, 232 R2, 232 R3. **Ardon Armstrong:** 152 RB. **David Belda:** 299 C1. **Kathleen Brenzel:** 299 C2, 242. **Claire Curran:** 255LB. **Cheryl Sales Dalton:** 187 B. **Colleen Duffley:** 331. **Mick Hales:** 303R. **Lynne Harrison:** 303 L, 318 RM. **Philip Harvey:** 141 LB, 144 LB,144 RB, 144-145 C, 145 LB, 145 RB, 302-303 B, 339 B. **Saxon Holt:** 132 LB, 133 T, 204-205, 229 RT, 250. **James Housel:** 123 LB. **Mary Gray Hunter:** 123 RB, 194-195B, 237 CT, 239 LC, 245 B, 255 LT, 270, 271 L-RC-R, 284 RB. **Louis Joyner:** 305 LB. **judywhite:** 191 RB. **Allan Mandell:** 232 L1. **Charles Mann:** 251 C. **Beth Maynor:** 34, 34-35 T, 35. **David McDonald:** 311 LT, 313 C2. **Emily Minton:** 151 R, 167 T, 312 RB. **Nightscaping:** 317 LT. **Jerry Pavia:** 133 B, 135 B, 231 LB, 229 C3. **Norman Plate:** 231 RM, 307, 315 B. **Ian Reeves:** 361. **Michael S. Thompson:** 161 T, 302 T. **Trex, Inc.:** 340B. **Tom Woodward:** 3, 9, 7. **Deidra Walpole:** 310 RB.